RAMESSES II

THE JOHNS HOPKINS NEAR EASTERN STUDIES

Hans Goedicke, General Editor

Hans Goedicke, *The Report about the Dispute of a Man with His* Ba

J. J. M. Roberts, *The Earliest Semitic Pantheon*

John D. Schmidt, *Ramesses II: A Chronological Structure for His Reign*

RAMESSES II

A Chronological Structure for His Reign

John D. Schmidt

THE JOHNS HOPKINS UNIVERSITY PRESS
Baltimore and London

Manufactured in the United States of America

The Johns Hopkins University Press, Baltimore, Maryland 21218
The Johns Hopkins University Press Ltd., London

Library of Congress Catalog Card Number 72-6558
ISBN 0-8018-1455-3

Library of Congress Cataloging in Publication Data

Schmidt, John D
Ramesses II; a chronological structure for his reign.

(The Johns Hopkins University Near Eastern studies)
Originally presented as the author's thesis, Johns Hopkins, 1970.
Bibliography: p.
1. Ramesses II, King of Egypt. 2. Egypt—History—To 332 B.C.—Chronology. I. Title. II. Series: Johns Hopkins University. Near Eastern studies.
DT88.S34 1973 932'.01'0924 72-6558
ISBN 0-8018-1455-3

CONTENTS

PREFACE

A reign as long and amply attested as that of Ramesses II offers the possibility of developing a chronological sequence of royal activities in a way similar to that which has been done for larger time periods. Though a general framework has been known, this study was undertaken to evolve a basic chronology of events for his reign and establish a structure into which the numerous undated material may subsequently be placed. Therefore the research is based upon those inscriptions and texts which contain regnal dates.

This endeavor began as a doctoral dissertation presented to The Johns Hopkins University in 1970, and I would like to thank Professor Hans Goedicke, who originally suggested an historical study of the reign of Ramesses II and who also helped towards its completion and publication. There are others who have also given assistance in various ways: Professor Ricardo A. Caminos supplied photographs and information of the Gebel Silsileh inscriptions, Mr. T. G. H. James sent a copy of the Sphinx Stela before it was available in his recent publication, Professor Charles F. Nims furnished a photograph of the Hittite Alliance, Professor Richard A. Parker kindly offered valuable chronological suggestions, Professor Edward F. Wente read the original dissertation, and not least of all, the late Professor Jaroslav Černý in his usual gracious way answered a number of inquiries. The help of those whose names are not mentioned is also greatly appreciated and will be remembered.

A grant from the Columbia University Council for Research in the Social Sciences has helped defray publication costs.

John D. Schmidt
Columbia University

CHAPTER I

THE ESTABLISHMENT OF AN ABSOLUTE CHRONOLOGY

Since this is a study of the internal chronology of the reign of Ramesses II, it is not the place to enter into a detailed exposition of ancient chronologies and dating methods.[1] However, one can not completely bypass the discussion concerning the absolute date of his reign,[2] for a number of historical considerations are involved which will also be an important part of this present work. There are two reasonable dates for the accession of Ramesses II, these being determined by astronomical considerations,[3] so it becomes necessary to point out the problems involved in choosing either before any conclusion may be reached.

The chronological structure of the entire New Kingdom is, in general, well defined but any absolute dates postulated for the period will contain a certain margin of error;[4] therefore any absolute date given for the reign of Ramesses II will be affected by such a margin. Nevertheless, by utilizing the historical and astronomical material not only from the New Kingdom, but from subsequent periods also, a reasonable date for his accession may be postulated. A possible secondary control for the date of his reign is the Mesopotamian chronological structure when brought into relationship with Egypt through synchronisms between Ramesses II and his eastern contemporaries.

It is fortunate that astronomical data is of particular help in establishing a Gregorian date for the accession of Ramesses II. Four astronomical references influence his date: a Sothic date belonging to the 9th year of Amenophis I, contained in Papyrus Ebers;[5] two lunar dates from the reign of Tuthmosis III;[6] and most important, a lunar reference in the 52nd year of Ramesses himself.[7] Each observation will permit only certain dates as possible solutions; hence one must decide which is the most reasonable according to the historical material available.[8]

The Sothic date in Papyrus Ebers cannot be used to produce one specific Gregorian date for the 9th year of Amenophis I, since a number of unknown factors prohibit such exactitude; certain unknowns are purely astronomical in nature and concern the length of the Egyptian year with regard to the Gregorian year, both differing from the sideral year and the solar year.[9] Another unknown is the actual time of the sighting with regard to the theoretical or astronomical observation.[10] In all, these considerations introduce an 8-year differential for the 9th year of Amenophis I.[11] Most of the unknowns mentioned above are inherent in any attempted equation of an ancient system of reckoning with that of the Gregorian; there is, however, one more unknown factor which would greatly influence the date of the Sothic observation and that factor is the site of the observation.[12] Because of the difference in latitude, an observation made in the Memphis-Heliopolis area would produce a date different from one made in Thebes, for the southern city would be able to observe the rising of Sirius before that of the north. The results are two different possible dates for the observation with a variable of 20 years.[13] If the observation were made in Memphis-Heliopolis, then the accession of Amenophis I would be 1553/1545, but if the observation were made in Thebes, then it would be 1534/1525.[14] Since there is no specific indication where the observation was made, historical considerations must determine which one is more likely correct; it must be noted that this Sothic observation permits one to posit a date where the variable is only 28 years at the most.[15]

Next, the lunar dates for Tuthmosis III, recorded in his 23rd and 24th regnal years, permit his accession to be placed in either 1515 or 1490, again a variable close to that mentioned for the reign of Amenophis I.[16] Year 1515 would agree with a Memphis-Heliopolis Sothic date, or "high" date, for Amenophis I and 1490 would agree with a Theban observation or "low" date. Consistency must be maintained in this respect; a "high" date for Amenophis I may not be combined with a "low" date for Tuthmosis III because such a combination would assign too many years to Tuthmosis II. Conversely, a "low" date for Amenophis I may not be combined with a "high" date for Tuthmosis III, since there would not be sufficient years for the intervening reigns, as required by the historical material.[17]

Finally, there is the lunar date of Ramesses II, listed on the *verso* of Papyrus Leiden I 350, which belongs to the 52nd year of his reign.[18] This sighting produces three dates for the accession of Ramesses II which would fit the historical situation: 1304, 1290 and 1279.[19] Of the three dates, that of 1279 has not received serious consideration, for according to present knowledge it would severely compress those reigns immediately following Ramesses II.[20] Since both the Sothic date belonging to the reign of Amenophis I and the lunar dates of the reign of Tuthmosis III allow a variable greater than the 14 years between 1304 and 1290, these earlier dates cannot determine which is the correct one.

Even if the lower date for the accession of Tuthmosis III were chosen, as is done by most historians,[21] this would not determine which of the two dates must be used for the accession of Ramesses II because of historical problems within the period separating Tuthmosis III and Ramesses II. Even though the earlier chronology of the Eighteenth Dynasty is well defined, the Amarna Period and beginning of the Nineteenth Dynasty is still unsettled. The basic historical problems which influence the chronology of this period are, first, the coregency question concerning Amenophis III and Amenophis IV[22] and then concerning Amenophis IV and Semenkhkare;[23] second, the true length of Horemhab's reign;[24] and third, the length of the reign of Seti I, for whom year 11 is the highest known, though he is usually given more based upon the figures in Manetho.[25] In terms of actual years, the coregency question between Amenophis III and Amenophis IV concerns 10 years and that of Amenophis IV and Semenkhkare, 3 years; with regard to Horemhab the amount is more difficult to define, but it involves a minimum 15-year range;[26] Seti's reign contains a variable equal to the amount of years one wishes to extend his reign beyond regnal year 11; since he is usually given 15 to 20 years, the variable is between 4 to 9 years.[27] It can be seen that there is a maximum variable of approximately 50 years between the accession of Amenophis I and the Sothic date in Papyrus Ebers[28] and up to 25-30 from the time of Tuthmosis III to Ramesses II,[29] if all the problems and variables are taken into consideration.

Though the unknowns listed above make it impossible to determine the accession of Ramesses II with precision, this does not mean that it is impossible to set a reasonable date for it. The variables represent the maximum years involved; one need not assume that each variable is of the same weight and historical value as the next, nor need one assume that the solutions for each are of equal difficulty. Furthermore, one is not limited to the period preceding Ramesses II, as that period which follows him can also be used as a guide and a check, proportionate to the validity of its historical materials.

The historical period immediately following Ramesses II contains no astronomically fixed date; the first "fixed" date belongs to the reign of Sheshonq I, whose reign may be reasonably established through Asiatic synchronisms. The date of this ruler can be determined through biblical chronology, for Sheshonq invaded Judah in the 5th year of Rehoboam,[30] who can be correlated with the Assyrian king lists which are sound at this period.[31] We know that he invaded Judah in Rehoboam's 5th year, but we do not know the exact regnal year of Sheshonq I in which this occurred, though it most likely happened in or very near his 21st year.[32] By this correlation the accession of Sheshonq I may be dated to the year 945 B. C. (actually 948/941 at the very most),[33] and from this one is able to work backwards to the reign of Ramesses II and have a second check upon his accession. However, this procedure is beset with difficulties for here the unknowns are even more numerous and less under control than those of the period prior to the reign of Ramesses II. The end of the Nineteenth Dynasty is uncertain, not only as to length, but as to succession; the length of Merneptah's reign is unknown, his highest dated inscription is that of regnal year 8 while Manetho accords him 20.[34] The length of the Twentieth Dynasty is fairly certain, with only a slight margin of error, but that of the Twenty-first is less sure.[35] Although the margin of error between the death of Ramesses II and the accession of Sheshonq I is too large to decide between 1304 and 1290 with certainty, the accepted results would tend to support the latter.[36]

Since the internal chronology of Egypt cannot precisely set one specific year for the accession of Ramesses II, synchronisms with foreign rulers, and hence with foreign chronological structures, become significant in the discussion of Egyptian chronology. The only direct synchronism between Ramesses and the ruler of any foreign land is with the land of Hatti. Even though this was an international period, there is no direct synchronism between Ramesses II and a Mesopotamian contemporary. This situation makes comparative chronology difficult and open to differences of interpretation, for Egypt must be correlated with either Babylon or Assyria and their respective king lists and chronicles, because Hatti kept no king lists and therefore cannot help determine an absolute date in Egypt.[37]

There is one important synchronism between Ramesses and a Hittite king; in regnal year 21, Ramesses and Hattushilish III formed an alliance,[38] thus providing a specific date for comparative chronology.[39] Hattushilish must have come to the throne shortly before the conclusion of the alliance; in fact his accession may be as closely dated as is possible through comparative chronology. In regnal year 5, Ramesses fought with Hatti at the battle of Qadesh; the Hittite king at that time must have been Muwatallish, though this is not certain for the name of Ramesses' Hittite opponent is never mentioned.[40] In his "Apology" Hattushilish states that Urkhi-Teshub, the son and successor of Muwatallish, reigned for seven years before he was deposed by Hattushilish;[41] therefore the earliest time by which Hattushilish could have achieved the Hittite throne would be regnal year 12.[42] This is the earliest possible; the actual date must have been some years later in order for the events mentioned in the "Apology" to have transpired between the battle of Qadesh and the accession of Urkhi-Teshub. The most likely year for the accession of Hattushilish is regnal year 17, as has recently been proposed by Rowton;[43] though this date is reached only through comparative chronology, it appears as accurate as possible by such methodology.[44]

Before proceeding to discuss possible synchronisms between Ramesses II and his eastern contemporaries, it must be pointed out that the Mesopotamian chronological systems contain three major factors which seriously affect their reliability at this period; each one could negate any attempt at a comparative chronology at the time of the Nineteenth Dynasty.[45]

A crucial factor is the length of the reign of Ninurta-apil-Ekur of Assyria, for it involves a 10-year differential.[46] The later king lists give three years as the length of his reign,[47] but the Nassouhi list, which is older, has 13.[48] Though the later Khorsabad and SDAS lists agree against the Nassouhi list, age alone is not enough to decide in favor of the Nassouhi date. A second problem is one of a lexicographical nature and concerns the *tuppšu*-reigns given in the king lists for two kings instead of listing the length of their reigns. Now Rowton has concluded that they have a chronological value of zero[49] but has been opposed in this by Landsberger.[50] If the *tuppšu*-reigns do not have a zero value, then they would represent an unknown length of time and invalidate the Assyrian king lists for any comparative chronological purposes.[51]

The third factor is the Babylonian interval between the Assyrian conquest of Babylon by Tukulti-Ninurta I and the accession of Adad-šuma-nazir.[52] In actual fact the key date for comparative purposes is the death of Kadashman-Turgu and the accession of Kadashman-Enlil II of Babylon;[53] the unknown factor of this interval would either raise or lower the date of his death. There are three reigns involved in this interval, with a total length of nine years; the question is whether these men ruled as governors of Assyria under Tukulti-Ninurta or whether they were independent rulers. If these men were merely Assyrian governors, then the lengths of their reigns given in the Babylonian king list would have to be included in the reign of Tukulti-Ninurta and simply considered as a zero factor chronologically. Rowton has concluded that these men were independent rulers, but his solution forces him to postulate some historical unknowns in order to explain why Assyria continued to claim the area of Babylonia and why Babylonian scribes considered the local rulers to be independent kings of that country.[54]

Though the number of years involved in two of the factors above are less than the 14-year differential between 1304 and 1290, they are both great enough to render the Mesopotamian systems useless for comparative purposes because there is no direct synchronism between a specific year of Ramesses' reign and a specific year of a contemporary ruler of either Assyria or Babylonia. And as mentioned, if the *tuppšu*-reigns indicate anything other than zero, it is only too evident that the Mesopotamian chronologies cannot help determine an Egyptian date.

Material from the Hittite archives at Boghazköy has been introduced as evidence for synchronisms between Ramesses and his Mesopotamian contemporaries. One of the most important is KBo I 10, a letter, or copy thereof, written by a ruler of Hatti to a ruler of Babylon.[55] A second letter, KBo I 14, was written by a Hittite to an Assyrian ruler.[56] In both instances neither sender nor recipient's name is extant, and though these may be postulated with varying degrees of certainty, it must be remembered that this fact, methodologically, places the synchronism in the realm of "probability" rather than established fact.

Letter KBo I 10 is from a Hittite king to a Babylonian ruler, and both have been identified with a measure of certainty. The sender was most likely Hattushilish III,[57] for he refers to Muwatallish as his brother (rev. 42), as he was; the very mention of Muwatallish gives a *terminus post quem* for the letter. The first ruler who followed him, his son Urkhi-Teshub, would not likely refer to Muwatallish as his "brother" nor would the successors of Hattushilish. Another indication that the sender is Hattushilish is the mention of Benteshina (rev. 26ff), who ruled Amurru during the reigns of Muwatallish and Hattushilish. The recipient is probably Kadashman-Enlil II, for Kadashman-Turgu is referred to as his father (obv. 55ff).[58]

In this letter the king of Hatti is attempting to establish diplomatic relations with Kadashman-Enlil of Babylon and recalls the good relations which he enjoyed with the present king's father, Kadashman-Turgu, whose death the Hittite king mourned and at which time he sent a message in support of Kadashman-Enlil, the Babylonian heir to the throne, and threatened to march into Babylonia with his army if the heir were opposed. Herein lies the Hittite king's complaint; apparently the new Babylonian ruler, Kadashman-Enlil, claims to have never seen such a letter, and so the Hittite ruler proceeds to accuse the vizier, Itti-Marduk-balatu, of having been anti-Hittite and of having concealed this letter from Kadashman-Enlil. After going on to discuss a few problems related to Assyria, the Hittite king then mentions the present political relationship with Egypt. He states that there once had been trouble between the two countries but an alliance had been formed and at the time when the letter was written there was only a minor disagreement between them. He declares that in the past the Babylonian and Hittite kings had a treaty and that during the major crisis between Hatti and Egypt, Kadashman-Turgu had even offered to lead troops to the aid of the king of Hatti.[59] The rest of the letter is concerned with the more mundane matters of business and is of no importance for the question of synchronisms.

Assuming that the two kings involved in this letter are Hattushilish III and Kadashman-Enlil II, a direct synchronism is established between Hatti and Babylon and thus, through Hatti, an indirect synchronism between Ramesses II and Kadashman-Enlil, for it is certain that the entire reign of Hattushilish was encompassed by the much longer reign of Ramesses II.[60] Only the date of this letter remains unknown; for it to be of any help in establishing the exact year of Ramesses' accession, it must be more specifically dated, because the variable would be greater than the 14-year difference.

Recent discussion centers upon two views: one, the letter belongs to the time prior to the alliance formed between Hatti and Egypt in regnal year 21, for it refers to trouble between the two countries which would not have existed after the alliance;[61] the other view suggests that the letter cannot be dated to the period prior to the alliance because historical facts mentioned in the letter show that it belongs to the time after the alliance.[62] Chronologically, the controversy revolves about Kadashman-Enlil and briefly stated simply means that if this letter is to be assigned to the period prior to the alliance of year 21, then the most reasonable date for Ramesses' accession would be 1290; however, if this letter belongs to the period after the formation of the alliance, then Ramesses' accession would be 1304.[63]

The basic point of disagreement is the interpretation of lines 55-74 on the obverse of the tablet; those who think it was written prior to the alliance, such as Tadmor, Edel and Helck,[64] see in this section a direct reference to hostilities between Egypt and Hatti and conclude that this could only refer to a time prior to year 21 when the alliance was formed. Rowton, who would date it after the alliance of year 21, contends that the above interpretation does not take into consideration all the historical references in KBo I 10, references which make it impossible to date this letter prior to the alliance since there would not be sufficient time for all the events to have transpired.[65]

Rowton maintains that there are two episodes mentioned in the letter which refer to difficulties between Hatti and Egypt; he also maintains that it is necessary to make this distinction between the two episodes in order to properly date the letter, though those who would date the letter prior to the alliance do not see this distinction. For Rowton there was a major crisis between Egypt and Hatti, referred to in lines 59-71, which occurred during the reign of Kadashman-Enlil's father, Kadashman-Turgu; this major crisis was finally solved by means of the alliance in regnal year 21. The second episode, lines 71-75, reflects only minor trouble between the two countries which had recently occurred during the reign of Kadashman-Enlil II, some time after the alliance had been concluded.[66] The fact that an alliance existed between Hatti and Egypt does not prohibit this interpretation according to Rowton, for minor difficulties were a constant in Near Eastern relations at that time;[67] further, he considers it quite likely that Urkhi-Teshub could have been the source of this difficulty between Hatti and Egypt, though this is only an inference and is not germane to his basic argument.[68]

Rowton does not rely upon this interpretation in order to date KBo I 10 but insists that the historical references within the letter demand the later dating.[69] He concludes that one must allow enough time for the period between the accession of Hattushilish and the date of KBo I 10 to include

a) a treaty of alliance between Hattushilish and Kadashman-Turgu,

b) the period between the formation of this treaty and the outbreak of warfare between Egypt and Hatti,

c) the time between this crisis and the death of Kadashman-Turgu,

d) the time between the outbreak of this crisis and the conclusion of the treaty with Egypt (there would be an overlap of unknown duration between c and d), and

e) a certain amount of time from the death of Kadashman-Turgu and the accession of Kadashman-Enlil until the writing of KBo I 10, during which time Kadashman-Enlil grew from childhood to adolescence;

and also if this letter were written before the alliance of year 21, then the period from Hattushilish's accession to the date of the alliance must not only include all the above but also the extra time element from the writing of the letter KBo I 10 to the conclusion of the alliance.[70]

Now Hattushilish's accession has been dated to years 16 or 17 of Ramesses II, for as mentioned earlier, enough time must be allowed for the historical material in the "Apology" to have transpired between Qadesh of year 5 and the accession of Urkhi-Teshub, who reigned 7 years. Therefore the date for Hattushilish's accession must include regnal year 5 plus X plus 7, and since X equals 4, or more likely 5, years, then his accession would correspond to Ramesses' regnal year 17.[71] Thus approximately 4 years are allowed for the historical material in this letter if it is to be dated prior to the alliance of regnal year 21. Of the allowances listed above, as propounded by Rowton, parts a, b and c do not of themselves demand a large amount of time, though they quite possibly could have encompassed many years. Part d, which partially overlaps part c, could represent any length of time as could that period between the writing of the letter and the conclusion of the alliance in year 21, if the letter pre-dates the Egypto-Hittite alliance. The parts listed above do not demand a period longer than 4 years, even though they could have taken place over a much longer time.

Rowton's main reason for dating this letter after the alliance is the statement that Kadashman-Enlil was a child at his accession to the throne and the vizier, Itti-Marduk-balatu, held sway over the young king. However, when this letter was written, Hattushilish refers to Kadashman-Enlil as a young man who now goes out hunting and no longer listens to the old vizier. Rowton concludes that 5 to 10 years must be allowed for this part (e) to have transpired in order for Kadashman-Enlil to grow from childhood into adolescence; therefore KBo I 10 could not have been written prior to Ramesses' 21st year but must belong to some time thereafter.[72]

If Rowton's interpretation of this letter be correct, then it must be dated after the formation of the alliance between Hatti and Egypt, but this later date for the letter becomes less probable when his interpretation of lines 34-35 and 71-75 are closely examined.[73] In this section the Hittite king refers to Kadashman-Enlil as having been a child and under the evil influence of Itti-Marduk-balatu, who was anti-Hittite. However, at the moment when the Hittite king is writing this letter, a time when the wicked vizier is apparently no longer able to influence the Babylonian king, he refers to Kadashman-Enlil as having become a man who goes out hunting (rev. 49).

Unfortunately for chronological purposes, this part may be understood as a diplomatic way of contrasting two views held by Kadashman-Enlil towards Hatti at different times; it need not necessarily refer simply to physical growth on the part of the Babylonian king. The Hittite king graciously gives reasons, perhaps a bit sarcastically, for the two views, but does not bluntly state that there had been a change of mind. The great thrust of this letter is to emphasize the good relations which existed between Babylon and Hatti during the reign of Kadashman-Turgu but were disrupted at his death;[74] whether physical immaturity on the part of Kadashman-Enlil was truly the reason for this disruption is impossible to say definitely.[75] Therefore the major evidence for placing this letter after the alliance in year 21 is not as sound as it would seem, and the letter is of questionable help in determining the accession date of Ramesses II.[76]

The second letter is KBo I 14, and though neither sender nor receiver are named in that which remains, it has been postulated that this is a letter from Hattushilish III to Adad-nerari I of Assyria.[77] The recipient must have been a king of Assyria because

a) the letter was written between kings of equal rank, and the only possibilities at that general period were the rulers of Hanigalbat, Assyria, Babylon and Egypt,[78]

b) but the recipient was not the king of Hanigalbat nor of Babylon for they are both referred to in the third person in the letter,[79]

c) nor was the recipient the king of Egypt, for it is unlikely that he would have been able to intervene between Hatti and Hanigalbat in order to settle difficulties occurring on their mutual border.[80]

Therefore it is not unreasonable to assume that the receiver of KBo I 14 was a king of Assyria.

The contents of KBo I 14 limit the number of possible Hittite rulers who could have written the letter and Hattushilish III has been proposed because

a) Urkhi-Teshub is referred to as having ruled Hatti, leaving only four Hittite kings between that reign and the final demise of the Hittite kingdom;[81] and

b) the last three Hittite kings are very unlikely candidates, for the country of Hanigalbat is mentioned in the letter and it has been demonstrated that Hanigalbat was no longer in existence in the reign of Tudhaliash IV, successor of Hattushilish III.[82]

Therefore, the only Hittite king who could have written this letter is Hattushilish III.

The point of contention centers upon the Assyrian king who received this letter; the possibilities are either Adad-nerari I or his son Shalmanezer I.[83] Now an established synchronism between Urkhi-Teshub and Shalmanezer I exists in a small fragment KUB XXVI 70 from the Boghazköy archives.[84] In this fragment a Hittite king refers to a letter which Urkhi-Teshub wrote to Shalmanezer, the father of Tukulti-Ninurta. The question is, did Urkhi-Teshub write this letter while he was king or during the time of his exile?[85] Rowton concludes that the letter most likely belongs to the time of his exile and therefore cannot be used to produce an indirect synchronism between Ramesses and Shalmanezer prior to regnal year 21.[86] Parker, however, has pointed out that it is unlikely that this letter would date to that period after the treaty had been concluded, for Urkhi-Teshub would not wish to offend his host and endanger the alliance by writing to Assyria; he therefore decides that KUB XXVI 70 can still be used to establish a synchronism between Ramesses and Shalmanezer.[87]

One key to the understanding and eventual dating of KBo I 14 lies in the reference to presents having been sent by the Hittite king's father to the Assyrian ruler upon his accession (lines 5ff). The Assyrian ruler must have been on the throne prior to the reign of Urkhi-Teshub, because the "father" or "brother" of Hattushilish could only be Murshilish or Muwatallish. This indicates that the Assyrian king had been ruling for 7 years at the very minimum prior to the writing of KBo I 14.[88] In itself, this does not determine which Assyrian ruler is being addressed, only that it must be one whose reign would span this period.

Since the question is still open as to the possible recipient of KBo I 14, other information must be utilized, especially the reference to Hanigalbath (lines 71-75). In this section it can be seen that the King of Hanigalbat is able to intervene on behalf of a border city; therefore this letter could only have been written at a time when there was a king in Hanigalbat and this sets a *terminus ante quem* for the letter. We know from the records of Adad-nerari I that he campaigned against Hanigalbat and defeated its king, Shattuara, who was not deposed but became an Assyrian vassal and paid tribute "annually, as long as he lived."[89] Later in the reign of

Adad-nerari, Washashatta, the son and successor of Shattuara, rebelled against Assyria; this time Adad-nerari defeated the king of Hanigalbat and incorporated the country into Assyria proper.[90] Consequently KBo I 14 should date to that time prior to the incorporation of Hanigalbat into Assyria, for after that there was no independent king in Hanigalbat for any length of time.[91]

Rowton concludes that the only Assyrian king who could have received this letter was Adad-nerari I and not Shalmanezer as Hornung states.[92] The point is, if it is Shalmanezer, then the 1290 date for the accession of Ramesses II is the only feasible one; but if it is Adad-nerari, the only date is 1304.[93] Rowton assumes that a number of years must have elapsed between the accession of Adad-nerari I and the defeat of Shattuara, who then for many years, at least 5-10, paid tribute faithfully to Assyria. Sometime in the second half of the reign of Adad-nerari, Washashatta rebelled and was defeated, at which time there was no longer a king of Hanigalbat; this sets the *terminus ante quem* for KBo I 14. Rowton states that there are two independent proofs that this letter was not written to Shalmanezer I; the first involves the reference of presents having been sent to the Assyrian king by the Hittite king's father, which means that the Assyrian king must have been on the throne for some 7 to 10 years prior to the accession of Hattushilish. According to Rowton, such a date is not permissible for Shalmanezer by Assyrian chronology; second, the situation with regard to Hanigalbat would not fit into the reign of Shalmanezer I.[94]

The interpretation proposed by Rowton raises serious questions. Outside of the fact that the correct identification of the sender is not an established fact, the section referring to "gifts" having been sent to the Assyrian king is not well preserved and requires restorations in order to complete the text;[95] here Rowton's better argument is built upon questionable restorations and interpretations. His second argument, concerning Hanigalbat, carries less weight, for we do know that this country was independent during a part of the reign of Shalmanezer I,[96] though the length of its independence is difficult to ascertain. His major proof that it remained an Assyrian vassal is an *ex silentio* argument.[97] It has even been stated by Kitchen that Hanigalbat exerted its independence later than the reign of Shalmanezer;[98] therefore it is not necessary to assign this letter to the reign of Adad-nerari just because there is a mention of a king of Hanigalbat. Rowton has introduced KBo I 14 into the discussion in order to disprove the synchronism between Ramesses II and Shalmanezer I proposed by Hornung[99] and supported by Parker, but he has not met with success; no reliable synchronism exists between Ramesses II and any Assyrian king.[100]

The difficulties involved in establishing and dating synchronisms between Mesopotamia and Egypt during the Nineteenth Dynasty negate any attempt to control the Egyptian material by either Assyrian or Babylonian chronology. Not only is the internal Mesopotamian chronology unsure because of the three basic problems discussed above[101]--namely, the reading of 3 or 13 years for Ninurta-apil-Ekur, the question of the *tuppšu*-reigns, and the Babylonian interval at the time of Tukulti-Ninurta--but the proposed synchronisms in these two letters from Baghazköy are not valid for comparative chronology.

In spite of the attempt to control Egyptian chronology by means of the Mesopotamian dating systems, the results show that both the Egyptian and Mesopotamian sources contain unknown time factors, which make them equally fallible. Beyond the basic question of reliability, the difficulty of establishing dated synchronisms limits the probability of control even more; hence Mesopotamian chronology cannot determine the accession date of Ramesses II.

Consequently, one must rely upon Egyptian material to set the accession of Ramesses. Assuming the date 1490 for the accession of Tuthmosis III,[102] disregarding, chronologically, the possible coregencies of Amenophis III and Amenophis IV and of Amenophis IV and Semenkhkare,[103] granting Horemhab a reign of 25-30 years as indicated by the inscription of Mes,[104] allowing Seti I a reign of approximately eleven years as indicated by the dated monuments,[105] then the more probable date for the accession of Ramesses II is 1290.[106]

NOTES TO CHAPTER I

THE ESTABLISHMENT OF AN ABSOLUTE CHRONOLOGY

Note: The abbreviations employed throughout the footnotes are the ones used in Janssen, Annual Egyptological Bibliography. In addition to these accepted abbreviations, a shortened form of an author's work may be given if the work occurs frequently; full titles of articles and works abbreviated because of frequency can be found under the author's name in the bibliography.

1 The most recent comprehensive work on Egyptian chronology is by E. Hornung, Untersuchungen zur Chronologie und Geschichte des Neuen Reiches, 1964, which updates and corrects Ludwig Borchardt's study, Die Mittel zur zeitlichen Festlegung von Punkten der aegyptischen Geschichte und ihre Anwendung, 1935. A select bibliography of works which deal with various parts of the Egyptian chronological system follows.

Edgerton, Critical Note on the Chronology of the Early Eighteenth Dynasty (Amenhotep I to Thutmose III), AJSL 53 (1936), 188-197.

Gardiner, The Coronation of King Haremhab, JEA 39 (1953), 13-31.

________, Regnal Years and Civil Calendar in Pharaonic Egypt, JEA 31 (1945), 11-28.

Ginzel, Handbuch der mathematischen und technischen Chronologie, Band 1.

Hayes-Rowton-Stubbings, Chronology, CAH^2 I vi.

Helck, Bemerkungen zu den Thronbesteigungsdaten im Neuen Reich, Analecta Biblica 12 (1959), 113-129.

________, Untersuchungen zu Manetho und den aegyptischen Koenigslisten = Untersuchungen zur Geschichte und Altertumskunde Aegyptens, Band 18.

Kitchen, On the Chronology and History of the New Kingdom, CdE 40 (1965), 310-322.

________, Further Notes on New Kingdom Chronology and History, CdE 43 (1968), 313-324.

________, Suppiluliuma and the Amarna Pharaohs.

van der Meer, The Chronology of Ancient Western Asia and Egypt.

Meyer, Aegyptische Chronologie.

Neugebauer, O., Die Bedeutungslosigkeit der 'Sothisperiode' fuer die aelteste aegyptische Chronologie, Acta Orientalia 17 (1939), 169-195.

________, The Chronology of the Hammurabi Age, JAOS 61 (1941), 58-61.

Neugebauer, P. V., Hilfstafeln zur technischen Chronologie.

Parker, The Calendars of Ancient Egypt.

_______, Sothic Dates and Calendar "Adjustment," Revue d'égyptologie 9 (1952), 101-108.

Schott, Altaegyptische Festdaten.

Sethe, Die Zeitrechnung der alten Aegypter im Verhaeltnis zur der andern Voelker.

2 The more recent studies are by Kitchen, CdE 40 (1965), 310-322; Rowton, JNES 25 (1966), 240-258; Redford, History and Chronology, 183-215, with a review by Kitchen, CdE 43 (1968), 313-324; and Parker, Revue d'égyptologie, 19 (1967), 185-189.
Considering Kitchen's remarks in CdE 43 (1968), 313 and 322, one treads cautiously into the discussion of an absolute chronology, but it will probably always be true that we need "new material rather than endless debate...for an eventual solution."
For this study, an absolute date for the accession of Ramesses II is not that important but synchronisms with foreign rulers are, and since such synchronisms are involved in the discussion of the accession of Ramesses II, the material will be reviewed here once again.

3 Parker, JNES 16 (1957), 42-43.

4 Hornung, *op. cit.*, 4-13, with references. Also see Read, JNES 29 (1970), 1-11, a recent study of dubious value which questions the entire chronological situation of the Eighteenth Dynasty.

5 Ebers, Papyros Ebers, plate preceding Tafel I, labeled "Rueckseite der Tafel I des Papyros Ebers." First recognized as a Sothic date by Brugsch, ZAeS 8 (1870), 108-111, and correctly dated to Amenophis I by Krall, Rec. Trav. 6 (1885), 57-63. Discussed most recently by Hornung, *op. cit.*, 12-23.

6 Regnal year 23, in the Karnak Annals, Urk. IV 657, 2 (Porter-Moss II 37 [75]), reading with Faulkner "day 20" instead of "day 21," JEA 28 (1942), 11 (hh). Regnal year 24, Karnak Stela, Urk. IV 836, 1-2 (Porter-Moss II 35).

7 Papyrus Leiden I 350, first published by Leemans, Monumens égyptiens du Musée d'antiquités des Pays-Bas à Leide, Pls. CLXIV-CLXVII, and most recently by Janssen, Two Ancient Egyptian Ship's Logs, 1-52, Pls. I-II. Hornung's proposal, ZDMG 117 (1967) 11-16, based upon Helck, Materialien, 629, of a lunar date for the 19th year of Amenophis II has been refuted by von Beckerath, ZDMG 118 (1968), 18-21, and Parker, in Studies in Honor of John A. Wilson, 75-82.

8 For example, Parker's method in JNES 16 (1957), 39-43. Rowton in JNES 25 (1966), 258, can say: "The present article was finished on 9 May 1966. On that day the balance of probability unmistakably favoured the higher chronology with Egypt." With less authority, his article in JCS 13 (1959), 10, with note 42.

9 The *tetraeteris* or Egyptian year of only 365 days falls behind the Julian one day every four years. For a comparison between Egyptian and Julian calendars, see Ginzel, Chronologie II, 576-585 (Tafel V); and Hornung, *op. cit.*, 17.
For a lucid discussion of dates in ancient history, see Bickerman, Chronology of the Ancient World, especially chapter I.

10 Edgerton, AJSL 53 (1936), 195. The *arcus visionis*, the visibility or invisibility of Sothis at its rising, Hornung, *op. cit.*, 19-20. This unknown is further complicated by the beginning and end of the Sothic period, *ibid.*, 17-19.

11 Hornung, *op. cit.*, 15-20.

12 Hornung, *op. cit.*, 20-21, with references.

13 Kitchen, CdE 40 (1965), 311; Hornung, *loc. cit.*

14 Hornung, *op. cit.*, 22.

15 Kitchen, CdE 40 (1965), 311; Hornung, *op. cit.*, 21-23. The 20-year variable is due to the unknown site of observation, while the 8-year variable results from the astronomical complexities involved in the different calendars.

16 Parker, JNES 16 (1957), 29-42; Hornung, *op. cit.*, 56-62.

17 Kitchen, CdE 40 (1965), 317-18; cf. Hornung, *loc. cit.*

18 Janssen, *op. cit.*, 33, *vs.* iii 6.

19 Parker, JNES 16 (1957), 43.

20 With regard to the two possible sites of observation for the Sothic date in the reign of Amenophis, there are two dates for the accession of Ramesses; the "high" date allows 1335/1296 and the "low" date, 1316/1276. If the "high" (Memphis-Heliopolis) date is correct, 1279 would then be impossible; it would be barely possible on the "low" (Theban) date. Hornung, *op. cit.*, 50 (and table at back of the book); Kitchen, CdE 40 (1965), 317.

21 Borchardt, *op. cit.*, 119; von Beckerath, 5000 Jahre aegyptische Kunst, 34f; Gardiner, Egypt of the Pharaohs, 443; Hayes, Scepter of Egypt, vol. 2, xv; Helck, Beziehungen, 99; Hornung, *op. cit.*, 108; Parker, JNES 16 (1957), 42; Rowton, CAH^2, Chronological Table; Wilson, The Burden of Egypt, viii.

22 Views concerning the coregency of Amenophis III and IV are still divided; for a thorough discussion to that date, see Fairman, in The City of Akhenaten III, 152-160, who upholds the coregency, but is opposed by Helck, MIO 2 (1954), 189-207. Others supporting the coregency are Aldred, JEA 43 (1957), 114-117, and 45 (1959), 19-23, JNES 18 (1959), 113-120; Fairman, JEA 46 (1960), 80-82 and 108-109; and Kitchen, Suppiluliuma and the Amarna Pharaohs, 7-8. But in CdE 43 (1968), 320, Kitchen states that the coregency has neither been disproved nor established. Those who deny the coregency are Campbell, The Chronology of the Amarna Letters, 6-30 and 136-137 (with reviews by Helck, OLZ 60 [1965], 559-563; and Kitchen, JEA 53 [1967], 178-182); Gardiner, JEA 43 (1957), 13, and Egypt of the Pharaohs, 213; Redford, History and Chronology, 88-169, and JEA 45 (1959), 34-37; Hornung, *op. cit.*, 76, allows only a few months coregency.

23 Gardiner, JEA 14 (1928), 10-11, and Newberry, JEA 14 (1928), 3-9. See also Campbell, *op. cit.*, 137-138; Kitchen, *op. cit.*, 8-9; and Hornung, *op. cit.*, 86-90. The question of a coregency between Tuthmosis III and Amenophis II is normally accepted but involves only a year or two, Hornung, *op. cit.*, 34; more thoroughly, Redford, JEA 51 (1965), 107-122, especially page 115

with note 4, and History and Chronology, 170-182; also von Beckerath, ZDMG 118 (1968), 18-21; most recently, Parker, in Studies in Honor of John A. Wilson, 75-82.

[24] Meyer, Aegyptische Chronologie, 90; von Beckerath, Tanis und Theben, 104; Sauneron, CdE 26 (1951), 46-49; Wilson, JNES 13 (1954), 126-129; Redford, JEA 45 (1959), 34-37, and History and Chronology, 183-208; Kitchen, *op. cit.*, 9-10; Hornung, *op. cit.*, 93-94; most recently, Harris, JEA 54 (1968), 95-99.

[25] Year 11, Gebel Barkal Stela, Reisner-Reisner, ZAeS 69 (1933), 73-78; cf. Waddell, Manetho, 100-153. Redford, History and Chronology, 208-215.

[26] Kitchen, CdE 40 (1965), 312-314; Hornung, *op. cit.*, 38-41, and ZDMG 117 (1967), 13; Harris, JEA 54 (1968), 99.

[27] As discussed below in chapter V, there is the possibility of co-regency between Seti I and Ramesses II of a little more than three years; this would raise the variable here.

[28] Kitchen, CdE 40 (1965), 314; Hornung, Chronologie, 22-23.

[29] Kitchen, *op. cit.*, 313-314.

[30] I Kings, 14:25; II Chronicles 12:2.

[31] Thiele, The Mysterious Numbers of the Hebrew Kings, 39-52, followed by Hornung, *op. cit.*, 24-29; for a different date, see Albright, BASOR 100 (1945) 20, note 14.

[32] Kitchen, *op. cit.*, 311-312; Hornung, *op. cit.*, 28-29.

[33] Kitchen, *loc. cit.*, proposes 945; Hornung, *op. cit.*, 29, suggests 948/941; while Uphill, JNES 26 (1967), 61, more recently has 940/939.

[34] For the succession at the end of the Nineteenth Dynasty, see Emery, Mélanges Maspero I 1, 353-356, and Helck, ZDMG 105 (1955), 39-52.

It is not clear what the highest regnal year for Merneptah is. An ostracon from the Valley of the Kings is dated to years 7 and 8, Daressy, ASAE 27 (1927), 167-168; and year 8 is recorded on the *verso* of Papyrus Bologna 1094. (Gardiner, LEM 12 and Caminos, LEM 34.) There is the possibility that Papyrus Sallier I is dated to his 10th regnal year, Caminos, LEM 303, but this is far from certain. Helck, Materialien, 590, refers to an 11th year but gives no reference for such. A much less likely year 12 has been thought his, Spiegelberg, Zwei Beitraege zur Geschichte der thebanischen Nekropolis; cf. Meyer, Nachtraege zur aegyptischen Chronologie, 39-40. Manetho accords him 20; Struve, ZAeS 63 (1928), 49-50, and Waddell, Manetho, 149-153.

[35] Hornung, *op. cit.*, 95-107, with a more recent study by Wente, JNES 26 (1967), 155-176.

[36] Hornung, *op. cit.*, 24-29, with references.

[37] Otten, MDOG 83 (1951), 47-71; Goetze, JCS 11 (1957), 53-61 and CAH^2 II, xvii, xxi(a) and xxiv, with references.

[38] Mueller, MVAG 7 (1902), no. 5; an English translation of both Akkadian and Egyptian versions by Langdon and Gardiner, JEA 6

(1920), 179-205.

[39] There is also a correlation between Ramesses and Hattushilish in regnal year 34, when Ramesses married a daughter of the Hittite king, but the historical significance of this date is less likely to be reflected in the correspondence between Hattushilish and Mesopotamian rulers.

[40] The cartouche containing the name of the Egyptian ruler with whom Muwatallish fought is destroyed, Alliance line 8. In the Qadesh inscriptions, the Hittite opponent is not specifically named; cf. Kuentz, MIFAO 55. There is a supposed reference to Qadesh in the "Apology" of Hattushilish, MVAG 29/3 (1924), ii 69ff, but Qadesh is not specifically mentioned.

[41] MVAG 29/3 (1924), iii 63.

[42] It should be noted at this point, whenever the phrase "regnal year X" or simply "year X" occurs with no specific ruler, it always refers to the reign of Ramesses II.

[43] For the latest chronological treatment of the "Apology" ii 74 - iii 44 (MVAG 29/3 [1924] and 34/2 [1930]), see Rowton, JNES 25 (1966), 244-249. He earlier proposed regnal year 16, JCS 13 (1954), 7 (note 32) and 9, and JEA 34 (1948), 68 (note 5), but changed to regnal year 17 in JNES 19 (1960), 18 and 22, and kept this date in his most recent work, JNES 25 (1966), 245.

[44] JNES 25 (1966), 245: "...If we date the accession of Ḫattušiliš III five years before the Treaty, that is in Year 17 of Ramesses II, we have a date which in terms of relative chronology is certain to be nearly correct and may very well be quite correct."

[45] For a slightly different approach but with much the same results, see Redford, History and Chronology, 185-195.

[46] As pointed out by Rowton, JNES 25 (1966), 241, where he says, "The question upon which the whole problem of the comparative chronology between Western Asia and Egypt depends is whether the correct figure for Ninurta-apil-Ekur is 13, as quoted in the oldest Assyrian king-list, or whether it is 3, as given in the two younger lists." Also see p. 254.

[47] Gelb, JNES 13 (1954), 209-230 (no. 82).

[48] Nassouhi, AfO 4 (1927), 1-11; Weidner, AfO 4 (1927), 11-17 (rev. i 40).

[49] JNES 18 (1959), 213-221.

[50] JNES 8 (1949), 248-297.

[51] Rowton, JNES 18 (1959), 213: "If on the other hand Landsberger is right, then Mesopotamian chronology prior to the seventh century has but little bearing on Egyptian chronology, and no attempt at close comparative chronology is justified."

[52] Rowton, JNES 19 (1960), 18-21.

[53] *Ibid.*, 15.

[54] *Ibid.*, 18-20. Also see J. M. Munn-Rankin, CAH^2 II, xxv 17-18.

[55] H. H. Figulla and E. F. Weidner, Keilschrifttexte aus Boghazköy, Wissenschaftliche Veroeffentlichung der deutschen Orient-Gesellschaft, vol. 30, no. 10.
First translated in part by Winckler, MDOG 35 (1907), 22-24, and then by Weidner, MDOG 58 (1917), 74-76; at the same time by Meissner, OLZ 20 (1917), 225-228, and ZDMG 72 (1918), 45-46 and 60-61; with an English translation by Luckenbill, AJSL 37 (1920-21), 200-205. The latest translation and commentary on part of the text is by Edel, JCS 12 (1958), 130-133, with a reply by Rowton, JNES 25 (1966), 243-249.

[56] Figulla and Weidner, *op. cit.*, no. 14. Translations by Meissner, ZDMG 72 (1918), 44-45 and 61; Luckenbill, AJSL 37 (1920-21), 205-207; Goetze, Kizzuwatna 27-31; Rowton, JCS 13 (1959), 6, and JNES 25 (1966), 249-252.

[57] Already proposed by Winckler, MDOG 35 (1907), 22.

[58] Also first proposed by Winckler, MDOG 35 (1907), 21, but incorrectly attributed to Kadashman-Turgu by Luckenbill, AJSL 37 (1920-21), 205.

[59] Obverse, lines 57-81.

[60] Goetze, CAH^2 II xxiv 48-49; and Hayes-Rowton-Stubbings, CAH^2 I vi 46.

[61] Most recently, Tadmor, JNES 17 (1958), 139-141; Edel, JCS 12 (1958), 130-133; Helck, Beziehungen, 231; Hornung, *op. cit.*, 60, with note 32.

[62] Rowton's recent affirmation, JNES 25 (1966), 243-249.

[63] Hornung, *op. cit.*, 60; Rowton, *op. cit.*, 243-249.

[64] See above, note 61.

[65] Rowton, JNES 25 (1966), 246-247.

[66] *Ibid.*, 243-249.

[67] *Ibid.*, 247.

[68] *Ibid.*, 249, note 41, and 250, note 42.

[69] JNES 19 (1960), 16-18, and 25 (1966), 247.

[70] JNES 19 (1960), 16 and 18.

[71] See above, note 43.

[72] JNES 19 (1960), 18, and 25 (1966), 246.

[73] Specifically, JNES 25 (1966), 246-247, and JNES 19 (1960), 16-17.

[74] Rowton, JNES 19 (1960), 17, and 25 (1966), 246.

[75] Lines 34-35 speak of the past and of the control the vizier once had over the Babylonian king "in those days." See also note 28 above.

[76] Also see Redford, History and Chronology, 195-199.

[77] Goetze, Kizzuwatna, 31-33; Rowton JCS 13 (1959), 3-5.

[78] Rev. 6-7; Rowton, JCS 13 (1959), 10 (note 43).

[79] Hanigalbat, obv. 8; Babylon, rev. 2.

[80] Obv. 6-13; Goetze, *op. cit.*, 32-33; Rowton, JCS 13 (1959), 3 (note 13).

[81] Goetze, *op. cit.*, 31-33; Rowton, JNES 25 (1966), 250-251.

[82] Otten, MDOG 94 (1964), 6, but also see note 98 below.

[83] Rowton, JCS 13 (1959), 5, and JNES 25 (1966), 249, proposes Adad-nerari.
Hornung, *op. cit.*, 50-51, with note 4, proposes Shalmanezer.

[84] Otten, in AfO Supp. 12 (1959), 67-68.

[85] Otten, *op. cit.*, 68, assumes that it was written while Urkhi-Teshub was king and is followed in this by Hornung, *loc. cit.* This view is opposed by Rowton, JNES 25 (1966), 249-250.

[86] Rowton, *loc. cit.*, has posited some reasons why KUB XXVI 70 could have been written while Urkhi-Teshub was in exile. However, his one reason (p. 250) why the letter was not found in Boghazköy is unsound, for we know that the Hittite kings sometimes moved their capitals; thus simply because the letter was not found in the archives this does not prove that Urkhi-Teshub was in exile when he wrote it.

[87] Revue d'égyptologie 19 (1967), 187-188, where he shows that if the accepted date of Shalmanezer is correct, then this synchronism between Ramesses II and Shalmanezer prior to regnal year 21 supports 1290 as the accession date.

[88] See above, note 43. The shortest interval possible between the reigns of Muwatallish and Hattushilish is 7 years, the length of Urkhi-Teshub's reign. Rowton, JNES 25 (1966), 251, wishes to allow a more reasonable 10-year minimum.

[89] Weidner, AfO 5 (1928-29), 91 (*vs.* 4-17).

[90] *Ibid.* (*vs.* 18-23), with AfO 6 (1929-30), 21-22.

[91] Rowton, JNES 25 (1966), 251 (with note 47), a view opposed by Kitchen, CdE 40 (1965), 316-317. Cf. J. M. Munn-Rankin, CAH^2 II, xxv 8.

[92] Rowton, *op. cit.*, 251-252; Hornung, *op. cit.*, 60.

[93] Kitchen, CdE 40 (1965), 316; Rowton, JCS 13 (1959), 8-9. See note 87 above.

[94] Rowton, JNES 25 (1966), 251-252; Weidner AfO 6 (1929-30), 21-22.

[95] Goetze, Kizzuwatna, 28-29 and 31-32; Rowton, JNES 25 (1966), 251.

[96] Weidner, AfO 5 (1928-29), 95-96; Rowton, JCS 13 (1959), 1-2; J. M. Munn-Rankin, CAH^2 II, xxv, 9-10.

[97] Rowton, *op. cit.*, 2.

[98] Kitchen, CdE 40 (1965), 317.

[99] *Op. cit.*, 50-52; and defended by Parker, in Revue d'égyptologie 19 (1967), 187-188.

[100] Thus also, Redford, History and Chronology, 199-208.

[101] See notes 46-54.

[102] See notes 16 and 21.

[103] See notes 22 and 23.

[104] See notes 24 and 26.

[105] See note 28 and also chap. V.

[106] Agreeing with Kitchen, CdE 43 (1968), 322, that "The ultimate result is that it is still impossible to decide as between 1304 and 1290 for the accession of Ramesses II." However, in this study 1290 will be the assumed date of his accession and the "lower" chronology will be employed whenever such dates are necessary.

CHAPTER II

EXAMINATION OF THE DATED INSCRIPTIONS

A chronological structure for the reign of Ramesses II should be based upon those inscriptions which bear regnal dates. But since a distinction must be made between those records which are definitely dated to his reign, be they royal or private, and those which might belong to his time, the method followed here is to distinguish between the two. In the first section, those royal and private records which date to his reign will be discussed to determine their reliability. In the second section, those questionable texts which have been attributed to Ramesses II for various reasons will be examined. An analysis and interpretation of this material will subsequently follow in the next chapters.

Section 1. Inscriptions with Ascertained Dates

Year 1

1-A. Abydos, Seti I Temple, Dedicatory Inscription

The great dedicatory inscription at Abydos[1] refers to regnal year 1 four times, but in each instance the date is retrospective. In line 22 it occurs in the phrase "...according to regnal year 1, on his first voyage to Thebes...," where the compound *ḫft rnpt* simply dates the voyage to the general time of year 1.[2] Line 26 is the only instance of an exact date within the entire inscription, "Once upon a time, it happened in regnal year 1, 3rd month of *3ḫt* day 23...."[3] This date is also mentioned in the tomb of *Nb-wnn.f*, though he only gives the year and month without mentioning the specific day.[4] In line 49, Ramesses says, "I fashioned my father anew in gold, in the first year of my appearing."[5] And in line 72, the last reference to year 1, "Behold he began to fashion his statue in year 1...," appears to refer to the same activity as in line 49.[6] In all four instances the reference to a regnal year is retrospective, and it is certain that this inscription was not composed nor inscribed in Ramesses' first year.[7] On the contrary, he makes it quite clear that he is reporting this in a later time by the manner in which he refers to the regnal year. Therefore this inscription, though it refers to year 1, must be assigned to a subsequent part of Ramesses' reign.

1-B. Gebel Silsileh, Rock Shrine Stela, "Hymn to the Nile"

At Gebel Silsileh there are three royal shrines with Nineteenth Dynasty stelae in them belonging to Seti I, Ramesses II and Merneptah. The depictions on the shrine of Ramesses II show him and Queen Nefertari performing religious functions before sundry deities.[8] As this shrine contains a stela dated to regnal year 1, it indicates that Queen Nefertari lived during the early years of Ramesses' reign.[9] This hymn to the Nile was reproduced in two later texts: one belonging to the first regnal year of Merneptah is located in his royal shrine next to that of Ramesses II at Gebel Silsileh;[10] the second is on a stela of Ramesses III located near these two shrines and records his 6th regnal year.[11] These texts of Merneptah and Ramesses III are almost exact duplicates of the earlier stela of Ramesses II.[12] The stela is dated to "Regnal year 1, 3rd month of *šmw* day 10," and extolls the bountiful fruits of the Nile through its inundation.

1-C. Giza, Sphinx Stela Fragment

A damaged fragment discovered by Caviglia near the Great Sphinx[13] consists of a "broken slab 40 inches long, with five lines of hieroglyphs dated in the first year of Ramesses II."[14] It is now in the British Museum (no. 440) and until recently had not been published since Sharpe's Second Series in 1853-55.[15] The date is well preserved, though only the regnal year is given without month or day, and is followed by the full five-fold titulary. Such a general method of dating indicates that no one specific event was being recorded and the remains of the stela bear out this assumption for the remnant is primarily composed of epithets and set-phrases describing the military ability of the king.

1-D. Abu Simbel, Door Thickness

Between the "Great Hall" and the "Second Hall" (Rooms E and F, respectively, of Lepsius) the thickness on the south (left) side contains a year date supposed to be that of Ramesses II.[16] There are five lines on this wall, but only the first few words of each are preserved; it is difficult to relate one line to the other, and thus one is reduced to treating each as an autonomous entity. This date is located in an unexpected place, for it is not likely that this part of the temple belongs to that period.[17] Furthermore, the date is not stated in the usual manner as being "under the Majesty of..." but reads, 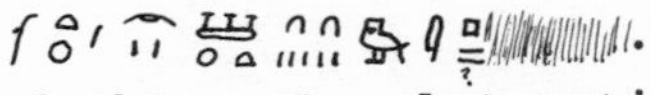. This is either a retrospective date placed there at a later time in his reign, or it was engraved by one of his successors.[18] As already noted above, such retrospective dating did occur during Ramesses' reign. As such this is little more than an isolated date which might represent the first regnal year of Ramesses II but could have been inscribed by one of his successors.

1-E. Theban Tomb 157, *Nb-wnn.f*

The appointment text of *Nb-wnn.f* as High Priest of Amun in Thebes was first published by Champollion and then by Lepsius; it was not further studied until Sethe's article in 1907 and since that time has received little attention except for some photographs.[19] Though the construction of the tomb of *Nb-wnn.f* certainly postdates regnal year 1, the composition of the text containing his appointment indicates that the original was composed in that first year; later this copy of the official pronouncement was included in the tomb. The date is abbreviated to year and month only (regnal year 1, 3rd month of *3ḫt*) but need not be questioned, for the date is not the day of his appointment but of the sailing of his Majesty downstream. The royal activity mentioned here in line 1, *m-ḫt ḫd ḥm.f m nỉwt rsyt* ("Afterwards his Majesty sailed downstream from the southern city"), is paralleled by the Abydos Dedicatory Inscription lines 28-29, *ỉỉ ḥm.f m nỉwt rsyt... dỉt ḥr m ḫd* ("His Majesty came from the southern city...sailing downstream"), though the Abydos text does not mention the appointment.[20]

1-F. Theban Graffito, No. 298

A graffito from the Theban necropolis records "Regnal year 1, 2nd month of *šmw* day 16 (of) King *Wsr-M3't-R' Stp-n-R' l.p.h.*"[21] This is followed by four names of scribes. Since these men do not seem to have come from the workmen's village of Deir el-Medineh, they might have been on a special mission to the necropolis.[22]

1-G. Luxor, Triple Shrine

An inscription assigned to year 1 of Ramesses II is on the outer side of the eastern wall of a shrine at Luxor.[23] This date might belong to Ramesses II, though it would be his earliest building inscription.[24]

Year 2

2-A. Aswan Stela

This stela located upon the eastern side of the ancient roadway leading south from Aswan was recorded by Lepsius and de Rougé,[25] but since that time no collation has been published.[26] Both these men date the inscription to regnal year 2 and write the form  but the date is suspect. This inscription suddenly portrays the king as mighty warrior and military defender of Egypt in a way much different from the Giza fragment of year 1. The king is presented as having overcome all the enemies of Egypt, both of the north and the south; this stela is situated near the border of Nubia, but it does not refer to a specific Nubian campaign, even though *T3-sty* is mentioned toward the end (line 10). The contents of the stela would better fit regnal year 10 from what we know of royal military activity at that time rather than year 2. There is only a slight difference between the writing of a "2" and a "10" and the position of the numeral in the inscription encourages one to read year 10 (∩) rather than 2 (||).[27] Therefore this stela should be assigned to regnal year 10, instead of the accepted year 2.

2-B. Sinai, Serabit el-Khadim, No. 252

The stela of *ʿŠ3-m-ḥbw-sd* and *Ỉmn-m-ỉpt*, both commanders of bowmen, was erected in the temple of Hathor at the Serabit el-Khadim.[28] These men were active at Sinai during the reign of Ramesses II; *ʿŠ3-m-ḥbw-sd* is also known from inscriptions 247, 250, 252, 253 and 260, while *Ỉmn-m-Ỉpt* is mentioned in nos. 260, 261 and 262.[29] This particular inscription, which begins with "Regnal year 2, live the Horus," consists primarily of the royal titulary but contains several phrases not found elsewhere.[30] *ʿŠ3-m-ḥbw-sd* also served in Sinai under Seti I, for he was, at least partially, responsible for the erection of the huge stela dated to Seti's 8th regnal year.[31] *Ỉmn-m-Ỉpt* also left an inscription on a side of that same stela, where he recorded his title as "Commander of bowmen of the Well-of-*Rʿ-ms.sw Mry-Ỉmn*."[32] One may therefore safely assume that their presence at Sinai occurred during the early part of Ramesses' reign and that the other stelae bearing his royal cartouches, nos. 253, 260 and 261, belong to that general period.[33] Though only one stela of Ramesses II at Sinai contains a regnal date, others may be dated approximately to the same period by means of the personal names recorded upon them.[34]

2-C. Nahr el-Kelb, South Stela

Though this stela is now in poor condition and the year date obscured,[35] Lepsius first read it as "year 2," but later admitted the possibility that it could be "year 10," "wenn die beiden Striche oben verbunden waren."[36] The loss of such a small curve on a stela as badly damaged as this can be easily understood. Fortunately, the stela can be dated to regnal year 10 with reasonable certainty. The Qadesh campaign of year 5 was Ramesses' second military campaign into Asia;[37] and since we know that he was also in Asia in the preceding year (the Middle Stela on the Nahr el-Kelb is dated to year 4), the South Stela cannot date to regnal year 2 but must belong to his 10th year.

2-D. Sai Island

A badly destroyed granite stela was found in a fortress on Sai Island with the regnal date "year 2."[38] Though "it was probably a record of Ramesses II"[39] there is no way to confirm this, and therefore it cannot be placed among those records which definitely belong to his reign.

2-E. Theban Graffito, No. 225

A second graffito was left by *Ỉmn-nḫt* in the Theban necropolis recording, "Regnal year 2, 1st month of *šmw* day 10."[40] In contrast to his simpler title of year 1, that of "scribe," he now states that he is a "royal scribe."

Year 3

3-A. Quban Stela

Discovered in 1843 by Prisse d'Avennes within the ruins of the fortress of Quban, this stela was transported from Egypt to Grenoble by Louis de Saint-Ferriol and set up in his château d'Uriage-les-Bains but was later transferred to the museum in Grenoble where it now rests.[41] The stela is broken and exists in two parts; the upper being the larger and more complete, is in very good condition, but the bottom is only represented by a large fragment, and consequently the latter third of the text is difficult to translate and to interpret. The stela is dated to "Regnal year 3, first month of *prt* day 4, under the Majesty of the Horus...," at which time Ramesses was holding court in Memphis. The object of royal concern was the gold mines in Nubia, particularly in the Wadi Allaki.[42] After a report by the Viceroy of Kush, the king recommended special measures in order to find water for the mining caravans. The latter part of the stela is a progress report by the Viceroy of Kush, in which he speaks of success--water was found. As such the stela dates a specific Nubian activity of Ramesses II to his 3rd regnal year.[43]

3-B. Luxor Pylon, East Wall

This appears to be the dedicatory inscription of the Luxor Pylon.[44] The date in the text reads: "Work was brought to an end (*'rḳ*) in regnal year 3, 4th month of *3ḫt*, day (?)." The inscription is similar to the Heliopolis stela (8-C and 9-D),[45] for it gives a report of the activities of the workmen, their performance and finally the day when the construction was brought to an end. Like the Abydos inscription, this date refers to a past activity in the reign of Ramesses II (*'rḳ k3t m rnpt 3...*)[46] and does not necessarily represent the time when the text was inscribed; however, there appears to be no reason to question the date of the activity recorded.[47]

Year 4

4-A. Nahr el-Kelb, Middle Stela

This stela is badly mutilated like its near neighbor, the South Stela discussed under year 2, but at least the year date is still legible and can be read with certainty as "Regnal year 4, 3rd month of *3ḫt* day 2(?)."[48] The rest of the stela is almost totally lost except for two lines on the right and left margins which give some broken epithets of the king along with his nomen and prenomen. Though most of the inscription is lost, enough is preserved to definitely date it to the reign of Ramesses II. This stela was probably executed during his first campaign into Asia.[49] Its existence upon the Nahr el-Kelb demonstrates the presence of Egyptians upon Asiatic soil during Ramesses' 4th year, though we know nothing of the activity which, presumably, it once reported.

4-B. Lachish, Hieratic Bowl Inscription

A bowl discovered during the excavations of Tell ed-Duweir in Palestine has a regnal date of year 4 written upon it in hieratic.[50] No king is mentioned, but it may be dated to the Ramesside period, or even more likely to the Nineteenth Dynasty, on paleographic grounds.[51] It has been suggested that the year belongs to Merneptah, but it could also refer to Ramesses since a carnelian scarab with the name of Ramesses II was found in the same deposit.[52] Even though this bowl may be assigned to Ramesses, the uncertainty involved makes it unreliable as a source for a chronology of his reign.

Year 5

5-A. The Qadesh Inscriptions

The inscriptions recording the battle of Qadesh have been collected by Kuentz in "La bataille de Qadech,"[53] and the most recent translation and commentary is by Gardiner.[54] Of the three major divisions of the inscriptions, the Poem, the Bulletin (Report) and the Captions,[55] only the Bulletin contains the regnal date of year 5. The Bulletin is found at seven sites in Egypt and Nubia: (1) at Abydos, on the walls of the temple of Ramesses II, where the year date is now lost;[56] (2) at the Ramesseum, on the inner face of the first pylon, where the date is preserved;[57] (3) also at the Ramesseum on the north wall of the second court, on its inner face, where the date is extant;[58] (4) at Luxor on the outer face of the first pylon, where the date is preserved;[59] (5) also at Luxor, on the exterior (west) side of the forecourt, where the date is destroyed;[60] (6) again at Luxor, the exterior (south) side of the forecourt, where the date is partially preserved;[61] (7) and finally at Abu Simbel, on the north wall of the Great Hall, where the date still exists.[62] The Poem, which does not bear a regnal date, is sometimes found in conjunction with the Bulletin and the Captions, or it may occur independently. It is found in association with the Bulletin at Abydos,[63] Luxor,[64] and Karnak (Temple of Amun, the outer, south wall of the Hypostyle Hall[65] and also on the exterior (west) wall of the court between the ninth and tenth pylons[66]). It stands independent of the Bulletin on the second pylon of the Ramesseum, where it accompanies some scenes of the battle.[67] Two other copies of the Poem exist: one is Papyrus Sallier III (to which Papyrus Raifé belongs), a copy made by the scribe *P3-n-t3-wrt* in the 9th year of Ramesses II;[68] the other is Papyrus Chester Beatty III.[69] This campaign is described as Ramesses' second one (B 3) and is securely dated to his 5th regnal year.[70]

5-B. Cairo Ostracon 25671

Ostracon 25671, which was discovered by the Carnarvon-Carter excavation in the Valley of the Kings in 1917-18,[71] is atypical for it contains notations both in hieroglyphs and hieratic. Two lines written in different styles but containing the same information comprise the hieroglyphic part, "Made for the scribe *R'-ms* of the domain of *Mn-ḫprw-R'-ḫ'w-Ḏḥwty-šrī-R'* (Tuthmosis IV)."[72] Beneath in hieratic script is a statement, "He repeated it for the scribe in the Place of Truth[73] in regnal year 5, 3rd month of *3ḫt* day 10, (of) King *Wsr-M3't-R' Stp-n-R'*, life, prosperity, health, son of Re,

R'-ms.sw Mry...." What appears to have been a practice piece has furnished a reference to a specific regnal year of Ramesses II; it also indicates that this temple of Tuthmosis IV, to which the scribe *R'-ms* belonged, was still in existence.

5-C. Thebes, Graffito of *R'-ms*

A graffito from the Valley of the Queens at Thebes may be assigned to the reign of Ramesses II even though only the prenomen is given.[74] The scribe in the Place of Truth, *R'-ms*, who executed the record in "Regnal year 5, 2nd month of *3ḫt* day 20," is probably the same person mentioned in the preceding inscription of year 5. Though this name was common at that time, *R'-ms* is quite likely the owner of Theban tombs 7, 212 and 250[75] and the person represented on the stela dedicated to the goddess Hathor, belonging to regnal year 9 of Ramesses II.[76] In each instance the person, *R'-ms*, has the title of *sš m St-M3't*, which limits the number of possible candidates from Deir el-Medineh.[77]

5-D. Louvre Leather Manuscript

A leather roll in the Louvre contains the date "regnal year 5, first (month) of *šmw* day 2" which would appear to belong to Ramesses II.[78] The text primarily consists of names with accompanying lists of bricks, to which dates are sometimes added in the usual accounting procedure. Since the regnal date is not compounded with the royal name, which occurs in the phrase *p3 iḥw pr '3 n R'-ms.sw Mry-Imn*, one cannot be certain that it refers to the reign of Ramesses II; however, internal evidence, such as the names listed, would indicate that it should be assigned to him.

Year 7

7-A. Aniba, Stela Fragment

Discovered during the excavations of Aniba under the direction of George Steindorff,[79] this sandstone fragment has a very short text which reads, "Regnal year 7, 3rd month of *prt* day 9, under the Majesty of King[80] *Wsr...R'....*" Since only a part of the prenomen is preserved one cannot be certain that the name is that of Ramesses II, though Steindorff attributed the inscription to him.[81] Other inscriptions of his were found at Aniba,[82] and these would indicate that this too might be his; certainty, however, cannot be established on such grounds and this date may be considered no more than a probability.

Year 8

8-A. Ramesseum, First Pylon, Asiatic Campaign

The only preserved records of the year 8 campaign are found upon schematic drawings of fortresses captured in that year and recorded upon the first pylon of the Ramesseum.[83] Each city captured is represented by a fortress, upon which is a vertical label. Most have "The town which his Majesty captured in regnal year 8...," to which the city and its location is appended. Out of fifteen towns now extant, with inscriptions, at least seven and possibly eight are recorded as having been taken in this campaign of year 8, four others have no date and the rest have fragmentary texts. There is no indication which number this campaign was; it might have been the third, since Qadesh was the second, but there might have been another between year 5 and that of year 8, as indicated by the North Stela at the Nahr el-Kelb which is now so mutilated as to be completely illegible.[84] The brief superscription on the pylon adds very little to our knowledge of events and reads in part, "[Who sets] his boundary where he wills, without his arm being repulsed, who puts an end to the unruly rebels so that every land comes in peace [to his Majesty]." It is sometimes assumed that all these cities recorded upon the pylon, whether specifically dated to the campaign of year 8 or not, belong to that year. Though this is our only direct reference to any military activity in regnal year 8, it is sufficient to show that Ramesses was again active in Asia sometime during his 8th year.

8-B. Turin Papyrus

The workman papyrus in Turin, Pleyte-Rossi Pl. XXIX,[85] is dated to "Regnal year 8, 4th month of *šmw* day 25" of a king with a prenomen "*Wsr-(M3't?)-*[*R'*] *Stp-n-R'*." The hieratic is not carefully written. The anticipated sign for *R'* in the prenomen does not appear, while the sign following *Wsr* looks more like the phonetic compliment  than the  sign; the  for might best be explained as a mistake on the scribe's part and was probably meant to stand for *M3't*. The *Stp-n-R'* is well written and presents no difficulties. The name can therefore be reasonably read as "*Wsr-M3't-*[*R'*] *Stp-n-R'*," and the papyrus should belong to the 8th regnal year of Ramesses II.

8-C. Heliopolis Stela

This stela was found in 1907 at Manshîyet-eṣ-Ṣadr, just to the south of Heliopolis and is now in the Cairo Museum, no. 34504.[86]

The content of the stela is of particular interest, for though it first refers to the king's discovery of a suitable piece of stone for a statue near Heliopolis, the content quickly moves to statements concerning working conditions and supplies (lines 8ff). A large part of the stela records assurances by Ramesses II to his craftsmen, not only about supplies of food and clothing, which would equal their pay, but also raw materials for their craft (cf. lines 18ff). The calendrical references upon this stela span parts of two regnal years, though they refer to a period of 363 days. The newly discovered stone was given to the stonemasons and sculptors in year 8, 3rd month of *šmw* day 21, and then in the 9th year, 3rd month of *šmw* day 18, the statue was completed. Though there was some doubt concerning the date when the stone was given to the artisans--Kamal read year 7--Hamada is correct in reading year 8, for the strokes are positioned above each other and thus must be an equal number; besides it would be difficult to give the stone to the workmen before it had been discovered. Even though the stela is dated to regnal year 8, it also furnishes a reference to the 9th year of Ramesses II.

Year 9

9-A. Papyrus Sallier III, Colophon

The short notation at the end of Papyrus Sallier III states that this copy was made in "Regnal year 9, 2nd month of *šmw*" of Ramesses II.[87] The papyrus, sometimes referred to as the "Poem of Pentawer," contains a description of the battle of Qadesh. Since it was once thought that this was written in poetic form, it was called a "poem" and the scribe who made this specific copy was considered the author.[88] This view has been abandoned; the scribe is recognized as that person who made the copy which now exists in two manuscripts (Papyrus Raifé and Sallier III) which were originally one.[89] The composition is no longer thought to be in poetic form either, and hence the word "poem" is a misnomer, though often retained for convenience.[90] The papyrus was divided in modern times; Papyrus Raifé is by far the smaller and consists of eleven lines, while the larger and more complete is Papyrus Sallier III, now in the British Museum.[91] The colophon at the end of Sallier III demonstrates that this "literary" (epic) composition was in existence a few years after the actual battle of Qadesh.

9-B. Deir el-Medineh, Hathor Stela

This stela, discovered by Bruyère in the temple at Deir el-

Medineh in 1939, records the stipulated offerings for a specific part of the cult of Hathor in the temple at that site.[92] The rather crude stela is dated to the 9th year of the reign of Ramesses II (regnal year 9, 3rd month of *3ḫt* day 8?) and was executed under the authority of the scribe in the Place of Truth,[93] *Rˁms*, who has been mentioned in connection with a graffito in the Valley of the Queens and the Cairo Ostracon 25671, both of regnal year 5.[94]

9-C. Beisan Stela

The stela of Ramesses II found at Tell el-Hosn (ancient Beth Shan) was originally dated to year 9 by Rowe[95] but more recently has been assigned to year 18 by Černý,[96] under which date it is discussed below.

9-D. Heliopolis Stela

The stela from Heliopolis referring to both regnal years 8 and 9 has been discussed under year 8-C.

9-E. Cairo Papyrus 86637, "Cairo Calendar"

This papyrus of "lucky and unlucky days"[97] has "regnal year 9, 4th month of *3ḫt* day 9" on the *verso* (XIII 9) and also records the nomen and prenomen of Ramesses II on the same side (*vs.* XIX 1) in a colophon. The papyrus is a collection of works, separated into different sections. It begins on the *recto* with two columns written upon a sheet which has been added, anciently, to the roll (Part I). The main text (Part II) then begins and continues on the *verso*. When the scribe reached the end of the *recto*, he turned the roll over and began writing upon the *verso*, back towards the "beginning" of the scroll. Thus Part II takes up most of the *recto* and about two-thirds of the *verso*. The third section (Part III) is written in the remaining third of the *verso*, though it does not cover all of the available space. This Part III is written "upside down" with respect to the other texts on the papyrus. It also begins towards the front of the roll, just after the place where the added sheet (Part I) joins the papyrus. It is, therefore, written towards the end of Part II; there is, however, considerable empty space between the ends of these two texts. The date given above is recorded in Part II on the *verso* while the royal name is in Part III, and, as can be seen, these two texts have no direct relationship. Within Part III there is a difference between the colophon, containing the name, and the other text written upon this part. Most of Part III is a palimpsest (*vs.* XXI-XXIV),[98] and it seems quite likely that the colophon was a part of the original and for some reason was not destroyed when the rest of the text was prepared for the new copy.[99] There are further problems regarding the date. It is written at the end of the "extra" (13th) month in Part II and probably does not represent the time when the text was copied but rather a date in the original which was included in this copy. Further, if this month were to be used when an extra month was intercalcated into the Egyptian year,[100] then it might represent a time when such an event occurred and thus its relationship to the royal name of Ramesses II (in Part III) would be even more tenuous. Thus we cannot be certain that the regnal date is that of Ramesses II.

Year 10

10-A. Nahr el-Kelb, South Stela

The South Stela has been mentioned under year 2, where it was concluded that it must be assigned to year 10 rather than the earlier date. Today the stela is in such bad condition that it is impossible to check the date.[101]

There is one more stela of Ramesses II on the Nahr el-Kelb, referred to as the North Stela, which is now obliterated. This stela was reinscribed by the French to commemorate their occupation of the country in 1860-61.[102]

10-B. Aswan Stela

Discussed under 2-A, this stela was assigned to year 10, instead of the accepted year 2.

Year 13

13-A. Serapeum, Apis Stela, Louvre 3

Brugsch, in his Thesaurus, 964, gives regnal year 13 as the earliest date on this stela;[103] for the full discussion, see below under year 16.[104]

Year 14

14-A. Abydos, Stela of *P3-sr*

The stela of *P3-sr*, now in the Cairo Museum (JdE) no.43649,[105] records the settlement of a property dispute by means of an oracular response and contains a reference to "Regnal year 14" of Ramesses II.[106] The stela is not a well-executed piece but reminds one of work from a later period.[107] We have dated records of lawsuits from the reign of Ramesses II,[108] but this is the first report of a dispute having been settled by divine intervention and as such is unique for his reign. An oracle is thought to have been responsible for the appointment of the High Priest *Nb-wnn.f* in year 1 of Ramesses II,[109] but the use of oracles in legal matters is more characteristic of the end of the New Kingdom and Late Period rather than the Nineteenth Dynasty.[110] Because this would be the only certain example of such from the reign of Ramesses II, the stela is not above suspicion; there are also other indications that this might have been executed at a time later than that of the Nineteenth Dynasty. For example, the main text is introduced by *hrw pn*, "this day," but it is written in a form not attested at this time.[111] The names of some of the people who witnessed the oracle are also more typical of a period later than the Nineteenth Dynasty.[112] Taking into consideration that, outside of this example, oracles of this nature are first found in the Twentieth Dynasty and become popular in the Late Period,[113] and combining this with the orthography employed and the atypical names, it is highly unlikely that this stela was executed in the reign of Ramesses II. Hence this stela cannot be considered contemporaneous with the regnal date it records. Because of these problems it is difficult to ascertain whether or not the date truly represents one of Ramesses' regnal years, but for chronological purposes this stela should be held in abeyance and not be included among those which definitely belong to his reign.[114]

Year 15

15-A. Papyrus Cairo 65739

In an article titled "A Lawsuit Arising from the Purchase of Two Slaves,"[115] Gardiner published Papyrus Cairo 65739, which has a reference to a regnal year 15 of an unnamed king. The papyrus records litigation between *Iryt-nfrt* and *N3hy*, in which *Iryt-nfrt* states that in "Regnal year 15, (that is) seven years after I had entered the house of the district supervisor *S3-mwt*," she purchased a Syrian girl from the merchant *R'-ỉ3*.[116] Because the year is mentioned in the testimony of *Iryt-nfrt*, it is not the date of the lawsuit; Gardiner wished to assign the papyrus to the reign of Ramesses II: "As regards date, the probabilities point to the beginning or middle of the reign of Ramesses II."[117] Since the reference is retrospective and there is no mention of a royal name, this regnal date cannot be considered sound enough for inclusion within a chronological framework for the reign of Ramesses II. Even if one might assume that the papyrus belongs to his reign, the date is not contemporary with the actual lawsuit.[118]

Year 16

16-A. Serapeum, Apis Stela, Louvre 3

The Louvre stela of *Py-ỉ3y* and *Ḏḥwty-ms* (called *R'-ms*) belongs to regnal year 30 though it mentions two earlier dates in the apex above the text.[119] Brugsch gave these dates as 13 and 23,[120] while Mariette recorded them as 16 and 26.[121] Year 26 refers to the burial of a *Mn-wr* bull,[122] while the other, year 16, refers to an Apis burial.[123] As mentioned above, the number 16 was given as 13 by Brugsch but is to be correctly read as 16.[124] The date recorded in the body of the text is "regnal year 30," which is the actual date of the stela; the references to two earlier burials, made in the stela's lunette, are therefore commemorative.

Year 17

17-A. Theban Tomb 311, Deir el-Bahri, Graffito

During the Metropolitan Museum's fourth season of excavations at Deir el-Bahri, a notation containing the name of a High Priest of Amun, *Nb-nṯrw*, was discovered in the Eleventh Dynasty tomb of *Ḫty*.[125] Originally the inscription was probably written upon the wall of the tomb, but it is now on a fragment of limestone, for the tomb was badly damaged in later times by people quarrying for good stone.[126] Unlike most visitor's inscriptions, which are in hieratic, this one is written in hieroglyphs by a well-trained hand and reads, "Regnal year 17 of the King *Wsr-M3't-R'*...the High Priest of Amun, *Nb-nṯrw*, justified...(?) for the father [of his father?], *Ḫty*...."[127] Winlock assigned the inscription to the reign of Ramesses II[128] and was followed by Kees, who places *Nb-nṯrw* between *Nb-wnn.f* and *B3k-n-Ḫnsw* as High Priest of Amun, though this is his only evidence for the existence of such a High Priest at that time.[129] The script is difficult, if not impossible, to date on paleographic grounds, as it is written in hieroglyphs instead of hieratic; however, there is no reason why it need be assigned to the reign of Ramesses II. The last half of the prenomen is lost and therefore any king whose name began with *Wsr-M3't-R'* is a possible candidate. Since the name *Wsr-M3't-R'* was a popular beginning of a prenomen from the Nineteenth through the Twenty-second Dynasty,[130] this inscription could belong to a number of kings. The Twenty-second Dynasty itself would be a more likely date for this *Nb-nṯrw* because that is the time of the influential family of *Nb-nṯrw's* who held numerous high positions at Thebes. So far there is only evidence for a *Nb-nṯrw* as Third Prophet of Amun,[131] but this graffito could represent that person's highest achievement. Also, the interest which the Twenty-second Dynasty took in the Deir el-Bahri area might be reflected by this text.[132] Since he would better fit this later period, there is no reason to postulate the existence of an otherwise unknown *Nb-nṯrw* as High Priest of Amun in the reign of Ramesses II.

Year 18

18-A. Deir el-Medineh, Ostracon No. 77

This ostracon, containing a very brief notation, has been attributed by Černý to Ramesses II.[133] The text consists of the date and one entry: "Regnal year 18, 4th month of *šmw* day 8(?), 200 *r(w)'*-fish." Since the paleography is Ramesside, the only kings to whom this could refer are Ramesses II and III, for no other king reigned this long at that time. Because of the similarity between this ostracon and No. 72,[134] which is attributed to Ramesses III, it should be assigned to that latter king rather than Ramesses II.[135]

18-B. Saqqara, The Inscription of Mes

The litigation between *Nb-nfrt* and *Ḫ'y*, as recorded in the tomb of *Ms* at Saqqara, contains two references to regnal years of Ramesses.[136] The first is partially destroyed, but the second is in good condition and is written 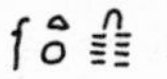 .[137] This writing of the units as if they were hieratic notations of the days of the month rather than the year is unusual but occurs elsewhere.[138] The two regnal dates of Ramesses are in a section which mentions past litigation; they are not the date of the legal proceedings which this text records.[139] This same text also refers to action taken in the reign of Horemhab's 58th or 59th regnal year (S8).[140] In spite of the questions raised concerning the Horemhab date, there seems to be no reason to doubt those attributed to Ramesses II, even with their unusual writing; it should be noted, however, that this, too, like Papyrus Cairo 65739 (15-A), is a retrospective date which is not contemporary with the lawsuit recorded.[141]

18-C. Beisan Stela

During the excavations conducted by the University of Pennsylvania at the site of biblical Beth-Shan (Arabic, Beisan, Tell el-Hosn), a large basalt stela belonging to the reign of Ramesses II was discovered; this stela is now in the Pennsylvania University Museum, Philadelphia, no. 29.107.958.[142] The accepted date of the stela had been "Regnal year 9" until Černý's study in Eretz Israel, in which he read it as year 18.[143] Though broken into two parts, the stela is nearly complete and little of the text is lost. However, it is made of Palestinian basalt, which can be very porous, and the area where the year date was carved is pitted with numerous small holes. In spite of this difficulty a reasonable reading may be given for the regnal year. If it were meant to be "year 9," then the formation of the strokes ⁞⁞⁞⁞ would be unusual; even the reading "year 18" creates some problems. The 10 (∩) is very close to the ☉ of *rnpt*[144] and is written beneath a unit stroke; for either reading, 9 or 18, the farthest stroke to the left is squeezed in close to its nearest neighbor. Aside from the porous stone, this "tight" writing is the major difficulty one must overcome in order to ascertain the correct reading. Upon examination of the original, "Regnal year 18" appeared to be correct, and therefore this stela should be assigned to that time in the reign of Ramesses II.[145]

Year 19

19-A. Deir el-Medineh, Ostracon No. 31

Not only does this ostracon have a regnal date; it also retains part of a royal prenomen, "*Wsr...R'....*"[146] A number of kings of the Ramesside period began their prenomens with "*Wsr...R'...*," but the high regnal year eliminates all but Ramesses II and Ramesses III. Identification is complicated in that apparently "*Wsr...R'...*" is all that was originally written; it seems the scribe reached the end of the stone and did not complete the name. Černý has ascribed this piece to Ramesses II, though the paleography would suit either the reign of Ramesses II or that of Ramesses III. Relying upon Černý's dating, this ostracon may be tentatively assigned to Ramesses II, but not with certainty.

Year 20

20-A. Giza, Chephren Fragment

This inscription has been dated to regnal year 20 by Hoelscher; however, since the year is uncertain it has been placed with those inscriptions with questionable dates which are discussed together at the end of this chapter in section 2.

Year 21

21-A. Thebes, The Hittite Alliance

The record of the Alliance between Ramesses II and Hattushilish III is preserved in two places; the more complete text is at the Temple of Amun in Karnak on the exterior (west) wall of the traverse section between the Hypostyle Hall and the Seventh Pylon.[147] This Karnak text is located among scenes of battle and the storming of Askalon. The second text, merely a fragment, is on the outer face of the Second Pylon at the Ramesseum, and what remains is almost an exact duplicate of the Karnak one.[148] The date mentioned in the introduction to the Alliance represents the day when the envoy from Hatti arrived at *Pr-R'-ms.sw Mry-Imn*, presumably with a copy of the text; the Alliance itself contains no specific date. Since the document is important for the chronology of this period, it will be examined later in chapter IV.

Year 23

23-A. The Bentresh Stela, Louvre C 284

Louvre C 284 is a stela of the Late Period presuming to report an activity which occurred during the reign of Ramesses II, and contains references to the three regnal years: 23, 26 and 33.[149] None of these dates may be considered accurate references to regnal years of Ramesses II, for even though the tale might be based upon historical fact, one cannot be certain that the dates are trustworthy. This stela and its dates, therefore, may not be used to establish a chronological structure for Ramesses' reign.

23-B. Serapeum, Apis Stela, Louvre 3

Brugsch, in his Thesaurus, 964, gives regnal year 23 for the second date on this stela;[150] the correct reading is year 26, under which it is discussed.[151]

Year 26

26-A. Heliopolis, Mnevis Tomb, Stela

In regnal year 26 Ramesses II erected a stela before the tomb of a Mnevis bull located just south of Heliopolis; the text begins, "Regnal year 26, live the Horus: *K3-nḫt Mry-M3't....*"[152] Only the regnal year is given and it seems that this does not refer to the actual burial of this bull but to the completion or restoration of the tomb, for the east wall still retains the nomen and prenomen of Horemhab.[153] The stela itself speaks only of Ramesses making this tomb as a monument for his father out of fine stone from the Tura quarries; it does not mention the burial itself, as do two stelae of year 30 which record an Apis burial.[154] Hence it appears that in year 26 Ramesses restored a *Mn-wr* tomb begun in the reign of one of his predecessors, Horemhab.

26-B. Deir el-Medineh, Ostracon No. 250

"Regnal year 26, 3rd month of *3ḫt* day 9, under the Majesty of King *Wsr-M3't-R' Stp-n-R'*, day of receiving the things for the necropolis...."[155] As the entire prenomen is given, this ostracon belongs to the time of Ramesses II; in the fragmented list there is no mention of any scribe or workman, only the enumeration of goods supplied to the necropolis crew.[156]

26-C. Theban Ostracon

Inscribed on the "Upper portion of a cream-coloured oil-jar" from Thebes are the following words, "Regnal year 26, *nḥḥ*-oil of the garden (*k3mw*) [of] King *Wsr-M3't-R' Stp-n-R'*, may he live(?) [for-ever]."[157] This notation must have once indicated the contents of the jar, but the actual date remains uncertain, for the royal name of Ramesses forms a compound with "garden" to indicate a location and is not a true royal date.[158] Therefore this inscription cannot be assigned to the reign of Ramesses II with certainty.

26-D. Serapeum, Apis Burial "No. III"

Mariette's dating of "Apis III" to regnal year 26 of Ramesses II[159] is incorrect; the date on Louvre Stela 3 distinctly refers to a *Mn-wr* burial,[160] the tomb of which has since been discovered by Daressy just south of Heliopolis.[161] As indicated above (16-A), Mariette's dates for "Apis II & III" can no longer be maintained, nor can one assign those officials, whose shabtis were found with these burials, to the early part of Ramesses' reign.[162]

26-E. Bentresh Stela

This stela has been discussed under year 23-A. It contains references to three regnal years of Ramesses II: 23, 26 and 33, but the text was written in a much later time.

Year 27

27-A. Medinet Habu, Ay and Horemhab Temple, Graffito

A statue fragment discovered in the mortuary temple of Ay and Horemhab has a short inscription written upon it in black ink, "Regnal year 27, 1st month of *šmw* day 9, the day when Horemhab, l.p.h., beloved of Amun, who hates his enemies and loves...entered..."[163] This controversial piece has played an important role in the chronology of the Eighteenth Dynasty, since some assign the date to Horemhab[164] while others consider it Ramesside, particularly Ramesses II.[165] Those who attribute it to Horemhab assume that this records a visit by the king to his mortuary temple; those who consider it Ramesside say it must refer to the mortuary temple of Horemhab.[166]

If this inscription does not belong to Horemhab, then it can only be dated to Ramesses II or III because of the high regnal year. The style of writing would fit the Ramesside period quite well, but this alone cannot date it to that time. The controversy centers upon two words at the end of the first line, which have been read either *ỉr n* or *pr n*.[167] If the line is to be read, *hrw n 'ḳ pr n Ḥr-m-ḥb*, then it could be translated, "the day of entering the domain of Horemhab" and could refer to the entry of the statue into the mortuary temple or be a notation left by some visitor.[168] However, if it is to be read, as Anthes does, *hrw n 'ḳ ỉr n Ḥr-m-ḥb*, "The day of entry which Horemhab made," then it must refer to an activity of Horemhab himself and consequently the graffito would belong to his reign. The first facsimile printed encourages the reading of *pr n*;[169] the second, however, looks much different and appears to read *ỉr n*.[170] Those who wish to assign this to the Ramesside period take the earlier reading and see it as another visitor's inscription, possibly written in the time of Ramesses II.[171] However, for our purposes here, the specific date of this graffito is too dubious to be used in a chronological structure for the reign of Ramesses II.

Year 30

30-A. Bigeh Inscription, First *Ḥb-Sd*

Prince *Ḫ'-m-W3st* recorded three of Ramesses' Jubilees in this short inscription at Bigeh; the *Ḥb-Sd*'s represented are years 30, 34 and 36, that is, his first three.[172] The text accompanying the dates along with the nomen and prenomen of Ramesses II reads, "His Majesty directed the *Sm*-priest and Prince, *Ḫ'-m-W3st* [to] announce the Jubilee throughout the entire land."[173] From this one may conclude that *Ḫ'-m-W3st* was active in all three Jubilees and not just the third, when this inscription was carved. Since the latest date is regnal year 36, it must represent the actual time when the record was made; though the two earlier dates are retrospective, one need not question their authenticity.[174]

30-B. Gebel Silsileh, Great Speos Stela (Duplicates)

Among the many inscriptions of Ramesses II at Gebel Silsileh are a number which record his Jubilees; of the six in the Gallery of the Great Speos which mention his *Ḥb-Sd*'s, only three list his first *Ḥb-Sd*-festival.[175] Two are almost exact duplicate texts, while the other is a later inscription which mentions Ramesses' sixth *Ḥb-Sd*.[176] The duplicates under discussion here record the Jubilees of Regnal years 30, 34, 37 and 40 and were carved under the authority of

Prince *Ḫ'-m-W3st*. In the upper part of the first stela, Ramesses II, followed by *Ḫ'-m-W3st*, is offering an image of Ma'at to Ptah and Amun-Re, while in the duplicate the king offers the same to Ptah and Sobek.[177] This text indicates that *Ḫ'-m-W3st* was involved not only in the first three, but also in the fourth Jubilee and that he was still living in regnal year 40. Since the last date is year 40, this represents the time when the inscription was carved.[178]

30-C. Gebel Silsileh, Great Speos, Vizier *Ḫ'y*

In this stela Ramesses II offers an image of Ma'at to a number of deities, Amun-Re, Re-Herakhty, Ma'at, Ptah-tenen and Sobek, while the Vizier *Ḫ'y* kneels below.[179] The inscription records Ramesses' first four Jubilees of years 30, 34, 37 and 40 and has a short reference to the Vizier, "His Majesty ordered...the Vizier *Ḫ'y* be appointed to announce the...Jubilee [in the] entire [land], throughout Upper and Lower Egypt." This text uses almost the same words to describe the Vizier's activities with regard to the Jubilee as the inscription of Prince *Ḫ'-m-W3st* in this same chamber at Silsileh.[180] Like the stela of *Ḫ'-m-W3st*, this too dates from regnal year 40 and shows that *Ḫ'y* may have been active in the earlier Jubilees but in what capacity we do not know. Though this inscription refers to him as Vizier, we cannot be certain that he was Vizier in regnal year 30, since it is only natural that his latest and highest titles would be used when the inscription was engraved.[181] This text then reflects the circumstances and conditions of Ramesses' regnal year 40.

30-D. Gebel Silsileh, Great Speos, Niche in Facade

Prince *Ḫ'-m-W3st*, in the regalia of a *Sm*-priest of Memphis, stands next to another record of Ramesses' first Jubilee.[182] The text records only the first *Ḥb-Sd* and reads, "Regnal year 30, the occasion of the first *Ḥb-Sd* of the Lord of the Two Lands, *Wsr-M3't-R' Stp-n-R'*...to announce the *Ḥb-Sd* in the entire land. The *Sm*-priest and Prince, *Ḫ'-m-W3st*." This inscription assures us that *Ḫ'-m-W3st* did participate in the first royal Jubilee as his other records suggest, even though they were completed at least a decade after that first occasion.[183] The same phraseology is found here as in the other inscriptions, and it would appear that he held the same position at each successive Jubilee as he did during the first.

30-E. Ostracon Gardiner 28

Though no definite regnal year is stated upon this ostracon, it can be assigned to Ramesses' 30th year because of the reference to his "first *Ḥb-Sd*."[184] The text records the wonders which occurred at the time of Ramesses' first Jubilee; it begins by referring to the great inundation of that year and continues by extolling the foodstuffs and drink which were thus available. The gods were festive and Egypt was pleased in his reign, no one was ashamed of any excess (*tḫt*); the land came (back) to its proper place after the Ennead had reassembled Upper Egypt. The king's treasuries were full of all good things; his granaries reached heaven and food supplies were as plentiful as sand. After Amun had done this for the king, all the gods and goddesses were pleased with the king's bounty; not only people but deities spent the entire day lauding the king's goodness. Though this "literary" composition may not date exactly to year 30, it was probably composed not long thereafter. It was quite likely written before year 34, when his second Jubilee was celebrated, for after that time one would expect a reference to Jubilees in general rather than the specific first one. Even though this piece naturally extolls the wonders of the king's first Jubilee with certain set phrases, its uniqueness forces one to consider it for historical purposes rather than reject it as a literary fantasia.[185]

30-F. Serapeum, Apis Stela, Louvre 3

The stela of *Py-ỉ3y* and *Ḏḥwty-ms*, called *R'-ms*, discovered by Mariette in the Serapeum[186] contains several regnal dates in different positions; in the lunette of the stela, years 16[187] and 26[188] are mentioned, while the body of the text begins with regnal year 30. It is evident that the stela commemorates the Apis bull which was buried in Ramesses' thirtieth year. "Regnal year 30, 3rd month of *šmw* day 21," was the day of the burial of this particular Apis,[189] sometimes referred to as the fourth Apis of the Nineteenth Dynasty.[190] Like its companion, Louvre 4, this stela was erected by private individuals to commemorate the auspicious occasion.

30-G. Serapeum, Apis Stela, Louvre 4

The stela of *Py-ỉ3y* and *Ry-ỉ3y*, like the Louvre 3 just mentioned, is dated to regnal year 30, but unlike Louvre 3, it does not have a reference to earlier years upon it.[191] Both Louvre 3 and 4 record regnal year 30, 3rd month of *šmw* day 21, as the day of the Apis burial.[192] The body of this text is basically the same as that of Louvre 3, and these two stelae give us year 30 as the first sure date of an Apis burial during the reign of Ramesses II.[193]

Year 33

33-A. Sehel Inscription

According to de Morgan, this Sehel inscription belongs to regnal year 33, *rnpt 33 wḥm Ḥb-Sd nb t3wy Wsr-M3't-R'*.[194] Unfortunately, the name of the person who left this carving at Sehel has not been properly recorded, but we know that he was a *ḥ3ty-' n 3bw*.[195] This is the only record of Ramesses' second Jubilee bearing the year 33 date; all the others have year 34.[196] At first one would see this as a possible mistake for year 34, if it were not for the statue fragment from Sinai which has the short inscription *rnpt 33 nfr nṯr nb Ḥbw-Sd* on its back.[197] This regnal date, then, may be kept as a reference to Ramesses' second Jubilee.

33-B. Sinai, Serabit el-Khadim, Statue Fragment, No. 298

The bust of a queen in sandstone from Sinai, now in the Manchester University Museum (no. 982) has a very short inscription on its back, *rnpt 33 nfr nṯr nb Ḥbw-Sd....*[198] In the Ramesside period there is only one king to whom this statement could refer and that is Ramesses II, for the reign of Ramesses III lasted only 32 regnal years.[199] This, unfortunately, appears to be the only inscription on the fragment and therefore affords no specific date for a particular queen of his. The statue is presumably dated to the Ramesside period by style[200] and then by default to Ramesses II; as such it may be employed in a chronological structure, but with caution for historical purposes.

33-C. Bentresh Stela

The Bentresh stela has been discussed previously under years 23-A and 26-E.

33-D. Ramesseum, Wine Jar Inscription No. 275

A jar inscription dated to regnal year 33, found during the excavations of the Ramesseum's storerooms,[201] has no royal cartouche but must belong to the reign of Ramesses II, because he is the only king whose reign could encompass this high date within the limits set by paleographic considerations.

33-E. Papyrus Anastasi V

"Regnal year 33, 2nd month of *Šmw* day 23" of Ramesses II is referred to in Papyrus Anastasi V 24, 7.[202] The date occurs in a letter of *3ny* and *B3k-n-Imn* written to the royal butler, *M3't-mn*; the date given is the time when the two passed the fortress of

R'-ms.sw Mry-Imn at Tjet, modern Et-Tell el-Ahmar, near Qantarah.[203] The men were directed by the king to hasten and overtake the royal butler, that he might direct the erection of three stelae which these men were transporting for his Majesty. The letter is a report by these two men, after they presumably accomplished his Majesty's commands. Though the date is retrospective it specifically refers to an event in the reign of Ramesses II.[204]

Year 34

34-A. Bigeh Inscription

Ramesses' second Jubilee is recorded at Bigeh in an inscription which mentions years 30 and 36 also.[205] This text, which was inscribed under the auspices of Prince *Ḫ'-m-W3st*, has been discussed under regnal year 30.

34-B. Gebel Silsileh, Great Speos (Duplicates)

The duplicate texts of Prince *Ḫ'-m-W3st* recording the Jubilees of regnal years 30, 34, 37 and 40 have been discussed under year 30.[206]

34-C. Gebel Silsileh, Great Speos, Vizier *Ḫ'y*

The stela of the Vizier *Ḫ'y*, which lists the Jubilees of years 30, 34, 37 and 40, has been discussed under regnal year 30, where it was concluded that this Vizier probably participated in each of these Jubilees, though we may not be certain that he was Vizier during the entire period.[207]

34-D. Marriage Stela

The texts of the marriage between Ramesses II and a Hittite princess in his 34th year are found at a number of sites throughout Egypt and Nubia.[208] At Abu Simbel there are two inscriptions which record this text,[209] and another was inscribed on a stela erected before the temple at Amarah West.[210] A number of fragments come from Elephantine[211] and also one from Karnak.[212] The incident was popular, for another stela at Karnak has an abbreviated version[213] and a broken Coptos stela also contains a variant on the same theme.[214] Ramesses' 34th regnal year was a momentous one, for not only was it his second Jubilee, but it also witnessed this royal marriage. The records do not give the exact day of the marriage but state that it occurred in year 34;[215] this date pertains not only to the actual marriage but also to the activity prior to the marriage. The text begins by relating the grievances of the Hittite king, who decided to send his eldest daughter to Egypt to become the wife of Pharaoh. After giving a detailed account of the protocol and procedures along the way to Egypt, the king finally received his bride-to-be and gave a sumptuous banquet in her honor. After she became Queen, she was given the Egyptian name of *M33-nfrw-R'* (or *Wr-m33-nfrw-R'*) and as such, she bore the title of *ḥmt wrt nswt*, that is, she was the official Queen.[216]

34-E. Deir el-Medineh, Ostracon No. 447

There are two reasons why this ostracon from Deir el-Medineh is to be assigned to the reign of Ramesses II.[217] Since the paleography dates this sherd to the Nineteenth Dynasty,[218] the high regnal year should refer to Ramesses II; second, and more conclusively, there is the remnant of a cartouche on the *verso*, ...*M3't*...*Stp-n-R'*, which can only refer to Ramesses II. The ostracon records a payment, "Regnal year 34, 2nd month of *3ḫt* day 17, paid for the tomb (*ḫr*) from the *w'b*-priest, *Ḥy*, of the Temple of Tuthmosis I, life, prosperity, health, pieces (of money), 152 bits."[219] Besides the simple business transaction, the relevant historical information concerns a *w'b*-priest with the common name of *Ḥy*, who belonged to the (mortuary?) temple of Tuthmosis I, which must have still been functioning at that time. One may safely assume that this date belongs to the reign of Ramesses, in spite of the fragmentary prenomen.

34-F. Saqqara, Pyramid Chapel, Graffito

At Saqqara, the Second Intermediate pyramid of *Ḫnḏr* contains a graffito of the scribe *N3-šwyw*.[220] The scribblings of this person are typical of those comments left in conspicuous places by tourists both ancient and modern.[221] According to paleography this may be attributed to the Ramesside period, and to Ramesses II because of the high regnal year. The graffito records a festival of Ptah, "Regnal year 34, 4th month of *šmw* day 24, the day of the festival of Ptah, south-of-his-wall and Lord-of-life-of-the-two-lands." The rest of the text has been interpreted as a reference to *N3-šwyw*'s disreputable activities at the pyramid. Jéquier understood the phrase *wp ỉnr* to indicate quarrying in the pyramid complex, but it is grammatically impossible to separate this phrase from the preceding word, *ḏsr*. The combination, *ḏsr wp ỉnr*, occurs in both lines 2 and 3. The meaning in line 2 is not immediately clear, but in line 3 there is no difficulty; it reads, "A coming by the scribe *N3-šwyw* to the pyramid of *Ttỉ*, *Mr-n-Ptḥ* and the pyramid of *ḏsr wp ỉnr*." Due to the parallelism in this sentence, *ḏsr wp ỉnr* can only designate a pyramid in the same way as *Tti*, Beloved-of-Ptah, and could be understood as the name of the pyramid of *Ḫnḏr*.[222] Though we know that Ramesses II did reuse older material, this graffito does not indicate that. Consequently, one can say that the chapel of *Ḫnḏr* was still in existence and available to visitors during the reign of Ramesses II.[223]

Year 35

35-A. Abu Simbel, The Decree of Ptah

The decree, or blessing, of Ptah is found in two texts, one from the time of Ramesses II and the other from the reign of Ramesses III.[224] Just as he copied the "Hymn to the Nile" at Gebel Silsileh, so Ramesses III also copied the decree of Ptah but dated it to his 12th regnal year.[225] The stela containing the decree of Ptah was erected by Ramesses II in his temple at Abu Simbel next to the stela recording his marriage to the Hittite princess.[226] The same relationship is found at Amarah West, where the niche with the decree of Ptah is next to the niche with the marriage stela.[227] The "decree" is a lengthy text which begins with Ptah enumerating the various gifts and blessings which he has bestowed upon Ramesses; he ends his speech with a reference to the land of Hatti (line 25) and to that ruler's eldest daughter who came to satisfy the heart of the Egyptian king (line 26). Ramesses then replies to Ptah's speech (lines 29ff) by listing the numerous gifts which have become the god's through the king's beneficence. Ramesses claims to have enlarged the temple at Memphis, a royal effort which has been substantiated by excavations.[228] He ends his oration by saying that he, the king, has conquered the foreign lands by and for the god Ptah.[229] When Ramesses III copied this text, he took it almost verbatim, with two interesting exceptions. In line 25 he does not speak of the "land of Hatti" but alters this to simply "the (foreign) lands"; in line 26, Ramesses III does not pretend to have married the daughter of the Hittite king but instead says, "their (the foreign lands) sons and their daughters come as slaves to your palace." Interestingly enough, Ramesses III recognized the historical reference and altered it in his own text.[230] Year 35, then, contains a text confirming the activity of regnal year 34, both of which center upon the royal marriage.[231]

35-B. Faiyum, Fragment, Cairo 42783

A block of grey granite bearing regnal year 35 of Ramesses II has been discovered at Medinet el-Faiyum and is now in the Cairo

Museum (no. 42783).[232] The date reads, "Regnal year 35, first month of *prt* under the majest of...," with little else remaining outside of the beginning of the Horus-name, the prenomen and the beginning of the nomen, all of which definitely date this piece to Ramesses II. The remainder of the text reads, "...his fear (?) in their hearts forever, king...."[233] This block gives evidence of royal activity in the Faiyum, particularly in regnal year 35 of Ramesses II, but does not say what type of activity it was or how long it endured.[234]

35-C. Ostracon Gardiner 24

The date on this limestone flake is given as year 35, though the five strokes are not well preserved; according to the traces, the number must be five or above and therefore the date belongs to the reign of Ramesses II.[235] It reads, "Regnal year 35, 4th month of *šmw* day 16; from the scribe *Imn-m-Ipt*...510, and on this day, from the scribe *Mry-R'*...250...." The text then continues in the same form with only the days changing; the items received from these scribes are not specified, though fish has been suggested.[236] This ostracon is one of a number of dated inscriptions which have no royal name but are assigned to the Ramesside period by paleography and by default to Ramesses II, for he alone reigned longer than 32 years at that time.

35-D. Graffito 988, Theban Necropolis

This brief text reads: "Regnal year 35, 4th month of *prt* day 13, excursion made by the scribe *Ḥy*."[237] Because of the high date, this might be assigned to the reign of Ramesses II; the scribe's name is also common at that time, but it is so common, it is impossible to identify him.

Year 36

36-A. Bigeh Inscription

In his inscription at Bigeh, *Ḫ'-m-W3st* lists the first three Jubilees of years 30, 34 and 36.[238] As regnal year 36 is the latest date given, it must represent the time when the inscription was carved on this island near the first cataract. This, however, is the only text pertaining to the third Jubilee dated to year 36; the rest have regnal year 37.[239] Since the major evidence points to year 37 as the year of the Jubilee, this situation is similar to that of the second *Ḥb-Sd* of years 33/34.[240]

36-B. Papyrus Gardiner 9

An unpublished papyrus belonging to the late Sir Alan Gardiner mentions a regnal year 36 on the *recto*.[241] The papyrus contains an itemized list of goods which were sold for three *deben* and eight pieces of silver; it is another business document which belongs to the reign of Ramesses II, since "the Eighteenth Dynasty is excluded on paleographical grounds."[242]

36-C. Deir el-Medineh, Wine Jar Inscription

"Regnal year 36, select wine...(of) the vineyard of the domain...(of) *Wsr-M3't-R' Stp-n-R'*, life, prosperity, health."[243] The hieratic inscription on the red-ware wine jug from Deir el-Medineh must have been written during the reign of Ramesses II. Even though the royal prenomen surely is part of a place name and cannot indicate the person of the king himself, the high regnal date combined with the paleography leaves Ramesses II as the only possibility.[244]

36-D. Saqqara, Step Pyramid, Graffito

A graffito from the South Mastaba in the Step Pyramid complex records, "Regnal year 36, month 3 of *Shomu*, day 10; the first (day) of the work of the stone-hewers(?) from the quarry."[245] This brief remark has been assigned to the reign of Ramesses II.[246]

Year 37

37-A. Gebel Silsileh, Great Speos (Duplicates)

The third regnal date on the duplicate stelae of *Ḫ'-m-W3st* at Gebel Silsileh is year 37; the text also refers to the Jubilees of years 30, 34 and 40 and was discussed under 30-B.[247]

37-B. Gebel Silsileh, Great Speos, Vizier *Ḫ'y*

The Vizier *Ḫ'y* commemorated the first four Jubilees of Ramesses II of years 30, 34, 37 and 40; these, like the preceding of *Ḫ'-m-W3st*, have been treated under year 30 (30-C).[248]

37-C. Thebes, Graffito

An unpublished graffito from the Valley of the Kings has a regnal year 37, which has been assigned to Ramesses II.[249] The person responsible for this record, *Ḥy*, the son of *Ḏḥwty-ḥr-mkt.f*, is impossible to identify further.[250]

37-D. Deir el-Medineh, Ostracon No. 333

Another limestone flake from Thebes bears a regnal date but

has no royal name; by paleography this ostracon belongs to the Nineteenth Dynasty and therefore because of the year date must represent regnal year 37 of Ramesses II.[251] Even though the left side is partially broken away, it is clear that this is another daily account of items received from two different people, *B3ky* and *'ḥ3-nẖt*. Since no titles are given for these two men, it is difficult to identify them. The ostracon is similar in format to that discussed under regnal year 35.

37-E. British Museum Stela 164, *B3k-'3*

This private stela is difficult to date properly. James says, "The arc of the stela contains the date: 'Regnal year 37, being the fifth *sed*-festival...'" and notes that year 37 was that of the third Jubilee and not the fifth.[252] This stela is similar to British Museum no. 166, which, unfortunately, does not retain the complete regnal year though it does refer to the third Jubilee.[253] These two stelae are not only similar in style, but a number of the same people are represented on both of them; however, this does not help solve the date of Stela 164. There seems to be no solution to the problem but to hold this text in abeyance and not include it within a chronological structure.[254]

37-F. British Museum Stela 166, *Imn-ḥtp*

As stated above (37-E) the regnal year is not entirely preserved on this stela, though it mentions the third Jubilee.[255] If there were no problem with Stela 164, which is definitely related to this one, it would be possible to assign this one of *Imn-ḥtp* to year 37 of Ramesses II. However, since the date is lost and because of the questionable value of its associate (164), this reference to Ramesses' third *Ḥb-Sd* cannot be used as a chronological reference point for his reign.

Year 38

38-A. Abu Simbel Stelae of the Viceroy *St3w*

The Viceroy of Kush, *St3w*, had "duplicate stelae" carved on the face of the cliff near the temple of Ramesses II at Abu Simbel.[256] The inscriptions consist of two almost identical texts,[257] each dated to "Regnal year 38, under the Majesty of the Horus...." Since this is the earliest dated record of the Viceroy *St3w*, it is tempting to see it as a commemoration of his installation, but this is only conjecture as the texts do not specify why they were made.[258]

38-B. Ostracon Michaelides 47

Unlike many ostraca belonging to the reign of Ramesses II, this one is a legal document, not a business transaction.[259] It begins with the heading, "Regnal year 38, 1st month of *3ḫt* day 3 under the Majesty of the King *Wsr-M3't-R' Stp-n-R'...R'-ms.sw Mry-Imn*, may he live forever and ever, as *P3-R'* endures in heaven." It then continues to relate an action taken by the necropolis lawcourt according to the laws of *M3't*; several names are specifically stated, *Ḳ3-ḥ3*, *R'-ms* and also *Ḥrî*, son of *Mr-W3st*. *Ḳ3-ḥ3* must be the same person who built Theban tomb 360, for both had the title, *'3 n(y) t3 ỉst m St-M3't*; because the name *R'-ms* is very common, it is almost impossible to identify him, as a number of persons at Deir el-Medineh bore that name at this time and held the title of "scribe."[260] The father of *Ḥrî*, *Mr-W3st*, is quite likely the same person who is mentioned on two stelae of *Ḳ3-ḥ3* now in the British Museum (nos. 144 and 291)[261] and whose name was found on a cover in the debris of *Ḳ3-ḥ3*'s tomb at Deir el-Medineh.[262] *Ḥrî* himself remains unknown.[263] That part of the ostracon which recorded the legal dispute is badly damaged by salt crystalizing on the surface of the stone so that little can be drawn from it; however, the dispute does record another regnal year of Ramesses II.

38-C. Cairo Ostracon 25809

Like a number of ostraca, this too is assigned to Ramesses II by paleography and high regnal year.[264] *Recto* and *verso* are dated, "Regnal year 38, 1st month of...day 2," and "Regnal year 38, 3rd month of *prt*" (with no day given). The brief notation concerns grain rations given to the crews working in the necropolis.

Year 39

39-A. Ramesseum, Wine Jar Inscription No. 321

Like inscription no. 275, discussed under regnal year 33, this too must belong to the reign of Ramesses II.[265] The entire selection of dated texts from the Ramesseum are combined in a later section.[266]

Year 40

40-A. Gebel Silsileh, Great Speos (Duplicates)

Regnal year 40 is the highest date on this inscription of Prince *Ḫ'-m-W3st*, which also contains years 30, 34 and 37, and represents the time when the stela was carved, as discussed under 30-B.[267]

40-B. Gebel Silsileh, Great Speos, Vizier *Ḫ'y*

As in the preceding text of *Ḫ'-m-W3st*, the stela of the Vizier *Ḫ'y* has year 40 as its highest regnal date and also lists the earlier years of 30, 34 and 37.[268] It was discussed under 30-C.

40-C. Sehel Inscription, *Ḫ'-m-W3st*

Prince *Ḫ'-m-W3st* left a brief inscription on the island of Sehel recording a Jubilee dated to Ramesses' 40th year.[269] The text reads, "Regnal year 40, the royal son and *Sm*-priest of Ptah, who propitiates the heart of the Lord of the two lands, *Ḫ'-m-W3st*, came to announce the fourth Jubilee throughout the entire land."[270] The few short vertical lines above this text are composed of the nomen and prenomen of Ramesses II and the titles and name of *Ḫ'-m-W3st*. There is only a slight change in the wording of this text from that at Gebel Silsileh, which belongs to the same year of Ramesses II.[271]

40-D. Gebel Silsileh, Great Speos, *Ḥy* Text

Ramesses' fourth *Ḥb-Sd* is also recorded in the Hall of the Great Speos at Gebel Silsileh by *Ḥy*, the son of *Ḫ'-m-W3st*.[272] This text adds little to the other Jubilee inscriptions which have been recorded in the Speos at Silsileh, except that a son of *Ḫ'-m-W3st*, and therefore a grandson of Ramesses II, was associated with the celebrations of that particular year.

40-E. Ostracon British Museum 5634

This ostracon departs somewhat from the usual style of a business receipt; it records a list of necropolis workmen, notes their days of absence from work and appends the reason for such absences.[273] At the top of the *recto* there is a simple "Regnal year 40"; the months and days are noted after each person's name in the list itself. This list, therefore, dates certain necropolis workmen to year 40 of Ramesses II.[274]

40-F. Wadi Allaqi, Graffito

At Huqab el-'Askar, about two-days journey up the Wadi Allaqi from the Nile valley, is the only known dated graffito in the wadi.[275] The brief text reads, "Regnal year 40, made by the scribe of the treasury, who records gold, *Ḫ'-[m]-W3st*." It has been suggested that the Huqab el-'Askar is the site of the well excavated by Ramesses II, as recorded in the Quban stela.[276] Though this is the only dated graffito in the wadi, all the others, except for three peculiar ones, can be assigned to the Nineteenth and Twentieth Dynasties on paleographic grounds.[277]

Year 41

41-A. El-Kab, Temple of Amenophis III

On the facade of the Eighteenth Dynasty temple of Amenophis III at el-Kab, the Prince and *Sm*-priest of Ptah, *Ḫ'-m-W3st*, left an inscription supposedly dated to regnal year 41, recording Ramesses' fifth Jubilee.[278] This poses a problem, for the stela of the Vizier *Ḫ'y* at Gebel Silsileh lists regnal year 42 as the time of the fifth Jubilee.[279] There are certain indications that the el-Kab text also belongs to regnal year 42. In his Thesaurus,[280] Brugsch has a shaded area over the sign for "one" which means that a second stroke above the remaining "one" was lost and consequently the year should be read 42 instead of 41. Nestor L'Hôte[281] and Lepsius[282] both have year 41 but place the "one" stroke in the lower half of the line. According to Egyptian symmetry, this lower stroke indicates that another should be directly above it. There seems little doubt, then, that this inscription should be assigned to the 42nd regnal year of Ramesses II.[283]

Year 42

42-A. Gebel Silsileh, Stela of *Ḫ'y*

This inscription records the Jubilee of year 42 only but is similar to other *Ḥb-Sd* inscriptions at Gebel Silsileh.[284] "Regnal year 42, the first (month) of *prt* day 1, (of) the King *Wsr-M3't-R' Stp-n-R'*, the son of Re, *R'-ms.sw Mry-Imn*, may he live forever and ever. His Majesty directed the Vizier, *Ḫ'y*, to announce the fifth Jubilee of King *Wsr-M3't-R' Stp-n-R'*, the son of Re, *R'-ms.sw Mry-Imn* throughout the entire land."[285] Here is evidence that *Ḫ'y*, who according to his other inscription at Gebel Silsileh was active in the first four Jubilees of Ramesses II, also took part in the fifth and thus paralleled the participation of Prince *Ḫ'-m-W3st* in these festivities. Since the inscription of *Ḫ'-m-W3st* on the temple of Amenophis III at el-Kab has a supposed regnal date of 42, this text from Silsileh is the only sure record of the fifth *Ḥb-Sd* being celebrated in year 42 of Ramesses II.[286]

42-B. Abydos, Stela of *Wn-nfr*

The First Prophet of Osiris, *Wn-nfr*, erected a typical "family stela" for posterity at Abydos,[287] which besides the usual filiation also records regnal year 42. Since *Wn-nfr* had some influential members in his family, his stela helps date certain high officials to a specific regnal year of Ramesses II. The stela names *P3-R'-ḥtp* as Mayor of Thebes and Vizier, *Mîn-ms* as First Prophet of Onuris, and *Ḳny* as Overseer of the granaries of Upper and Lower Egypt.[288] Thus this stela gives a fixed date for a number of administrative officials and indicates the general period of their activity in the reign of Ramesses II.

42-C. Ostracon Louvre 2262

The Louvre ostracon, published by Spiegelberg in 1894, is dated to "Regnal year 42, 4th month of *prt* of King...the son of Re, *R'-ms.sw Mry-Imn ḥḳ3-Iwnw*."[289] Even though the royal prenomen is lost, this notation can be assigned to Ramesses II by means of the longer nomen, which no other king employed.[290] The text then continues with some information of more historical interest than the usual business matters, "*Iryt*, the daughter of the *mnš*-captain, *Bn-'nty* (בן־ענת), (is?) the wife of the royal son, *S3-Mnṯw*, (it is she) who is with (?) the vineyard of the domain of *Wsr-M3't-R' Stp-n-R'* life, prosperity, health, in *Mn-nfr*." The royal son is known from the Abydos list of Ramesses II,[291] if this refers to the same person. It has been thought that this refers to the marriage between *Iryt* and *S3-Mnṯw*,[292] but this is not certain from the text.[293] Thus we have a regnal date for an obscure younger son of Ramesses, who married the daughter of a person with a Semitic name.[294]

42-D. Aswan *Ḥb-Sd* Inscription

An unpublished inscription of *Ḫ'-m-W3st*, "At the foot of the Public Garden lying to the north of Cataract Hotel in Aswan,"[295] records the announcement of the fifth *Ḥb-Sd* in regnal year 42.

Year 44

44-A. Gebel Silsileh, Stela of *Ḫ'y*

The Vizier *Ḫ'y* left a second inscription in the Great Speos of Gebel Silsileh; this one contains only the date of the sixth *Ḥb-Sd*.[296] The text differs little from his stela in the same chamber which records the first four Jubilees,[297] but this date is uncertain, for it could be read 44, 45 or 46. Brugsch indicates a small lacuna after the regnal year number.[298] Champollion read year 45, which was followed by Legrain[299] and Erman,[300] while Petrie proposed year 46.[301] Thus the only record of Ramesses' sixth Jubilee cannot be dated precisely.[302]

44-B. Wadi es-Sebua', Stela of *St3w*

Discovered in 1909 and now in the Cairo Museum, this sandstone stela of the Viceroy of Kush contains the date of year 44 and a short directive from the king.[303] The surface has suffered considerable weathering so that the inscription is difficult to read, but one is able to ascertain that the king ordered the Viceroy of Kush and a number of people to perform a specific activity. The text of the directive is now lost but must have been of sufficient importance for a stela to commemorate the deed. This monument further indicates that *St3w* was Viceroy during the latter part of the reign of Ramesses II.[304]

44-C. Abydos, Jar Inscription

Amélineau discovered a number of hieratic inscriptions at the Umm el-Qa'ab at Abydos, one of which is attributed to regnal year 44 of Ramesses II.[305]

Year 45

45-A. Graffito, Valley of the Kings, No. 1401

A brief notation left by the scribe *Ḳn-ḫpš.f* records "Regnal year 45, 1st of *prt* day 20."[306] Because of the high regnal date, this has been assigned to Ramesses II.

Year 46

46-A. Papyrus Berlin 3047

A judicial papyrus at Berlin has the heading "Regnal year 46, 2nd month of *3ḫt* day 14, under the Majesty of the King and Lord of the two lands *Wsr-M3't-R' Stp-n-R'*, life, prosperity, health, the son of Re and Lord of appearances, *R'-ms.sw Mry-Imn Nṯr-ḥḳ3-Iwnw*, life, prosperity, health, beloved of Amun-Re, King of the gods, may he live forever and ever."[307] The text then continues, "Today, (in) the law court of Pharaoh, life, prosperity, health, which is in the Southern City (Thebes) near 'Satisfied with *M3't*'[308] the great portal of *R'-ms.sw Mry-Imn*, life, prosperity, health, at *Hry-ḥr-Imn*.[309] The court of this day...." The record continues by listing the officials who sat to hear the case: *B3k-n-Ḫnsw*, the High Priest of Amun; *Wsr-Mnṯw*, a prophet of Amun; *R3m*, a prophet of Amun; *Wnn-nfr*, a prophet of the domain of Mut; *Imn-m-ḥb*, prophet of the domain of Khonsu; *Imn-m-ἰpt*, administrator of Amun; *Imn-ḥtp*, a *w'b* and lector priest of Amun; *3ny*, a *w'b* and lector priest of Amun; *Ḥy*, a *w'b*-priest of the domain of Amun.[310] At the end is the name of the court-recorder, *Ḥy*. The dispute was between the scribe *Nfr-'bt* and

Ny-ỉ3, who was legal representative for his relatives. Like the *Wn-nfr* stela of Abydos,[311] this document indicates the general period when a number of high officials were active during the reign of Ramesses II.

46-B. Deir el-Medineh, Wine Jar Inscription

Another wine jar from Thebes bears the short notation, "Regnal year 46, wine of...from the overseer of the vineyard...."[312] For similar inscriptions on pottery from Deir el-Medineh, see under years 36-C, 47-A and 49-A; like those, this too must belong to the reign of Ramesses II.

46-C. Ostracon British Museum 5634

This ostracon was discussed under year 40-E, though it has been suggested that the date is higher than 40 and more likely 46.[313]

Year 47

47-A. Deir el-Medineh, Wine Jar Inscription

Similar to the preceding inscription, this also comes from Deir el-Medineh; like those mentioned earlier, this dates to the reign of Ramesses II.[314] The text reads, "Regnal year 47, wine of the vineyard of the domain of the temple of Millions of Years of King *Wsr-M3't-R' Stp-n-R'*, life, prosperity, health, in the domain of Amun which is in...from the overseer of the vintagers, *'ḫy-pt*."[315]

47-B. Saqqara, Step Pyramid Graffito

A graffito on the South Chapel of the Step Pyramid complex has the date, "Regnal year 47, 2nd month of *prt* day 25" and is assigned to the reign of Ramesses II.[316] The scribe of the Treasury, *H3d-nḫt*, son of *Sw-n-r3*, whose mother was *T3-wsr(t)*, came with his brother *P3-nḫty*[317] on an excursion to the West of Memphis. These men invoke the gods in their inscription, asking for a fine burial in the Memphis cemetery. This, then, is another example of the interest taken in the Saqqara area during the reign of Ramesses II.[318]

Year 48

48-A. Deir el-Medineh, Wine Jar Inscription

Another wine inscription from Thebes, which reads, "Regnal year 48, wine...which is on the west of the..." belongs to the reign of Ramesses II.[319]

48-B. Deir el-Medineh, Ostracon No. 294

This fragmentary piece contains the beginnings of four lines of script, all of which are very short; line one starts with "Regnal year 48, these herbs, which were brought...."[320] The units are written as one would write the numbers for the days of the month; otherwise the year date is quite clear. There is no royal name, but this too must belong to the reign of Ramesses II.[321]

48-C. Saqqara, Step Pyramid Graffito

Like that of the preceding year, this graffito is also on the south chapel wall of the Step Pyramid but in contrast is only a very short inscription consisting of "Regnal year 48, 2nd month of *3ḫt* day...son of *Ḥrỉ*...."[322] Like the other graffiti from Saqqara of years 36-D and 47-B, this too must be assigned to the reign of Ramesses II.[323]

Year 49

49-A. Deir el-Medineh, Jar Inscription

From tomb 369 comes another jar inscription dated to a regnal year 49, which must date to Ramesses II.[324] The text reads, "Regnal year 49, honey of the Temple of Millions of Years of King *Wsr-M3't-R' Stp-n-R'*, life, prosperity, health...the overseer of bees, *Ḥy*; refined honey, 34 hin."

Year 50

50-A. Abu Sir, Mastaba of *Ptḥ-špss*, Graffito

Another New Kingdom visitor's inscription extolls the wonders seen in the necropolis at Abu Sir; it is dated to "Regnal year 50, 1st month of *prt* day 16."[325] Though Ramesses II is not mentioned in the body of the inscription, his prenomen and what remains of his nomen is written just to one side;[326] hence this graffito may be assigned to his reign not only by the high regnal date but also by the proximity of his royal name. The text records the names of two men, the scribe *Ptḥ-m-wỉ3* and his father, the scribe *Yw(?)-p3*; the son's name is a common New Kingdom one,[327] but the father's appears to be foreign.[328] These men praise the gods and request a full life of 110 years; as they announce themselves as scribes of Ptah, they are likely to be local inhabitants.[329]

Year 51

51-A. Armant, Temple Pylon Fragment

This fragmentary inscription from the temple at Armant has

been assigned to Ramesses II[330] because of its similarity to an inscription of his on the opposite wall.[331] Both texts begin with high regnal dates, and though the fragment contains little more, the parallel text on the opposite wall records three different Jubilees.[332] This text has the beginnings of three lines representing the years 51, 63 and 66(?),[333] and Drower has suggested that year 51 might be a mistake for year 61[334] because of the two dates which follow. The text on the opposite wall lists regnal years 54, 57 and 60, and it is thought that this fragment is a sequel to the other.[335] In both texts the month, where preserved, is *prt*; therefore we may assume that they record a similar event, that is, Ramesses' Jubilees. In order to establish the correct date for the first line of this fragment, it should be noted that in the parallel text on the opposite wall the first date belongs to a certain *Yw-p3*, while the lower two belong to the Vizier *Nfr-rnpt*. This could be the case here, too; the top line might belong to one person--perhaps *Yw-p3*--and the next two might have been added by another. If one is correct in assuming that all these dates refer to Ramesses' Jubilees, it would be unusual to find him celebrating one in year 60 and then another in year 61. All considered, the date should be kept as is, without emendation. Ramesses' last dated Jubilee before year 51 was held in regnal year 44; since he celebrated his ninth in year 54, it appears that regnal year 51 most likely represents his eighth Jubilee and may be so postulated.[336]

51-B. Asyut Stela

In 1922 a hoard of stelae, many of them badly damaged by salt, was discovered in the tomb of Hepdjefa III (the Great Salkhana) at Asyut.[337] This one, dated to the reign of Ramesses II, has either regnal year 51 or 61, with year 61 being more likely,[338] and depicts the cartouches of Ramesses' receiving adoration.[339]

Year 52

52-A. Papyrus Leiden I 350 *verso*

Papyrus Leiden I 350 contains hymns to Amun on the *recto* and a ship's log on the *verso*, which is dated to the 52nd year of Ramesses II.[340] This papyrus plays a key role in the establishment of an absolute chronology not only for the reign of Ramesses but for the whole New Kingdom and consequently Egyptian history in general, for it has a reference to a lunar date which is one of the few astronomical sightings from the New Kingdom.[341] The royal son *Ḫ'-m-W3st* is mentioned in lines II 2 and IV 16, which shows that he was still alive at that time. Most of the text is a listing of daily supplies and differs from the usual business document only in that it refers to several persons of royal rank.[342] Though the date is not compounded with the royal name of Ramesses II, there is no doubt that this part of the papyrus belongs to his reign.

52-B. Qantir, Wine Jar Inscription

A number of hieratic ostraca were discovered by Hamza at Qantir in 1928; among them was a jar inscription with a year date which reads, "Regnal year 52, wine of the vineyard which his Majesty, life, prosperity, health, made anew...."[343] The location of this vineyard, which Ramesses apparently had rejuvenated some years before, is unknown.[344]

Year 53

53-A. Ostracon Louvre 2261

"Regnal year 53, 3rd month of *3ḫt* day 23," is the date on Louvre 2261; the ostracon has both the nomen and prenomen of Ramesses II and thus is securely dated to his reign.[345] A royal son, *Sty*, is stated to have been born of *Nfrt-ỉry*, but the relationship between this *Sty* and a person mentioned later by the name of *Sty-ḥr-ḫpš.f* is not entirely clear.[346] The remainder of the text lists some names and titles: *Wsr-M3't-R'-nḫt*, a royal scribe; *R'-ms.sw-mn*,[347] a scribe; *P3y.tn-ḥb-p3-šd*;[348] *Imn-ms.sw*, an agent;[349] and finally *Ḥy3*,[350] an overseer of the *ḥtyw*. These persons, except for *Wsr-M3't-R'-nḫt* and *Imn-ms.sw-mn*, are found on another ostracon in the Louvre (no. 666),[351] which is primarily a list of the royal daughters of Ramesses II. Because of the similarity of names and titles on both ostraca, that family list may be dated approximately to the same time as Louvre 2261.

Year 54

54-A. Armant, Temple Pylon

A number of regnal dates listing the later Jubilees of Ramesses II were found at Armant; his ninth Jubilee was celebrated in year 54, as recorded in the inscription of the royal scribe *Yw-p3*.[352] The text reads, "[Regnal year] 54,[353] 1st month of *prt* day 1(?), under the Majesty of King *Wsr-M3't-R' Stp-n-R'*, the son of Re, *R'-ms.sw Mry-Imn*, given life. His Majesty directed the royal scribe and overseer of the *pr-wr* in *Ḥwt-Wsr-M3't-R' Stp-n-R'* in the domain of Amun, *Yw-p3*, to announce the ninth *Ḥb-Sd* of *Wsr-M3't-R' Stp-n-R'* ...."[354] *Yw-p3* appears in other texts belonging to the reign of

Ramesses II,[355] and his sarcophagus is now in Brussels.[356]

54-B. Papyrus British Museum 10447

Ramesses' regnal years 54 and 55 are represented by a papyrus of unknown provenance purchased by the British Museum in 1877.[357] The papyrus is an account listing the amount of grain from a particular estate near *Nfrw-sy* (Hermopolis) belonging to a statue of Ramesses. The location of this statue is unknown; it might have been in Hermopolis,[358] though Gardiner questions this.[359] The papyrus dates to year 55 but refers to the remaining grain of regnal year 54. It gives a brief insight into the economic world of the Nineteenth Dynasty, different from those account receipts of Deir el-Medineh.

54-C. Deir el-Medineh, Ostracon No. 351

"Regnal year 54, 2nd month of *prt* day 14," is the date of an ostracon from Deir el-Medineh[360] with a brief notation which mentions foodstuffs and water supplies.[361]

Year 55

55-A. Papyrus British Museum 10447

This papyrus, discussed above under year 54-B, properly belongs to regnal year 55 of Ramesses II, for year 54 is a retrospective date.[362]

55-B. Serapeum, Graffito

During his excavation of the Serapeum, Mariette found a graffito on the wall of an Apis burial chamber listing "regnal year 55," which he assigned to Ramesses II.[363] Within the sarcophagus of this chamber, Mariette found a body which he assumed to be that of the royal prince, *Ḫ'-m-W3st*, and therefore concluded that this regnal date must refer to the death of the prince.[364] It is unlikely that a royal son was buried in the Serapeum, even *Ḫ'-m-W3st*, who was closely associated with the Apis burials in his office as *Sm*-priest; however, it is even less likely that he was buried there since a tomb belonging to him has been found at Kafr el-Batran, near the Great Pyramid.[365] Though this date should be assigned to the reign of Ramesses II, it cannot be related to the death of *Ḫ'-m-W3st*.

Year 56

56-A. Papyrus Sallier IV *verso* 17, 1-4

"Regnal year 56, 4th month of *prt* [day 2]2, under the Majesty of the Horus: *K3-nḫt, Mry-M3't*, lord, l.p.h., of Jubilees like his father *Ptḥ-Tnn*. The Two Ladies: Protector of Egypt, who curbs the foreign lands, offspring of Re and the gods, who establishes the two lands. *Ḥr-nbw*: Rich of years and great of strength. The King, the Lord of the two lands, the Ruler of the Nine Bows, *Wsr-M3't-R' Stp-n-R'*, l.p.h., the son of Re, the Lord of appearances like *Itm*, the Lord of the two lands of Heliopolis, Re-Herakhty, *R'-ms.sw Mry-Imn Nṯr-ḥḳ3-Iwnw*, l.p.h., beloved of Suth-great-of-strength-of-*R'-ms.sw-Mry-Imn*, l.p.h., may he live forever and ever."[366] Thus Papyrus Sallier preserves the full titulary of Ramesses II with a specific regnal date, perhaps the day when this titulary became effective;[367] otherwise no historical reference is made within this section of the papyrus.

56-B. Aniba, Wine Jar Inscription

In contrast to many wine jar inscriptions assigned to the reign of Ramesses II, this one comes from Nubia instead of Egypt.[368] Though it contains no royal name, it is dated to Ramesses II by paleography and high regnal year. It was found in a New Kingdom shaft tomb (SA 14) in which were also some shabtis with the name of *Ḏḥwty-ms*, a *ḥ3ty-'* of *Mi-'m* (Aniba),[369] who is likely the same person depicted on the stela of the Viceroy *St3w* in regnal year 63, engraved at Tonqala.[370] This, along with the questionable Aniba date of regnal year 7,[371] indicates Egyptian activity at this site during the reign of Ramesses II.

56-C. Graffito No. 857, Theban Necropolis

This graffito contains the words "Regnal year 56 of King" and nothing more.[372] Because of the high date, it has been assigned to Ramesses II.

Year 57

57-A. Armant, Temple Pylon

Directly beneath the inscription of *Yw-p3* recording the ninth Jubilee of Ramesses II, the Vizier *Nfr-rnpt* left a record of the tenth celebration.[373] "[Regnal year] 57, first month of *prt* day 17, under the Majesty of the King *Wsr-M3't-R' Stp-n-R'*, son of Re, *R'-ms.sw Mry-Imn*, given life. His Majesty directed the Mayor of Thebes and Vizier, *Nfr-rnpt*, to announce the tenth *Ḥb-Sd* of King *Wsr-M3't-R' Stp-n-R'*, son of Re, *R'-ms.sw Mry-Imn* in the entire land...." Except for name and titles, the inscription of *Nfr-rnpt* is almost an exact duplication of the one left by *Yw-p3* of year 54.[374] This is the only record of Ramesses' tenth Jubilee and one of the few dated inscriptions in which the Vizier *Nfr-rnpt* is mentioned.[375]

57-B. Ramesseum, Jar Inscription No. 323

As with inscriptions 275 and 321, discussed under years 33-D and 39-A, respectively, this too should be dated to the reign of Ramesses II.[376] The material from the Ramesseum bearing regnal dates is examined in section 2.

Year 58

58-A. Ramesseum, Jar Inscription, No. 300

This inscription, like no. 323 just mentioned, belongs to the reign of Ramesses II. It is nothing more than a regnal date on a potsherd,[377] and is discussed later.[378]

Year 59

59-A. Cairo Ostracon 25619

An ostracon found by Baraize in 1912 at the temple of Deir el-Medineh has a reference to regnal year 59; it is another account document, and no personal names are recorded.[379]

Year 60

60-A. Armant, Temple Pylon

As in year 57, so also in year 60, the Vizier, *Nfr-rnpt*, recorded a Jubilee of Ramesses II at the temple of Armant.[380] Though the first part of the year is lost, it must be read 60, for it is the eleventh Jubilee of Ramesses II and regnal year 57 was his tenth.[381] This inscription was written directly beneath that of year 57 and, except for the date, is an exact duplicate of the earlier record. It is the only dated evidence for Ramesses' eleventh Jubilee.[382]

Year 61

61-A. Papyrus Gurob, Fragment N

A papyrus fragment from Gurob,[383] the site of ancient *Mr-wr*,[384] contains regnal year 61; the *recto* has the remains of a report made in year 61 (*smỉ m rnpt* 61) while the *verso* records the delivery of fish. The same scribe probably wrote the undated Gurob Fragment U, which mentions Queen *M33-nfrw-R'*, the daughter of the chieftain of Hatti;[385] he probably also wrote Gurob Fragment L, which is dated to regnal year 67 of Ramesses II.[386] The temple of Ramesses called *Ḥwt-R'-ms.sw Mry-Ỉmn, mrwt mỉ R'* is only known from this and the Wilbour Papyrus;[387] hence its location has been assumed to be in the vicinity of *Mr-wr*.[388] A fragmentary part on the *recto* begins, "Regnal year 61 (?), One was in *Pr-R'-ms.sw Mry-Imn*, life, prosperity, health, the great *k3* of *P3-R'*...the report in regnal year 61, which was placed in a document..."; the rest is too incomplete to reconstruct the content of the report.[389]

61-B. Asyut Stela

This stela was discussed under year 51, for the date is either 51 or 61, the latter being more probable.[390] Since the date of this text is questionable, it is of little independent chronological value for the reign of Ramesses II.

61-C. Armant, Temple Pylon, Fragment

The first of three dates on the fragment from the temple at Armant reads "year 51," but it has been suggested that this could have been an ancient mistake for regnal year 61, since "one would expect the inscription to be a sequel to that on the opposite wall."[391] It has, however, been pointed out that "year 51" should be retained.[392]

Year 62

62-A. British Museum Stela 163, *Nfr-ḥr*

A typical "family stela" from the Salt collection, which probably came from Abydos, bears the regnal year 62.[393] At the very top of the stela is the date preceding an extended cartouche of Ramesses II, "Regnal year 62, 1st month of *šmw* day 29 of (the cartouche begins) King *Wsr-M3't-R' Stp-n-R' s3-R' R'-ms.sw Mry-Imn Wsỉr ḫnty ỉmntyw mry*" (here ends the cartouche).[394] *Nfr-ḥr*, a scribe in the office of letters of Pharaoh,[395] is depicted before his family, whose names are accompanied by general titles, making it difficult to identify them accurately.

Year 63

63-A. Armant, Temple Pylon Fragment

"Regnal year 63, 1st month of *prt* day 1, of King..." is all that remains of this inscription, which must belong to Ramesses II.[396] As mentioned above under year 51, this text possibly refers to a *Ḥb-Sd* of Ramesses, either his twelfth or thirteenth, depending upon the exact date of the text directly above it.[397] Unfortunately, the inscription is so short that it furnishes nothing more than the regnal year.

63-B. Deir el-Medineh, Ostracon No. 285

A fragmentary list of goods, apparently taxes (*b3kw*), with "Regnal year 63, 1st month of *šmw*, day...," was discovered at Deir el-Medineh.[398] No royal or private names are given; all it contains is a list of foodstuffs.

63-C. Tonqala (Tomas), Stela of *St3w*

Just to the south of Tomas on the opposite bank, there is a stela of the Viceroy of Kush, *St3w*, which most likely belongs to regnal year 63 of Ramesses II.[399] The date is partially destroyed, but year 63 has been suggested by Weigall as the only reasonable restoration.[400] The text records the donations to a statue of Ramesses given by the *ḥ3ty-'* of *Mỉ'm* (Aniba), *Ḏḥwty-ms*.[401] Beneath this is a short notation that the stela was made by the Viceroy of Kush, *St3w*.[402]

Year 64

64-A. Deir el-Medineh, Ostracon No. 621

Ostracon 621 from Deir el-Medineh foreshadows the end of Ramesses' reign, for it not only lists regnal year 64, but also records a year 2, which can only belong to his successor.[403] The *recto* contains a list of accounts and supplies and has the date, "Regnal year 64, 1st month of *šmw* day 12," while the *verso* begins with "Regnal year 2, 3rd month of *3ḫt* day 2." The *verso* mentions several names, but without titles except for *Nfr-ḥtp*, an *'3-n-ỉst*; therefore it is difficult to identify these persons.[404]

Year 65

65-A. Sesebi, Votive Tablet

From the sanctuary of the South Temple at Sesebi in Nubia comes a fragment of a votive tablet recording regnal year 65 of Ramesses II.[405] The tablet, discovered during the excavations of 1936-37, was dedicated by an *ỉmy-r mš'* and is made of blue faience. The purpose of the tablet remains unknown; perhaps it was to commemorate one of Ramesses' Jubilees.[406]

Year 66

66-A. Armant, Temple Pylon, Fragment

This fragment has been discussed under years 51-A, 61-A and 63-A where it was proposed that it records Ramesses' last Jubilees.[407] The third year date on this block is only partially preserved and therefore must in part be restored. Since it is the lowest in position of the three dates, we may assume it is the latest one, if the other inscription recording the Jubilees of Ramesses II at Armant be any indication.[408] The possible readings are: 65(',','), 66(¦¦¦) or, least likely, 67(¦'¦'¦'¦),[409] assuming that the first group should read 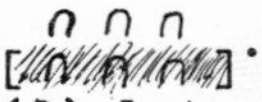. If this is a Jubilee date, it should be "Regnal year 66 (?) 1st month of *prt* day 1 (?) of King...." If it does represent a *Ḥb-Sd*, it must have been Ramesses' last.[410]

66-B. Cairo Ostracon 25237

An ostracon from Abydos, which Mariette records as having been found at the Shunet el-Zebib,[411] is dated to a year 66 which can only refer to Ramesses II.[412] "Regnal year 66, 1st month of *3ḫt* day 1," is on the *verso*, while the third month of *3ḫt* day 5 is given for the *recto*.[413] Because of its poor condition, much of the text is lost, though several names and titles are still legible: *Inpw-m-ḥb*, a scribe; *Nḫt-Mîn*, chief of police; and *Nfr-ḥtp*, an *'3 n îst*. This *Nfr-ḥtp* is mentioned on Papyrus Salt 124,[414] but the other men are less well known.[415]

66-C. Coptos Stela, *B3k-wr*

The private stela of *B3k-wr*, discovered by Maspero at Coptos in 1886, is dated to "Regnal year 66 under the King, the Lord of the two lands, *Wsr-M3't-R' Stp-n-R'*, may he live, the son of Re and Lord of appearances, *R'-ms.sw Mry-Imn*, may he live like Re."[416] According to the copy available, the sentence which follows is very difficult to translate.[417] The text apparently records a transfer of property which was presumably made in regnal year 66 of Ramesses II. Because of the orthographic peculiarities, it would be best to hold this inscription in abeyance, since it does not appear to be contemporaneous with the date it records.[418]

Year 67

67-A. Papyrus Gurob, Fragment L

Ramesses' 67th and last regnal year is attested in a tax document found by Petrie at Gurob.[419] "Regnal year 67, 1st month of *3ḫt* day 18," is the first date listed; a few lines beneath is another, "Regnal year 1, 2nd month (?) of *3ḫt*(?) day 19."[420] It is unfortunate that the exact month is not clearly preserved in the second date; otherwise one could say that Ramesses died after the 1st month of *3ḫt* day 18 and before the 2nd month of *3ḫt* day 19.[421] This is the highest regnal date in any record from the reign of Ramesses II, and it supports the 66 years and 2 months given him by Manetho, as recorded by Josephus.[422]

67-B. Abydos Stela, Ramesses IV

A stela belonging to the 4th regnal year of Ramesses IV contains a reference to the length of Ramesses II's reign.[423] In lines 22-23 Ramesses IV states, "Oh greater...are the benefactions which I have done for your (the gods) domain, in order to endow your divine offerings and to seek every excellent thing and every beneficial thing, that they be done at your temple-court every day, during these four years, than that which *Wsr-M3't-R' Stp-n-R'*, the great god, did for you during his 67 years. And so may you give to me the long lifetime and the great reign which you gave (him)...." Though Ramesses IV did not receive all the blessings from the gods which he desired, he did furnish a second reference to Ramesses' 67th year as the year of his death.[424]

Section 2. Inscriptions with Questionable Dates

Within the corpus of dated inscriptions belonging to the reign of Ramesses II, there are some which no longer retain the regnal year; either it has been partially destroyed, broken off or obliterated and is no longer legible. At times restorations are feasible; in such an instance the inscription has been discussed under the restored date. But when the traces are too questionable for any sound restoration, there is no one year to which the text may be assigned. Such inscriptions should be classified in a special category established for those records which once were dated but no longer retain a legible regnal year.

A. Deir el-Medineh, Ostracon No. 233

Like many from Deir el-Medineh, this ostracon is a terse business document and records the payments made by one *P3y* to a person with the name *Ḏḥwty-ḥr-mkt.f*.[425] Unlike many business forms, which give only month and day, this one was specifically dated to a regnal year. Unfortunately, the actual year number has been lost and all that remains is "Regnal year 1+...*nswt-bît Wsr-M3't-R' Stp-n-R'*."[426] Though only the prenomen is given, it must represent Ramesses II for no other king in this period bore the same prenomen.[427] In this instance the names are not much help in dating the ostracon precisely. The name *P3y* must be an abbreviation, and though the name *Ḏḥwty-ḥr-mkt.f* is less common, the person cannot be established with certainty.

There is a *Ḏḥwty-ḥr-mkt.f* mentioned in Theban Tomb 357,[428] whose wife is called *Wr-n-r3*, but that *Ḏḥwty* has the title of *sḏmw 'š m St-M3't* (Servant in the Place of Truth) rather than the title of *w'w* ("soldier") found on this ostracon. However, one may assume that this ostracon belongs to the reign of Ramesses II, though the precise year remains unknown.

B. Giza, Chephren Complex, Stela Fragment

This badly weathered limestone fragment was discovered during the excavations of the Chephren mortuary complex; the piece containing two (fragmentary) lines is 90-100 cm. long. Hoelscher originally read the date as "year 20 under the Majesty of...,"[429] but this was questioned by Sethe. Because the prenomen was written *Wsr-M3't-R'* only, Sethe placed this inscription in the early part of regnal year 1.[430] According to the published photograph, which is not very clear, the numeral is certainly 20, but that which precedes it is more likely a month rather than the word *rnpt*. Sethe restored the month *prt*, even though it could also be read *3ḫt*.[431] In either case, the traces above the circle do not appear to be a *t* (⌂), and consequently the word is not likely *rnpt*. Since the date is lost, this brief inscription may not be assigned to any specific regnal year, not even by means of the abbreviated prenomen.[432]

C. Graffito, Theban Necropolis, No. 18

A badly preserved inscription from the Theban necropolis has "Regnal year 39(?), 4th month of *3ḫt* day 20(?)," which is followed by "death(?) of *Pn-t3-[wrt]*."[433] Unfortunately, this graffito is in such poor condition, neither the date nor the person's name can be read with certainty.[434]

D. Deir el-Medineh, Wine Jar Inscriptions

From Theban tomb 359 come two wine jars with similar notations, each with the same incomplete year date, "Regnal year 40+...."[435] Though the tomb is assigned to the reign of Ramesses IV,[436] it contained a wine jug inscription recording year 2 of Horemhab.[437] Since an Eighteenth Dynasty record appeared in this tomb, it is not surprising to find dates which belong to Ramesses II.[438] Both inscriptions consist of this short notation and nothing more.[439]

There are certain inscriptions which could possibly belong to the reign of Ramesses II, even though there is no reference to him within these texts themselves; any inscription generally dated to the Ramesside period or even more specifically to the Nineteenth Dynasty could belong to his reign. It is not necessary to discuss in detail those inscriptions which have been wrongly dated in the past, for they have been corrected;[440] it would also be superfluous to list the stelae with regnal years which belong to the Ramesside period in general if they cannot be more closely dated.[441] On the other hand, the New Kingdom material from Sinai forms a special corpus; most of the Ramesside texts with regnal years can be correctly dated except for four inscriptions with low regnal years. In view of the later discussion of the Sinai material, these four texts will be investigated in this section.[442]

Year 3

Sinai, Serabit el-Khadim, No. 301

The stela of *Sty-nḫt*, with year 3 of an unknown king, has been assigned to either the Nineteenth or the Twentieth Dynasty.[443] Since the style of this text is unlike those with *'š3-m-ḥbw-sd* and *Imn-m-Ipt*, who are dated to the early reign of Ramesses II,[444] and because the phraseology is similar to that found on two stelae dated to regnal year 5 of Ramesses IV (nos. 275 and 276),[445] this stela probably belongs to the Twentieth Dynasty, approximately the time of Ramesses IV.

Sinai, Serabit el-Khadim, No. 302

On this stela, *Sbk-ḥtp* states that this was his fourth journey to Sinai, though it is his only record now extant there.[446] If this man were active during the reign of Ramesses II, he might have been a contemporary of *'š3-m-ḥbw-sd* and *Imn-m-Ipt*, though there is no indication of this.[447] The similarity in style between it and nos. 275 and 276, which were mentioned in the preceding paragraph, is the best indication of its date; like no. 301, this too should be assigned to the Twentieth Dynasty and not to the reign of Ramesses II.

Year 4

Sinai, Serabit el-Khadim, No. 304

On the upper face of this stela, the name *R'-ms.sw* is written without a cartouche, just beneath a winged sun disk.[448] The few remaining words of the original text comprise little more than the date, "Regnal year 4, 2nd month of *šmw*...." This fragment is too vague to be assigned to the reign of Ramesses II.

Year 5

Sinai, Serabit el-Khadim, No. 294

The stela of *Wsr-ḫ'w* bears the date, "Regnal year 5, 2nd month of *šmw*...."[449] Though the inscription is very brief, similarities between it and the stelae of year 5 of Ramesses IV can be established and also between it and no. 302 mentioned above. These similarities point to a date within the Twentieth Dynasty and thus this record does not pertain to the reign of Ramesses II.[450]

There are a number of ostraca, papyri and wine jar inscriptions which do not contain a royal name by which the text may be dated to a specific period; many of these are assigned to the Nineteenth Dynasty in general, though some are more specifically attributed to the reign of Ramesses. As has been mentioned in the previous section, any inscription assigned to this period on paleographic grounds with a regnal date higher than year 32 should belong to Ramesses II; these have been treated under the regnal date in the earlier section.[451]

The list given in Chart I is a representative body of ostraca, papyri and jar inscriptions as found in the major publications of such material.[452] These have been assembled in order to present a group of texts which could be assigned to Ramesses II according to the general dates given by the different authors of these works. The "attributed date" given in the chart is that of the author of the publication, unless indicated;[453] only those texts which could possibly belong to the time of Ramesses II have been included. For example, if an author assigned an ostraca to the second half of the Nineteenth Dynasty, it will not be given in this list, though something dated to the Nineteenth Dynasty in general has been listed, since it could possibly belong to the reign of Ramesses II. Because of the difficulties involved in dating a text by paleography alone, it is impossible to be certain about the specific date of any of these inscriptions; therefore they cannot be used for a chronological structure of this reign.[454]

CHART I

Ostraca, Papyri and Wine Jar Inscriptions of Questionable Date

Abbreviations:

CG:HO = Černý-Gardiner, Hieratic Ostraca
C:DeM = Černý, Doc. de fouilles 3-7 (with ostracon number)
C:OH = Černý, Ostraca hiératiques (with ostracon number)
G:RAD = Gardiner, Ramesside Administrative Documents
N:DeF = Nagel, Doc. de fouilles 10 (with page number)
D:O = Daressy, Ostraca (with ostracon number)

Year	Publication	Attributed Date
1	C:DeM 30	19th Dynasty
1	C:DeM 215	19th Dynasty
1	G:RAD 27	*Ramesses II?
2	C:OH 25676	19th Dynasty
2	C:DeM 209	19th Dynasty
2	CG:HO XXV (2)	*
2	CG:HO CVI (1)	*
2	G:RAD 60-63	Ramesses II or Merneptah?
3	C:DeM 5	19th Dynasty
3	C:DeM 7	19th Dynasty
3	C:DeM 8	19th Dynasty
3	C:DeM 9	19th Dynasty
3	C:DeM 13	19th Dynasty
3	C:DeM 18	19th Dynasty
3	C:DeM 23	19th Dynasty
3	C:DeM 24	19th Dynasty
3	CG:HO XXVI (2)	19th Dynasty
3	CG:HO LIV (1)	*
3	CG:HO LVI (3)	*
3	C:OH 25552	19th Dynasty
4	N:DeF 18 (30)	* Ramesside
4	CG:HO XVI (3)	*
4	CG:HO LIX (2)	*
5	CG:HO XX (1)	*
5	CG:HO XX (3)	*
5	CG:HO XXVII (3)	Ramesside
6	N:DeF 15 (2)	* Ramesside
6	CG:HO XVI (2)	*

*Not assigned to any specific period by the author(s).

Year	Publication	Attributed Date
6	CG:HO XXXII (3)	*
7	CG:HO XXXVI (1)	*
11	C:DeM 354	19th Dynasty
15	CG:HO XXXIX (2)	* Ramesses II or III?
17	CG:HO LXVIII (3)	* Ramesses III?
19	N:DeF 50 (b)	* Ramesside
19	C:DeM 192	19th Dynasty
20+	C:OH 25594	Ramesses II?
20+	C:OH 25502	19th Dynasty
22	G:RAD 34	Ramesses II or III
23	C:DeM 140	19th Dynasty
23	CG:HO LXIV (2)	* Ramesses III?
24	CG:HO LXXXI-II	* Ramesses III?
24	C:OH 25803	19th Dynasty
24	N:DeF 64 (11)	* Ramesside
26	C:OH 25681	19th Dynasty
26	CG:HO III (3)	* Ramesses II or III?
27	C:DeM 334	19th Dynasty
27	D:O 25365	Ramesses II or III
28	CG:HO LXIII (2)	* Ramesses III?
29(?)	C:OH 25798	19th Dynasty
31	CG:HO LXVII (3)	* Ramesses II or III?

Ramesseum

The ostraca and wine jar inscriptions from the Ramesseum[455] present a particular problem, for though one might assume that most of the regnal dates which they represent would refer to the reign of Ramesses II, such is apparently not the case.[456] As the following chart indicates, most of the inscriptions belong to regnal years 3 to 8 of unspecified rulers. Though many of them contain references to the *Ḥwt-Wsr-M3ʿt-Rʿ-Stp-n-Rʿ*, this is only an indication of origin or destination, not of date; the Ramesseum remained in use many years after the death of its owner, as shown by the various ostraca and papyri which date as late as the Twenty-sixth Dynasty.[457] The different names of vineyards and their overseers also allude to reigns of kings other than Ramesses himself; this has been recognized and an attempt has been made to distribute these labels throughout the Nineteenth and Twentieth Dynasties.[458] The four inscriptions which have dates higher than year 32 must belong to Ramesses II, as their paleography generally dates them; thus only four sherds represent the last thirty-five years of his rule.[459] Such a sparsity of material for that period indicates that most of the earlier material must belong to other reigns. Since the majority of the labels are confined to years 3 to 8, it is most likely that they belong to different Ramesside kings, with no particular ruler being responsible for the majority. Thus these inscriptions are of no significance in constructing a chronological structure for Ramesses' reign.

CHART II

Ramesseum Jar Inscriptions

Year	Spiegelberg Number
2	157
3	174
	177
	253
	313
	318
	325*
4	178
	219
	227
	254
	279
	303
5	148
	152
	155
	160
	180
	204
	224
	239
	248
	362*
6	149
	217
	218
	229
	235
	255*
	265

Year	Spiegelberg Number
7	153
	176
	201
	211
	216
	221
	243
	251*
	261
8	145
	192
	197
	225*
	257
	291
9	269
10	319*
13	285
17	311
19	241
29	240
33	275
39	321
57	323
58	300

* Questionable, since the year is not well preserved.

N. B. The regnal dates higher than year 32 have been discussed previously in the corpus of dated inscriptions.

NOTES TO CHAPTER II

EXAMINATION OF DATED INSCRIPTIONS

[1] Gauthier, Bibl. d'étude 4; Porter-Moss VI 3 (34-37); Kitchen, Ramesside Inscriptions II 323-326.

[2] For the use of *ḫft* to equate one year date with another, see Newberry, Beni Hasan I, Pl. 8; similarly, Papyrus Abbott, *verso*, A 1 and 19; cf. Černý, JEA 15 (1929), 194, note 3.

[3] This part begins with a general temporal introduction (*w' m nn hrw*) and then gives the specific date.

[4] See below under year 1, Theban tomb 157; Sethe, ZAeS 44 (1907-8), 30-35; Porter-Moss I^2 267 (8).

[5] The text reads, *m rnpt tpy n ḫ''.ἰ*, and reminds one of the statement attributed to Seti I in the dedicatory inscription line 45, which reads, *ḏd.n.f r.ἰ sḫ' sw m nswt....* For *ḫ'ἰ*, see Redford, History and Chronology, 3-27.

[6] The words are different but could refer to the same activity, as understood by Breasted, ARE III, p. 110, note a.

[7] For other retrospective dates, see below 1-D(?), 8-C, 15-A, 16-A, 18-B, 26-A, 30-A, 30-B, 30-C, 33-A, 33-E, 34-A, 34-B, 34-C, 37-A, 55-A, 56-A, 66-C, and 67-B.

[8] Porter-Moss V 217; Champollion, Mon. cxxii bis (3), ciii (i).

[9] For a recent discussion of this Queen, see Thausing and Goedicke, Nofertari, where in the commentary (p. 31) this dated reference is omitted, but see note 5 on p. 32.

[10] Porter-Moss V 217.

[11] Porter-Moss V 216-217.

[12] Collation by Stern, ZAeS 11 (1873), 129-135.

[13] Sethe, ZAeS 62 (1927), 112; Gauthier, Livre des rois III 35; Porter-Moss III 9.

[14] Sharpe, Egyptian Antiquities in the British Museum, 1862, p. 63.

[15] Sharpe, Egyptian Inscriptions from the British Museum and Other Sources, Pl. 33 (B). Before his recent work, Hieroglyphic Tests from Egyptian Stelae, etc., Part 9, appeared, a copy was kindly supplied by T. G. H. James of the Department of Egyptian Antiquities, The British Museum. For this inscription, see his Pl. VII and p. 13, and also Kitchen, *op. cit.*, 337.

[16] L. D. III 189 a; Weigall, Report, 124; Porter-Moss VII 108 (92-3).

[17] Christophe, La Revue du Caire 47 (1961), 303-333. Also Habachi, Abh. DAIK 5 (1969), 7-8, who quotes an unpublished work by Christophe.

[18] Christophe, *op. cit.*, 311, states that this date must belong to some king other than Ramesses II, possibly Seti II.

[19] Champollion, Not. descr. I 851-852; L. D. Text III 239 (a); Sethe,

ZAeS 44 (1907-8), 30-35; Porter-Moss I² 267 (8).

20 Gauthier, Bibl. d'étude 4 (Abydos inscription). Also see Sethe, ZAeS 58 (1923), 54; Edgerton, JNES 6 (1947), 157-158; Kees, Das Priestertum im aegyptischen Staat, 90-91 and 100-101; and Wente, JNES 25 (1966), 73-87, for a similar text from the Twentieth Dynasty.

21 Spiegelberg, Aegyptische und andere Graffiti, no. 298, p. 26. The scribes names are *Ỉmn-nḫt* (son of *Ỉpwy*) and his sons *Ḥr-(šrỉ?)*, *Ỉmn-ḥtp* and *Pn-t3-wr*. *Ỉmn-nḫt* also left a second inscription in the necropolis, see year 2-E.

22 The names are not uncommon for workmen at Deir el-Medineh, but the parentage rules out those commonly found there at that time.

23 el-Razik, MDAIK 22 (1967), 68-69, Pl. 28 (b); Kitchen, JEA 57 (1971), 110.

24 See 3-B, below.

25 L. D. III 175 g; Text IV 119 (5); de Rougé, Inscr. hiéro. cclii-ccliii. It is also recorded in de Morgan, etc., Cat. des mon. I 6, who appears to have followed de Rougé and Lepsius.

26 Porter-Moss V 245; Kitchen *op. cit.*, 334-335, not collated with the original.

27 Since Qadesh was Ramesses' second campaign and we know of one in the year preceding it, it appears impossible to presume that he conducted one as early as year 2; for this also, see Redford, JEA 57 (1971), 118-119. With regard to the date, it is quite likely that both de Rougé and de Morgan were dependent upon Lepsius for the regnal year.

The number 2 is commonly written after *rnpt* (𓆳𓇳𓏻) and with longer strokes than is usual with higher units, perhaps to distinguish 𓏻 from 𓎆 . For an inscription with similar problems, see year 2-C below.

28 Gardiner-Peet-Černý, Inscriptions of Sinai I 177-178 and II, Pl. LXX; Kitchen, *op. cit.*, 339-340; Porter-Moss VII 349-350. For *ḥry pḏt(yw)*, see Shulman, Military Rank, Title and Organization in the Egyptian New Kingdom, 53-56.

29 Gardiner-Peet-Černý, *op. cit.*, no. 247 = I 175-176 and II, Pl. LXVIII; no. 250 = I 176-177 and II, Pl. LXXI; no. 253 = I 178 and II, Pl. LXX; no. 260 = I 180 and II, Pl. LXXI; no. 261 = I 181 and II, Pl. LXXI; no. 262 = I 181 (that is, I 175-176 and II, Pl. LXVIII, the south side of no. 247); Kitchen, *op. cit.*, 339-341.

30 See Gauthier, Livre des rois III *passim*.

31 Gardiner-Peet-Černý, *op. cit.*, I 175-176 and II, Pl. LXVIII.

32 *Ibid.*, I 176 and II, Pl. LXVIII. See also below, chap. V.

33 These texts do not contain much information; no. 253 has only the prenomen with the name of *ʿš3-m-ḥbw-sd*, while no. 260 is very fragmentary, as is no. 216.

34 Particularly nos. 250, 253, 254(?), 260 and 261.

35 L. D. III 197 c; Kitchen, *op. cit.*, 149; Porter-Moss VII 385.

36 Lepsius, Briefe aus Aegypten, 403. Kitchen, *loc. cit.*, gives the date as "year 10" with no comment upon the possible variant. A similar problem was discussed in year 2-A above, the Aswan Stela.

37 Qadesh B 3.

38 Breasted, AJSL 25 (1908-9), 98.

39 *Ibid.*

40 Spiegelberg, Aegyptische und andere Graffiti, no. 225, p. 21. This year *Imn-nḫt* was accompanied by only one other person, the scribe *'nḫ.f-n-Imn*. One cannot be certain if this is the same person whose name was found in a graffito in Theban Tomb 291; Bruyère and Kuentz, MIFAO 55, 57.
For the earlier graffito of *Imn-nḫt*, see year 1-F.

41 Tresson, Bibl. d'étude 9, vii-xvi and 1-11, with Pls. I-III for the text. Also see Porter-Moss VII 83.

42 The Wadi Allaki touches the Nile valley at Quban, hence the erection of the stela at that site. For an interesting and early translation, see Birch, Archaeologia 34 (1852), 357-391; later, Breasted, ARE III §§285-293.

43 For a similar activity in the reign of Seti I, see Schott, Kanais, der Tempel Sethos I. im Wadi Mia, 134-135 and 139. For a description of the area, Weigall, ASAE 9 (1908), 71-77.

44 Redford, JEA 57 (1971) 110-119, with Pl. XXXI A; Kitchen, *op. cit.*, 345-347. The text is not well preserved.

45 The intent and purpose of the two texts are not the same. The Heliopolis stela records an agreement between the king and workmen; the Luxor text is dedicatory.

46 Unlike the Abydos inscription, the one at Luxor appears to be more directly related to the building upon which it is found; that at Abydos is more general.

47 The first part of the inscription is written in horizontal lines, while the latter part--containing the date--is vertical. Some of the signs employed, particularly in the first part, are not common in most of the texts left by Ramesses II, though this is, perhaps, no good reason to question its authenticity.

48 L. D. III 197 b; Kitchen, Ramesside Inscriptions II 1, Porter-Moss VII 385. The day is uncertain; it is at least "day 2," though it could be "day 3" if a stroke has been lost.

49 As stated under year 2 above, Qadesh was his second military campaign (B 3). The battle of Qadesh is discussed under year 5-A.

50 Starkey, PEFQS 1937, 238, Pl. VII; Illustrated London News, Nov. 27, 1937, 944-945, figs. 1 and 7; Porter-Moss VII 371.

51 Gardiner and Černý quoted by Starkey, *op. cit.*, and interpreted by Albright, BASOR 69 (1938), 7, note 2, to mean that it must date to Merneptah.

[52] Starkey, *op. cit.*, 237-239. Albright's objections in BASOR 68 (1937), 23, to such a date are not conclusive.

[53] Kuentz, MIFAO 55. Also see Kitchen, Ramesside Inscriptions II, 2-147.

[54] The Ḳadesh Inscriptions of Ramesses II.

[55] Gardiner, *op. cit.*, discusses these terms and proposes new ones; however, for convenience the older terms will be retained since the changes are not completely adequate.

[56] Kuentz, *op. cit.*, 328; Porter-Moss VI 39-41.

[57] Kuentz, *op. cit.*; Porter-Moss II 151 (6-12).

[58] Kuentz, *op. cit.*; Porter-Moss II 152.

[59] Kuentz, *op. cit.*; Porter-Moss II 100 (6-9).

[60] Kuentz, *op. cit.*; Porter-Moss II 109 (130-131).

[61] Kuentz, *op. cit.*; Porter-Moss II 110 (136-141).

[62] Kuentz, *op. cit.*; Porter-Moss VII 103-104 (41-42).

[63] Kuentz, *op. cit.*, 1-13; Porter-Moss VI 39-41.

[64] Kuentz, *op. cit.*, 67-108, 115-143 and 144-149; Porter-Moss II 100 (6-9), 109 (130-131), and 110 (136-141).

[65] Kuentz, *op. cit.*, 21-52; Porter-Moss II 24 (69-70).

[66] Kuentz, *op. cit.*, 52-66; Porter-Moss II 61.

[67] Kuentz, *op. cit.*, 169-180; Porter-Moss II 152.

[68] Kuentz, *op. cit.*, 205-208[8], first published by Hawkins, Select Papyri in the British Museum, Pls. XXIV-XXXIV.

[69] Gardiner, Hieratic Papyri in the British Museum, Third Series, I 23-24 and II, Pls. 9-10; Kitchen, Ramesside Inscriptions II 2-101.

[70] For the most recent discussion of the battle itself, see Goedicke, JEA 52 (1966), 71-80.

[71] Černý, Cairo Cat., I 55 (p. 75*) and II, Pl. LXX. Also see Bruyère, FIFAO 20 iii 19 (Report, 1935-40).

[72] For a reference to this temple, note Helck, Materialien, 202.

[73] Černý, Revue de l'Égypte ancienne 2 (1929), 200-209.

[74] Černý, Doc. de fouilles 9, 6 (no. 1140), Pl. 13; Porter-Moss I^2 771. The paleography is typically Ramesside, and Ramesses II is the only king of this period with that prenomen.

[75] Porter-Moss I^2 15-16, 309 and 336, respectively.

[76] Bruyère, FIFAO 20 ii 56, Pl. XII (no. 115), discussed below under regnal year 9-B.

77 This same *R'-ms* is represented on a stela with the Vizier *P3-sr*, a correlation which helps date *P3-sr* to the early years of Ramesses II. Bruyère, *op. cit.*, 129; Helck, Verwaltung, 447-51.

78 Virey, Mission archéologique francaise au Caire, Mémoires, I 481-510; see Pl. IV for the date and Pl. I for the royal name. Reference is also made to this date by Černý in Le fonti indirette della storia egiziana, 38-39.

79 Steindorff, Aniba II 1, 27 (54); II 2, Tafel 13, 52.

80 Written 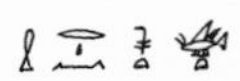 which must stand for 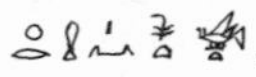.

81 *Ibid.*, II 1, 27 (54).

82 *Ibid.*, II 1, 21 and 23.

83 Ramesseum, west face of the north tower of the first pylon. Porter-Moss II 151; Wreszinski, Atlas II 90-91; Kitchen, *op. cit.*, 148-149.

84 It is quite possible that this stela was erected in year 8 itself.

85 Pleyte-Rossi, Papyrus de Turin I 41 and II, Pl. XXIX; not listed in Gauthier, Livre des rois III unless this is the source for the one on III 226, which has the same spelling.

86 Kamal, Rec. Trav. 30 (1908), 213-214; with a more recent publication and commentary by Hamada, ASAE 38 (1938), 217-230; cf. Porter-Moss IV 62. For further commentaries, see Sethe, ZAeS 62 (1927), 113; Schaefer, ZAeS 67 (1931), 93-94; Loret, Mélanges Maspero I 2, 873; Helck, Materialien 205; and Hermann, Die aegyptische Koenigsnovelle, 53-56 and Tafel II.

87 Kuentz, MIFAO 55, 208^{7-8}; Kitchen, *op. cit.*, 101.

88 de Rougé, Revue égyptologique 3 (1885), 149.

89 Kuentz, *op. cit.*, $203\text{-}208^{8}$.

90 See Gardiner, The Ḳadesh Inscriptions of Ramesses II, 1-6, for a recent view on prevailing terminology.

91 Hawkins, Select Papyri in the Hieratic Character from the Collections of the British Museum, Pl. XXXIV; Moeller, Hieratische Palaeographie II, Tafel V (Papyrus Raifé).

92 Bruyère, FIFAO 20 ii 56-57, Pl. XII (no. 115).

93 For the phrase *St-M3't* and titles compounded therewith, see Černý, Revue de l'Égypte ancienne 2 (1929), 200-209, and note 73 above.

94 See years 5-B and 5-C above.

95 Rowe, Pennsylvania University Museum Journal 20 (1929), 94-95.

96 Černý, Eretz Israel 5 (ת), 76* and 80* (a), followed by Kitchen, *op. cit.*, 150.

97 First announced by Bakir, ASAE 48 (1948), 425-31, and fully published by him as The Cairo Calendar, Cairo, 1966.

98 Bakir, Cairo Calendar, 2 and 4. Pages of Part II are also reused;

Ibid., 2 and 3.

99 Between *vs.* XX and XXI (Pl. L) there are some traces which could have been written by the same hand which wrote the colophon (also see the other traces on Pls. LI-LIV).

100 Parker, Calendars, 26-29.

101 Porter-Moss VII 385; Kitchen, *op. cit.*, 149.

102 Boscawen, TSBA 7 (1882), 336. Also see Virolleaud, L'Ethnographie 50 (1955), 4, with note 1, and Kitchen, *op. cit.*, 1.

103 Revillout, in Catalogue de la sculpture égyptienne, follows Brugsch.

104 The reading "16" is certain; Mariette, Sérapéum (1857) III 12 and 15, has year 16, as does Chassinat, Rec. Trav. 21 (1899), 70-72. Also see Gauthier, Livre des rois III 42, note 1; Porter-Moss III 206; and recently, Malinine, Posener, Vercoutter, Catalogue, 4, Pl. II.

105 Legrain, ASAE 16 (1916), 161-170, with plate. Translations by Legrain, *ibid.*; Thomas, Ancient Egypt 1921, 76-78; Roeder, Kulte, Orakel und Naturverehrung im alten Aegypten, 239-241; Černý, *op. cit.*, 43; Wilson, ANET[3], 448-449.

106 The date given is "Regnal year 14, 2nd month of *3ḫt* day 24(?)." It is not clearly written, particularly the day-number, which can be read 14 or 24, with the latter being more likely.

107 There is not much to indicate a particular date according to artistic style, but there is a very close similarity between this and the depiction of the oracular response which belongs to the reign of Ramesses XI, the major difference being this stela's simplification of detail. See Nims, JNES 7 (1948), 157-162, with references, and also Foucart, BIFAO 24 (1924), with plates.

108 See years 15-A, 18-B, 38-B and 46-A.

109 There is a difference between a legal dispute being settled by means of an oracle and the appointment of a particular person, such as *Nb-wnn.f*, to an office (1-E); cf. Lods, Mélanges Maspero I, 91-100.

110 For this, see Černý in Parker, A Saite Oracle Papyrus from Thebes, 35-48.

111 I can find no example of *hrw pn* being written  in this period. One can find examples of the being omitted: 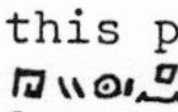 (Černý, Cairo Ostraca, 25557); 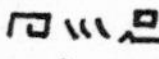 (Černý, Cairo Ostraca, 25613); 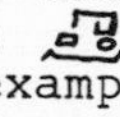 (Alliance, line 2); but none without the . A later example, from the time of Takelotis, does omit the : 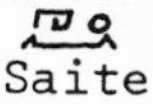 (Brugsch, Thesaurus, 1072). For *hrw pn*, see Parker, Saite Oracle Papyrus, 7.

112 The uncommon names are

P3-ỉr (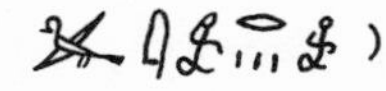), Ranke, Personennamen I 101 (23);

Yn-ḏ3-bw (), Ranke, *op. cit.*, 56 (10);

Sdm.n.f (), Ranke, *op. cit.*, 323 (22);

T3y (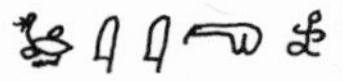), Ranke, *op. cit.*, 386 (22).

113 Černý, *op. cit.*, 38-43; Kaiser, Zeitschrift fuer Religions und Geistgeschichte 10 (1958), 193-208. A stela from Coptos has been assigned to his reign; Černý, *op. cit.*, 40, with note 1.

114 Retrospective dating is not unusual in the reign of Ramesses II; for such, see years 1-A, 8-C, 15-A, 16-A, 18-B, 26-A, 30-A, 30-B, 30-C, 33-A, 33-E, 34-A, 34-B, 34-C, 37-B, 55-A, 56-A, 66-C and 67-B.

115 Gardiner, JEA 21 (1935), 140-146, discovered by H. E. Winlock in Theban tomb 48, along with a number of other papyrus fragments, ranging in date from the Eighteenth Dynasty to Ptolemaic times.

116 *Ibid.*, lines 1-5.

117 *Ibid.*, 141. Dating by paleography and grammar cannot be that precise as we do not have sufficient material for comparison; for example, Černý in Cahiers d'histoire mondiale I (1953-54), 905, with note 12, says that "of perhaps approximately the same date (as Cairo 65739) is a Vienna papyrus (No. 34)." His wording illustrates the caution one must use when attempting a specific date by such criteria, for the style of handwriting only shows when the scribe learned his art, not the actual date of the papyrus.

118 It is, of course, recognized that a certain amount of time must elapse between the erection of a stela and the date recorded upon it; this, however, is not considered a "retrospective date."

119 The upper part of the stela with the two dates reads,

See Mariette, Sérapéum III 12 and 15; Chassinat, Rec. Trav. 21 (1899), 70-72; Malinine, Posener, Vercoutte, Catalogue, 4, Pl. II; Porter-Moss III 206. Also see year 30-F.

120 Thesaurus 964-966.

121 *Op. cit.*, 12.

122 This burial has been discovered, and it contained a royal stela dated to regnal year 26 of Ramesses II; Daressy, ASAE 18 (1919), 196-210. See year 26-A.

123 Mariette, *op. cit.*, used these two earlier dates, years 16 and 26, in order to date several Apis burials; this has caused chronological confusion with regard to some officials belonging to the reign of Ramesses II, especially with regard to private stelae and shabtis found in the Apis burial. Yoyotte, Orientalia, N. S. 23 (1954), 227; Helck, Verwaltung, 312; Hornung, ZDMG 117 (1967), 12, note 4; Harris, JEA 54 (1968), 98, note 6.

124 The number 16 can be clearly seen in the recent publication of Malinine, Posener, Vercoutter, Catalogue, 4, Pl. II.

125 Winlock, Bulletin of the Metropolitan Museum of Art, Part II,

The Egyptian Expedition 1922-1923, 16, fig. 9; Porter-Moss I^2 387 (no. 311).

126 Winlock, *op. cit.*, 16-17. It is not known how much of the inscription is lost; we can only assume that the title, *ḥm-nṯr tpy n Ỉmn*, is the title of *Nb-nṯrw* and not part of a longer title or something which belongs to a preceding phrase or name of someone else, now lost.

127 One may question if this is truly a "visitor's inscription." Since it is a fragment we do not know how much information is lost and hence do not know the relationship between the remaining lines. A similar situation was encountered in the Abu Simbel text (1-D).
The fragment, which is on display at the Metropolitan Museum, perhaps has a trace of one sign from the second part of the prenomen. One might wish to see this as the top part of the *stp*-sign. I, myself, cannot be certain of that reading; though if it were true, it would limit the number of candidates (see note 130 below).

128 *Ibid.*, 16, where he reads "Ramesses II" in his translation of the incomplete prenomen.

129 Das Priestertum im aegyptischen Staat, 118; not listed by Lefebvre, Histoire des Grands Prêtres.

130 Gauthier, Livre des rois III *passim.*

131 Kees, *op. cit.*, 223-229 and 319; Die Hohenpriester des Amun von Karnak von Herihor bis zum Ende der Aethiopenzeit, 115. This name becomes very common in the Late Period; Ranke, Personennamen I 185 (27).

132 A number of tombs belonging to important personnel of Amun have been found there; Porter-Moss I^2 628-30.

133 Doc. de fouilles 3, 21.

134 This ostracon, attributed to Ramesses III by Černý, *op. cit.*, 19, Pl. 49A, also contains the regnal year date 18.

135 In a private communication, the late Professor Černý kindly informed me that Ostracon no. 77 must date to the reign of Ramesses III, as does no. 72.

136 Loret, ZAeS 39 (1901), 1-10; Gardiner, The Inscription of Mes, lines N 6 and 7.

137 Line N 6, the date reads, 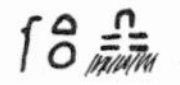.

138 Gardiner, Grammar^3 §259; Sethe, Die Entwicklung der Jahresdatierung bei den alten Aegypten, 91-92. Also see year 48-B.

139 They occur as part of the testimony given. For a similar situation, see year 15-A above.

140 See above chap. I.

141 The actual date of the trial is now lost. For a lawsuit belonging to the time of Ramesses II, containing a specific date, see regnal year 46-A; also one on an ostracon, year 38-B. For examples of specific dates in legal documents, see Peet, The

Great Tomb Robberies of the Twentieth Dynasty; for judicial procedure, Seidl, Einfuerhrung in die aegyptische Rechtsgeschichte bis zum Ende des Neuen Reiches. For similar texts dated retrospectively, see below, footnote 362.

142 Rowe, The History of Beth-Shan, 33-36. Also see Fischer, Pennsylvania University Museum Journal 14 (1923), 234 and fig. on p. 245; Rowe, Pennsylvania University Museum Journal 20 (1929), 94-98; Porter-Moss VII 379; Kitchen, *op. cit.*, 150-151.

143 Vol. 5 ([hieroglyph]), 76* and 80* (a).

144 For discussion of the word [hieroglyphs] , see Sethe, Die Entwicklung der Jahresdatierung bei den alten Aegypten, 95-100; Edel, JNES 8 (1949), 35-39; Gardiner, JNES 8 (1949), 165-171; Beckerath, ZAeS 84 (1959), 155-156, and ZAeS 95 (1969), 88-91. Following Edel, the reading *rnpt*, instead of *ḥ3t-sp*, will be employed.

145 Kitchen, *op. cit.*, 150, in note 10[a] says: "So, clearly, and not '9' (re-collated by D. O'Connor)." Unfortunately, the date is not as "clear" as this note would indicate.

146 Černý, Doc. de fouilles 3, 7, no. 31; Pl. 8A and 8.

147 Porter-Moss II 49 (2); Kitchen, *op. cit.*, 225-232.

148 Porter-Moss II 152 (14); Kitchen, *op. cit.*, 230-232. Earlier studies by W. M. Mueller, MVAG 1902, 5, and Sethe in JEA 6 (1920), Pl. XVIII, and a recent translation by Wilson, ANET[3], 199-201.

149 Most recently, Kitchen, *op. cit.*, 284-287, and a transcription in de Buck, Readingbook, 106-109. Also see de Rougé, Journal asiatique 5. Ser. T. 8, 1856-58; Tresson, Revue biblique 42 (1933), 57-78; Ranke, ZAeS 74 (1938), 49-51, Pl. V; Porter-Moss II 89; and translations by Breasted, ARE III §§429-447; Lefebvre, Romans et contes égyptiens, 221-232; E. Brunner-Traut, Altaegyptische Maerchen, 163-171; Wilson, ANET[3], 29-31.

150 Revillout in Catalogue de la sculpture égyptienne, follows Brugsch.

151 The reading "26" is corroborated by a royal stela found in the *Mn-wr* tomb near Heliopolis; see Daressy, ASAE 18 (1919), 207.

152 Daressy, ASAE 18 (1919), 207; Porter-Moss IV 59.

153 Daressy, *op. cit.*, 204-206.

154 See below under year 30, Louvre stelae 3 and 4. The year is referred to retrospectively in Louvre 3 by date, Chassiant, Rec. Trav. 21 (1899) 71. It is this burial which Mariette incorrectly applied to the Apis bull of the Serapeum, that is, "Apis III" which he dated to regnal year 26; Mariette, Sérapéum III, 12. Also see Otto, Beitraege zur Geschichte der Stierkulte in Aegypten, 34-40.

155 Černý, Doc. de fouilles 6, 3; Pl. 3, no. 250. The rest of the text contains a list of supplies.

156 For a different view, see E. Thomas, The Royal Necropoleis of Thebes, 108.

157 Gardiner, in Theban Ostraca, C. T. Currelly, ed., p. 8. For a discussion and references to *nḥḥ*-oil, see Helck, Materialien, 693-698.

158 For a similar ostracon with a reference to this same religious establishment, see year 47-A.

159 Mariette, Sérapéum, III 12.

160 Mariette, Sérapéum, III, Pl. 15; Chassinat, Rec. Trav. 21 (1899), 70-72.

161 ASAE 18 (1918), 207; see 26-A.

162 Officials such as the Vizier *P3-sr* have been placed in this period, because their names have been found connected with the tombs of "Apis II and III." However, Prince *Ḫ'-m-W3st*'s name is also found in conjunction with both "Apis II and III." It is impossible to associate him with a presumed burial in regnal year 16, since he first appears in dated inscriptions in year 30.

163 Hoelscher, O. I. C. 15 (1930-31), 51, fig. 35; Anthes in Hoelscher, Excavations of Medinet Habu II 107-108, fig. 90, Pl. 51 c. The translation follows Anthes' reading, *ibid.*

164 Hoelscher, O. I. C. 15 (1930-31), 51; Anthes, *op. cit.*, 107; von Beckerath, Tanis und Theben, 104; Wilson, JNES 13 (1954), 128; Redford, JEA 45 (1959), 36.

165 Fairman, CoA III 158; Helck, Manetho, 68, note 3, and MDAIK 17 (1961), 108; Kitchen, CdE 40 (1965), 313. Others tend in this direction but are not as explicit; Harris, JEA 54 (1968), 96, and Hornung, Chronologie, 39.

166 The difference of opinion is a result of a questionable reading; see the next note below.

167 Anthes, *op. cit.*, 107, reads *ỉr n*, but Fairman, *op. cit.*, 158, disagrees and reads *pr n*.

168 See Helck, ZDMG 102 (1952), 39-46.

169 Hoelscher, O. I. C. 15 (1930-31), 51, fig. 35.

170 Anthes, *op. cit.*, fig. 90; questioned by Fairman, *op. cit.*, 158, see Kitchen, CdE 40 (1965), 313.

171 It is dated to Ramesses II by default, because of the high regnal date and because it appears unlikely that the temple was functioning that late in the reign of Ramesses III.
The problem is further complicated by the fact that the inscription appears to have been written after the statue was broken, for the text seems to conform to the edges of the fragment.
Though the reading of *ỉr n* is more likely, either wording could refer to the entry of Horemhab into his mortuary temple after his death.

172 L. D. Text IV 175; Brugsch, Thesaurus 1127 I; Porter-Moss V 256; Habachi in ZAeS 97 (1971), 64, says "year 37."

173 The word *sr* (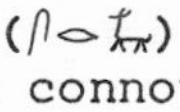) has been translated "announce" to fit the context as it connotes more the meaning of "announcing" rather

than "administrating" the festival. For a similar use of *sr*, cf. Wb. IV 190, 9. For *sr* and the coronation, see Gardiner, JEA 31 (1945), 23, note 4.

174 The Gebel Silsileh inscription of *Ḫ'-m-W3st* (Porter-Moss V 209) of regnal year 30 shows that he was active in the first Jubilee. See year 36-A below for the difficulties connected with the date of the third Jubilee.

175 Porter-Moss V 211-212. Photographs of these texts were kindly supplied by Professor Caminos of Brown University.

176 The duplicate texts, Porter-Moss V 212 (42-43); the other, V 212 (47). For others connected with the proclamation of this Jubilee, see Habachi, ZAeS 97 (1971), 65-67, fig. 2, Pl. V b, and fig. 3, Pl. V c.

177 Champollion, Mon. cxv-cxvi; Rosellini, Mon. d. Culto, xxxvii and xxxv.

178 It must have been carved before year 42, his fifth *Ḥb-Sd*, otherwise one would expect it to have been mentioned also.

179 Brugsch, Thesaurus, 1128 III; Habachi, ZAeS 97 (1971), 64; Porter-Moss V 212 (47). Professor Caminos also provided a photograph of this stela, as he did for the previous texts.

180 The use of the word *sr* appears to connote a special position and activity with regard to the *Ḥb-Sd* itself. See note 173 above. For others associated with this inscription, see Habachi, ZAeS 97 (1971), 66, and note 19.

181 Helck, Verwaltung, 456-458, incorrectly dates this to year 44, instead of year 40.

182 L. D. III 175 f; Brugsch, Thesaurus, 1127 II; Habachi, ZAeS 97 (1971), 64; Porter-Moss V 209 (4).

183 See above, 30-A and 30-B.

184 Černý-Gardiner, Hieratic Ostraca I 3, Pls. IX-IXA.

185 For literary products of a similar nature, see Papyrus Anastasi II 1, 1-2, 5, Praise of Per-Ramesses; on an ostracon from Thebes (Erman, ZAeS 38 [1900], 30-31) is a hymn of praise to Ramesses himself; also see the so-called poem on the king's chariot, Černý, Revue de l'Égypte ancienne 1 (1927), 224-226 and Dawson-Peet, JEA 19 (1933), 167-174.

186 Mariette, Sérapéum III 12 and 15; Chassinat, Rec. Trav. 21 (1899), 70-72; Porter-Moss III 206.

187 Under year 16-A, it was concluded that the reading "Regnal year 16" was correct and should be retained. The most recent publication is by Malinine, Posener, Vercoutter, Catalogue, 3-5, Pl. II.

188 Year 26 refers to a *Mn-wr* burial, the tomb of which has now been found (Daressy, ASAE 18 [1918], 196-210), and not an Apis; see year 26-A.

189 For such, see Otto, Beitraege zur Geschichte der Stierkulte in Aegypten, 19, 21 and 26.

190 Mariette, *loc. cit.*; Porter-Moss, *loc. cit.*

191 Mariette, Sérapéum III 15-16; Chassinat, Rec. Trav. 21 (1899), 72-73 (xxxv).

192 Mariette, Sérapéum III 12, calls this "Apis IV" and is followed in this by Porter-Moss III 206.

193 For further discussion of this problem, see under years 16-A and 26-A.

194 de Morgan, Cat. des mon. I 88 (62); Porter-Moss V 251 (137).

195 Habachi, ZAeS 97 (1971), 66, with note 21, gives the name as "Khnememwesekhet."

196 See below year 34-A, 34-B and 34-C.

197 See year 33-B.

198 Gardiner-Peet-Černý, Inscriptions of Sinai, I, Pl. LXXVII and II 194, no. 298; Porter-Moss VII 365. Since the date has been collated, it must be year 33, though one would expect year 34, because of the phrase *nb ḥbw-sd*. However, see year 33-A as a date for Ramesses' second Jubilee.

199 Černý, ZAeS 72 (1936), 109-118. Further see Goedicke, JEA 49 (1963), 71-92.

200 No photograph has been published; Gardiner-Peet-Černý (p. 194) have assigned it to Ramesses II. See Petrie, Researches in Sinai, 129.

201 Spiegelberg, Hieratic Ostraka and Papyri, Pl. XXXII, no. 275. The Ramesseum jar inscriptions are discussed together under a later section; only texts belonging to years 33, 39, 57 and 58 are included in this section.

202 Hawkins, Select Papyri in the Hieratic Character from the Collections of the British Museum, Pl. CXVIII; Gardiner, Late-Egyptian Miscellanies, 70; Caminos, Late-Egyptian Miscellanies, 266-269.

203 Gardiner, AEO II 202*-204*; JEA 5 (1918), 244, note 6; Hayes, JNES 10 (1951), 101. Also see Anastasi III *vs.* 6, 5.

204 The original letter might have been written only a few days after the date given, even though the copy we now have probably belongs to a later time and is the product of the Egyptian scribal schools.

205 Porter-Moss V 256.

206 Porter-Moss V 212 (42-43). Photographs provided by Professor Caminos.

207 Porter-Moss V 212 (47). Photograph provided by Professor Caminos.

208 Kuentz, ASAE 25 (1925), 181-185; Kitchen, *op. cit.*, 233-257.

209 Kuentz, *loc. cit.*; Porter-Moss VII 98 (8) and 106.

210 Fairman, JEA 24 (1938), 155 and 25 (1939), 140; Porter-Moss VII 159 (3).

211 Kuentz, *loc. cit.*, 181-185; Porter-Moss V 225.

212 Kuentz, *loc. cit.*; Porter-Moss II 59 (54). For texts from Amarah West and Aksha, which had hitherto been unpublished, see Kitchen, *op. cit.*, 233, with the texts on pp. 241-256.

213 Lefebvre, ASAE 25 (1925), 34-45; Kitchen, *op. cit.*, 256-257.

214 Petrie, Koptos 15, Pl. XVIII. A few lines also exist in the Seti Temple at Abydos; Kitchen, *op. cit.*, 282-284.

215 For a collection of the texts, see Kuentz, *op. cit.*, 181-238; Kitchen, *op. cit.*, 233-257 and 282-284.

216 This daughter of the Hittite king was still living in regnal year 61; Papyrus Gurob, Fragment N (61-A). Also see Gardiner, JNES 12 (1953), 145-149.

217 Černý, Doc. de fouilles 7, 29, Pl. 27 (no. 447).

218 Černý, *op. cit.*, 29.

219 The use of *rdyt* as a word for "payment" is common in the ostraca from Deir el-Medineh.
For the use of *š'y* as "money," see Černý, Cahiers d'histoire mondiale I (1953-54), 910-912.

220 Jéquier, Deux pyramides de Moyen Empire, 13-15.

221 This name is also found in a graffito in the Wadi Allaqi, whose father was *P3-rwḏy*, Černý, JEA 33 (1947), 54, no. 15. For a brief discussion of visitor inscriptions, see Helck, ZDMG 102 (1952), 39-46. For the name see Ranke, Personennamen I 170 (4-5).

222 The meaning of this name is obscure; *ḏsr* could be a nisbe referring to *Ḫnḏr* himself, but the *wpt ỉnr* (if the word is *ỉnr*) remains unclear. Professor Goedicke has suggested that *ḏsr* probably refers to Djoser and that the entire phrase refers to that mortuary complex instead of *Ḫnḏr*'s. See also Wildung, Die Rolle aegyptischer Koenige im Bewusztsein ihrer Nachwelt, 72-74.

223 For other visitors' inscriptions, see years 17-A, 36-D, 47-B, 48-C and 50-A; and years 5-C, 27-A, 37-D and 40-F for graffiti.

224 Four copies from the time of Ramesses II and one of Ramesses III; Kitchen, *op. cit.*, 258-281.

225 L. D. III 209 c and Text III 170; de Rougé, Inscr. hiero., cxxxi-cxxxviii; Porter-Moss II 179 (3).

226 Porter-Moss VII 106, between Pillars III and IV.

227 Porter-Moss VII 159 (2-3), where the niches are on either side of the entrance to the inner court of the temple of Ramesses II.

228 Anthes, Mit Rahineh 1955 and 1956, *passim*; Petrie, Memphis I-VI.

229 Again the relation between this king and the god Ptah may be seen; cf. Holmberg, Ptah, 204-250, particularly 235-40.

230 Ramesses III does not reproduce the text of the Marriage Stela, for obvious reasons, though it was more popular in the reign of Ramesses II than the Decree of Ptah.

231 See year 34-D for the Marriage Stela.

232 Gauthier, Livre des rois III 44 (xxxi); Porter-Moss IV 99.

233 Only  remains, which can reasonably be restored as *ḥryt*.

234 But note the "Harim" at Mi-wer, where the Hittite princess later lived; see 61-A.

235 Černý-Gardiner, Hieratic Ostraca I 7, Pls. XXIII-XXIIIA (2).

236 *Ibid.*, 7.

237 Spiegelberg, Aegyptische und andere Graffiti, no. 988, p. 82.

238 Porter-Moss V 256 (5B), discussed under 30-A.

239 See years 37-A and 37-B below.

240 Ramesses apparently followed the example set by Amenophis III who also celebrated his first three Jubilees in years 30, 34 and 37. However, Amenophis has a year 38 reference to his third Jubilee; see Hayes, JNES 10 (1951), fig. 11, no. 142. Also see years 33-A, 34-A, 34-B, 34-C. Habachi, ZAeS 97 (1971), 64, gives year 37.

241 Černý, Cahiers d'histoire mondiale I, 911, with note 26.

242 Černý, *op. cit.*, 911, note 27.

243 Nagel, Doc. de fouilles 10, 22 (37) and Pl. 25 (no. 37).

244 For a similar wine jar inscription so dated by this criteria, see regnal year 33-D above. In this instance, even though the date must belong to Ramesses II, the jug was found in tomb 359, which belongs to the reign of Ramesses IV; Nagel, *op. cit.*, 14. A wine label with regnal year 2 of Horemhab was also found in the same tomb; *ibid.*, 15 (6).

245 Firth-Quibell, The Step Pyramid, I 85, where only a translation is given without a text. Also see Wildung, MAeS 17, 68.

246 For other such visitors' inscriptions, see years 17-A, 34-F, 47-B, 48-C and 50-A; and years 5-C, 27-A, 37-C and 40-F for graffiti.

247 Porter-Moss V 212 (42-43). Professor Caminos has kindly informed me that the reading 37 is correct; he also supplied photographs of the stelae.

248 Porter-Moss V 212 (47). Professor Caminos also verified the reading 37 for this stela and provided a photograph.

249 Porter-Moss I^2 590. Professor Černý, in a private communication, sent a copy of this graffito, which will appear in a forthcoming publication of the "Centre de documentation."

250 *Ḏḥwty-ḥr-mkt.f* could be the owner of Theban tomb 357, but his

son cannot be identified for the name is too common. See Sethe ZAeS 44 (1907), 89, for a discussion of the name *Ḥy*.

251 Černý, Doc. de fouilles 6, 25, Pl. 31, no. 333.

252 James, Hieroglyphic Texts, 9, 25-26 and Pl. XXI. Gauthier, Livre des rois III, 45, note 1, gives the year as 38.

253 See year 37-F.

254 One might wish to read 𓎆𓎆𓎆𓏺𓏺𓏺𓏺𓏺𓏺𓏺 as a mistake for 𓎆𓎆𓎆𓎆𓏺𓏺𓏺𓏺𓏺, but this would not solve the problem, for year 45 was not his fifth Jubilee.

255 James, *op. cit.*, 26-27, with Pl. XXII.

256 L. E. III 195 b, c; Porter-Moss VII 118-119 (24).

257 The texts differ only slightly: the text to the right of the observer has the more complete titulary, while the short inscription accompanying the figure of the Viceroy contains slightly different titles in either stela.

258 For works on the Viceroys of Nubia, see Reisner, JEA 6 (1920), 28-55; Gauthier, Rec. Trav. 39 (1921), 179-238; Habachi, Kush 5 (1957), 13-36.

259 Goedicke-Wente, Ostraka Michaelides, 17, Pl. L.

260 There is no indication that this is the same person mentioned on the Hathor stela of year 9-B and on both the Cairo Ostracon 25671 and Theban graffito of regnal year 5-C.

261 Bruyère, FIFAO 8 (1930), 114.

262 *Ibid.*, 106.

263 The name in this shorter form and in compounds is common at Deir el-Medineh, but nowhere is *Mr-W3st* given as a father of *Ḥrỉ*, except in this instance.

264 Černý, Cairo Cat. I 95 (116*), II cxii.

265 Spiegelberg, Hieratic Ostraka and Papyri, Pl. XXXVIII, no. 321. For similar material from the Ramesseum, see years 33-D, 57-B and 58-A.

266 See below in section 2 of this chapter.

267 Porter-Moss V 212 (42-43). With photographs provided by Professor Caminos.

268 Porter-Moss V 212 (47). With photograph provided by Professor Caminos.

269 de Morgan, Cat. des mon. I 103 (33); Porter-Moss V 251 (137). The existence of this inscription has been questioned by Habachi, ZAeS 97 (1971), 64.

270 The word "fourth" can be safely restored even though de Morgan, *loc. cit.*, only gives three vertical strokes, since the texts from Gebel Silsileh (40-A and 40-B) date the fourth Jubilee to year 40.

271 The verb *ii* is used here in a narrative instead of *wḏ.n ḥm.f; Ḫ'-m-W3st* also adds a new title of *sḥtp ib n nb t3wy*. For the previous Jubilee inscriptions of *Ḫ'-m-W3st*, see years 30-A, 30-B, 30-D, 33-A, 34-A, 34-B, 36-A, 37-A, 37-B, 40-A.

272 Legrain, Bull. Inst. Ég., Third Series, 10 (1899), 133; Porter-Moss V 211 (30).
For a mention of the fourth Jubilee, but with no date given, see Habachi, ZAeS 97 (1971), 65, fig. 1, Pl. V a (=Porter-Moss V 211 [30]). This inscription is just above that of *Ḥy*, son of *Ḫ'-m-W3st*.

273 First published by Birch, Inscriptions in the Hieratic and Demotic Character, Pls. XX-XXI, and more recently by Černý-Gardiner, Hieratic Ostraca, I 22-23, Pls. LXXXIII-LXXXIV, with references to it by Erman, Aegypten and aegyptische Leben, 181-182; Spiegelberg, Rec. Trav. 15 (1893), 144-145, and Arbeiter und Arbeiterbewegung im Pharaonenreiche, 5-6; Černý, ASAE 27 (1927), 209-210, and JEA 15 (1929), 254; Helck, Analecta Biblica 12 (1959), 119.

274 See below (46-C) for a suggested reading of 46(?) for this ostracon, instead of 40.

275 Černý, JEA 33 (1947), 55 (no. 27) and 56; Porter-Moss VII 318.

276 Černý, *op. cit.*, 57; see also under year 3-A.

277 *Ibid.*, 56; paleography combined with the high regnal year, dates this to Ramesses II.

278 Porter-Moss V 188 (1). A view of the facade by Hall, JEA 13 (1927), Pl. II.

279 Porter-Moss V 212 (48).

280 Page 1128 (VI), called the tomb of *St3w*.

281 Vandier d'Abbadie, Nestor L'Hôte, Pl. XXXVIII 1.

282 L. D. III 174 d.

283 For similar problems on dating the Jubilees, see under year 33-A, Porter-Moss V 251 (137), and year 36-A, Porter-Moss V 256 (5B).
Habachi in ZAeS 97 (1971), 64, decides on year 41 for the date of this inscription and in footnote 5 says: "The year of this proclamation of the jubilee is sometimes taken as year 40, 41 or 42, but year 4 [sic] is certain; there is a hole in the place where a part of the numeral is engraved...."

284 Porter-Moss V 212 (48), but corrected by Habachi, ZAeS 97 (1971), 64, note 5. For similar ones, note the Bigeh inscription of *Ḫ'-m-W3st*, years 30, 34 and 36, Porter-Moss V 256; Gebel Silsileh stela of *Ḫ'-m-W3st*, years 30, 34, 37 and 40, Porter-Moss V 212 (42-43); and at Silsileh, year 30 of *Ḫ'-m-W3st*, Porter-Moss V 209 (4); the stela of *Ḫ'y* at Silsileh, with years 30, 34, 37 and 40, Porter-Moss V 212 (47); and finally also at Silsileh the text of *Ḫ'y* with regnal year 44 (?) only, Porter-Moss V 212 (47).

285 Legrain, Rec. Trav. 26 (1904), 219, note 3.

286 The el-Kab inscription has regnal year 41 preserved but most

likely should be read as 42, as concluded above, under year 41-A. Habachi, ZAeS 97 (1971), 64, following Borchardt, ZAeS 72 (1936), 54, says the actual celebration may have taken place in year 43.

287 Mariette, Abydos II, Pl. 41 and Catalogue 1126; Legrain, Rec. Trav. 31 (1909), 209-210; Porter-Moss V 70.

288 For *P3-R'-ḥtp*, see Helck, Verwaltung, 455-456; for *Ḳny*, *ibid.*, 503; for *Mìn-ms*, Ranke, Personennamen, I 152, 4.

289 Spiegelberg, Rec. Trav. 16 (1894), 64-65.

290 Gauthier, Livre des rois III, *passim*. Normally Ramesses' longer nomen reads ...*nṯr-ḥḳ3-Iwnw*; the only instances of the abbreviated form are in the two Louvre ostraca published by Spiegelberg, in Rec. Trav. 16 (1894), 64-66; cf. Gauthier, *op. cit.*, 46 and 48. This might be a result of a misreading, with an assimilation of the *nṯr*-sign into the divine determanitive and not a development in the royal name.

291 Seti Temple, no. 23; L. D. III 168; Gauthier, Livre des rois III 98 (xxiv); Lefebvre, ASAE 13 (1913), 207, with note 2; Porter-Moss VI 2-3.

292 Petrie, History III 37.

293 The ostracon only states that the person was the wife of the prince; there is no reference to an actual ceremony.

294 The name *Bn-'nt* occurs in the Ugarit material, cf. F. Groendahl, Die Personennamen der Texte aus Ugarit, 34, 111 and 321 (where the reference should read: III 11.839-12 and 16), and at a much later date in Egypt at Elephantine, cf. Cowley, Aramaic Papyri of the Fifth Century B.C., 70, line 108. For biblical reference, see Albright, AJSL 41 (1925), 73-101.

295 Habachi, ZAeS 97 (1971), 64; in note 4, he says, "There the prince is shown almost life-size, looking towards Elephantine and lifting his hands in adoration. This inscription we hope to publish with other inscriptions of Khaemweset."

296 Porter-Moss V 212 (49).

297 For the other stela of *Ḫ'y* at Silsileh, see under year 30-C, a stela which records years 30, 34, 37 and 40.

298 Thesaurus, 1128 IV.

299 Rec. Trav. 26 (1904), 219, note 3.

300 ZAeS 29 (1891), 128.

301 History III 39.

302 Habachi, ZAeS 97 (1971), 64-65, with note 9, says the Jubilee was announced in year 45, and on p. 67 he assumes it was celebrated in year 46. On p. 66 (with note 18), he lists another mention of the sixth Jubilee, which does not have a year date.

303 Barsanti and Gauthier, ASAE 11 (1911), 83-84, Pl. IV: Porter-Moss VII 55.

304 See under year 38-A for an earlier date of *St3w* and year 63-C for a later one.

305 Amélineau, Le Tombeau d'Osiris, 47; Porter-Moss V 80.

306 Černý, Graffiti, 28; on p. 37 he assigns it to Ramesses II, but omits it under his name on p. 29.

307 Erman, ZAeS 17 (1879), 72, Tafel I; Helck, JARCE 2 (1963), 65-73, Pls. IX-XII; photograph in Moeller, Hieratische Palaeographie II, Tafel IV.

308 Nims, JNES 14 (1955), 119, with notes 93 and 94, in a review of Otto, Topographie des Thebanischen Gaues, states that this place was apparently located in the Theban area, but its exact site is unknown. The phrase *hrw ḥr M3't* was also used as a part of Ramesses' prenomen, Spiegelberg, ZAeS 58 (1923), 31.

309 For the place *Hry-ḥr-Ỉmn*, located in Thebes-West, see Otto, *op. cit.*, 2, 16, 62 and 80 (especially 62).

310 For other references to these persons, see Helck, *op. cit.*, 66.

311 Of regnal year 42-B.

312 Nagel, Doc. de fouilles, 10, 50 (a).

313 James, Hieratic Texts, 9, 35, note 3, says, "40 can certainly be read, with some digits of uncertain number following." In the text above he states that the ostracon is "dated to a regnal year 46(?)."

314 Nagel, Doc. de fouilles 10, 18 (11); see also under years 36-C, 46-B, 48-A and 49-A.

315 For the name see Ranke, Personennamen I 71, 3.

316 Firth-Quibell, The Step Pyramid I 82-83. Also see Wildung, MAeS 17, 68.

317 Ranke, Personennamen I 231 (20), 355 (22).

318 For other visitors' inscriptions, see years 17-A, 34-E, 36-D, 48-C and 50-A; and years 5-C, 27-A, 37-C and 40-F for graffiti.

319 Nagel, Doc. de fouilles, 10, 50 (c). See also under years 36-C, 46-B, 47-A and 49-A.

320 Černý, Doc. de fouilles 6, 14, Pl. 15 (no. 294).

321 For similar ostraca so dated because of their paleography and high regnal year, see under years 35-C, 37-D, 38-B, 40-E, 48-A, 54-C, 59-A, 63-B, 64-A and 66-B. For units written as days, see year 18-B.

322 Firth-Quibell, The Step Pyramid I 83-84, where this inscription is distinguished from another on a different block nearby which Gunn had originally combined with it. Also see Wildung, MAeS 17, 68.

323 For other visitor inscriptions, see years 17-A, 34-F, 36-D, 47-B and 50-A; and years 5-C, 27-A, 37-C and 40-F for graffiti.

324 Nagel, Doc. de fouilles 10, 18 (28). It is assigned to Ramesses by the same means as those jar inscriptions of years 36-C, 46-B, 47-A and 48-A.

325 Spiegelberg, Rec. Trav. 26 (1904), 152-154; Porter-Moss III 79. See year 34-F for a similar inscription.

326 Spiegelberg, *op. cit.*, 154.

327 Ranke, Personennamen I 139, 18.

328 This name also occurs at Armant where the royal scribe *Yw-p3* records that he was sent there to announce the ninth Jubilee; see below year 54-A.

329 This is deduced only from the name compounded with the deity Ptah; at Thebes, specifically Deir el-Medineh, the equivalent would be *Imn-m-wỉ3*; cf. Theban tombs 163, 270 and 356 as examples. For a discussion of such visitor inscriptions, see Helck, ZDMG 102, 39-46.

330 Mond-Myers, Armant, 164, Pl. XCIII 3. The fragment consists of

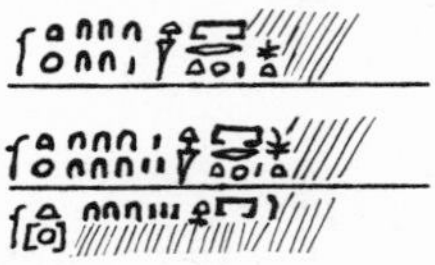

331 For the discussion of this text, see years 54-A, 57-A and 60-A.

332 The opposite wall records his ninth, tenth and eleventh Jubilees, the ninth recorded by *Yw-p3* and the tenth and eleventh by *Nfr-rnpt*.

333 The last date has been restored as 66; see there for the reasons.

334 Drower in Mond-Myers, *op. cit.*, 164.

335 *Ibid.*

336 Scarabs in London (Hall, B. M. 2117) and Berlin (Erman, ZAeS 29 [1891], 128) refer to Ramesses' eighth Jubilee by number and it is possible that they belong to year 51. Also see Habachi, ZAeS 97 (1971), 65, who says that nothing is known of this date but the Berlin scarab.

337 Wainwright, ASAE 28 (1928), 175; Porter-Moss IV 264.

338 Wainwright, *op. cit.*, 175.

339 Since either date is possible, this stela cannot be placed with exactitude within a chronological structure.

340 Most recently, Janssen, Two Ancient Egyptian Ship's Logs, 1-52 and Pls. I-II.

341 See chap. I for the discussion of this date.

342 The royal persons mentioned are Prince *R'-ms* (II2 and IV 16) and *3st-nfrt*, daughter of *Mr-n-ptḥ* (II 7 and IV 20). Janssen, *op. cit.*, 6, shows that this papyrus among others very probably came from Memphis and might have formed a part of *Ḫ'-m-W3st*'s

private archives.

343 Hamza, ASAE 30 (1930), 43-45. Instead of "anew" Hamza read "bank" and restored "on the west"; cf. page 43. He also refers to this as an "ostracon" even though it might be called a wine jar inscription.

344 For similar inscriptions from Thebes, see years 33-D, 36-C, 39-A, 44-C, 46-B, 47-A, 48-A, 49-A, 52-B, 56-B, 57-B and 58-A.

345 Spiegelberg, Rec. Trav. 16 (1894), 65-66.

346 The sentence appears to read, "The royal son, *Sty*, born of *Nfrt-ỉry*, became (*wnn...n* [for *m*] *r3-p't*) Crown Prince *Sty-ḥr-ḫpš.f*, of those born of his Majesty, life, prosperity, health, and (at this occasion) was accompanied by the royal scribe, *Wsr-M3't-R'-nḫt*, etc." Spiegelberg did not give a translation.
A stela found at Qantir, Habachi, ASAE 52 (1952), 501-507, must belong to this same *Sty-ḥr-ḫpš.f* and reads, *r3-p't, ḥ3ty-' mry ỉt-nṯr ḥry-sštз nt pr nswt ḥry-tp n(y) t3 r ḏr.f sm ỉt-nṯr-nfr r3-p't t3yty ḫrp t3w ḥ3w-nbw s3 nswt sm3 st-Ḥr r3-p't sš nswt.* ("Hereditary noble and count, beloved of the Father-of-the-god, confidant of the house of the king, one having authority over the entire land, *Sm*-priest of the Father-of-the-good-god; hereditary noble, the invested one, who administers the lands of the *ḥ3w-nbw*, the royal son who partakes of the throne of Horus; hereditary noble and royal scribe.")

347 Ranke, Personennamen, I 218, 13. The reading of *mn* for  is confirmed by Ostracon Louvre 666; Spiegelberg, *op. cit.*, 67.

348 *P3y.tn-ḥb-p3-šd* must be a compound name, not attested in Ranke, Personennamen, for this same compound occurs with the same title "scribe" in Louvre Ostracon 666 (Spiegelberg, *op. cit.*, 66-67). Helck, Verwaltung, 517, gives only the name *P3y.tn-ḥb*.

349 This translation, Gardiner, JEA 38 (1952), 28.

350 Ranke, Personennamen I 233, 27 and 234, 1. Apparently a foreign name built upon the familiar Semitic form יה or יהו.

351 Spiegelberg, *op. cit.*, 66-67.

352 Mond-Myers, Armant, 163, Pl. XCIII.

353 Though partially destroyed 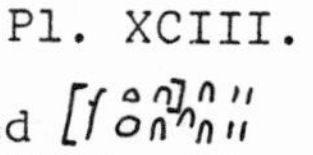 the date is certain; also see Habachi, ZAeS 97 (1971), 65.

354 For similar texts relating to the *Ḥb-Sd*'s, see under years 30, 34, 37, 40, 41, 42 and 44. Several scarabs also record Rameses' ninth Jubilee: Newberry, Scarab-shaped Seals, no. 37427, p. 358, Pl. xvii; and Rowe, A Catalogue of Egyptian Scarabs, no. 688, pp. 163-164, Pl. xviii.

355 The same name was encountered in the graffito of the Mastaba of *Ptḥ-špss* at Abu Sir of year 50-A, and it is probable that these two represent the same person. For other references to *Yw-p3*, see Helck, Verwaltung, 491.

356 Speleers, Recueil des inscriptions, 66, no. 278.

357 Glanville, JRAS 1929, 19-26, Pl. I; Gardiner, RAD xviii and 59. No royal name is given, but this papyrus is assigned to him on

paleographic grounds and because of the high regnal date.

358 For a colossus of Ramesses II at Hermopolis, see Roeder, Hermopolis 1929-1939, II 19 c, and Habachi, Features of the Deification of Ramesses II, 41, with note 152.

359 JEA 27 (1941), 59; also see Habachi, ASAE 52 (1952), 553.

360 Černý, Doc. de fouilles 7, 4, Pl. 3, no. 351.

361 Helck, Materialien, 846. For similar ostraca, see years 35-C, 37-D, 38-B, 40-E, 48-A, 59-A, 63-B, 64-A and 66-B.

362 For similar retrospective dates, see years 1-A, 8-C, 15-A, 16-A, 18-B, 26-A, 30-A, 30-B, 30-C, 33-A, 33-E, 34-A, 34-B, 34-C, 37-A, 37-B and below, 56-A, 66-C and 67-B.

363 Mariette, Sérapéum III 15.

364 *Ibid.*, 15-16.

365 Porter-Moss III 240 (Addendum to p. 66).

366 Hawkins, Select Papyri in the Hieratic Character from the Collections of the British Museum, Pl. CLXVI; Gardiner, Late-Egyptian Miscellanies, 98; Caminos, Late-Egyptian Miscellanies, 367-368.

367 A fuller discussion of the royal titulary and its changes will be made later in chap. VI.

368 Steindorff, Aniba II 1, 220, note 1.

369 *Ibid.*, 220 (7).

370 Discussed under regnal year 63-C below.

371 Discussed above under year 7-A. It is questionable whether this can safely be dated to Ramesses II for the prenomen is so badly destroyed; however, we do know of other undated inscriptions of his at Aniba. For these see under year 7-A.

372 Spiegelberg, Aegyptische und andere Graffiti, 70.

373 Mond-Myers, Armant, 163, Pl. XCIII.

374 The only paleographic differences are,  for  and  instead of 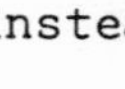.

375 Just beneath this inscription, there is one of his recording Ramesses' eleventh Jubilee in regnal year 60. Also see Weil, Die Veziere Aegyptens, 94-95; Helck, Verwaltung, 451-453; Habachi ZAeS 97 (1971), 65.

376 Spiegelberg, Hieratic Ostraka and Papyri, Pl. XXXVIII, no. 323. For similar material from the Ramesseum, see years 33-D, 39-A and 58-B.

377 Spiegelberg, *op. cit.*, Pl. XXXV, no. 300. For similar dated material from the Ramesseum, see under years 33-D, 39-A and 57-B.

378 See below in section 2 of this chapter.

379 Černý, Cairo Cat., I 40 and II, Pl. LVI. Only the regnal year is given. For similar ostraca, see years 35-C, 37-D, 38-B, 40-E, 48-A, 54-C, 63-B, 64-A and 66-B.

380 Mond-Myers, Armant, 164, Pl. XCIII.

381 The year date reads,  , and since Ramesses did not reign 70 or 80 years, this can only refer to his 60th year. The even spacing of one ∩ upon another indicates an even number.

382 A graffito from the Wadi Arbad mentions his eleventh Jubilee: "Bringing gold for the 11th *Ḥb-Sd* of *Wsr-M3't-R' Stp-n-R'*," L. D. Textband IV 82.

383 Gardiner, RAD xi and 27-28.

384 Gardiner, AEO II 115* (no. 392), JEA 29 (1943), 37-50, and JNES 12 (1953), 145-149.

385 Gardiner, RAD x-xi and 22-24.

386 Gardiner, *op. cit.*, xii and 30-32.

387 Gardiner, The Wilbour Papyrus, II 12, with note 4.

388 Since the papyrus is from Gurob; *ibid.*

389 A similar phrase is found in Gurob Fragment L 1, 8; Gardiner, RAD 30.

390 Wainwright, ASAE 28 (1928), 175.

391 Mond-Myers, Armant, 164.

392 For the discussion, see under year 51-A; for other references to this fragment, see years 63-A and 66-A.

393 Budge, A Guide to the Egyptian Galleries (Sculpture), 170, Pl. XXIII; James, Hieroglyphic Texts, 9, 30-31, Pl. XXVI.

394 This is the only example Gauthier gives of this particular form (Livre des rois III *passim*). The epithet "Beloved of Osiris, Foremost of the Westerners," suggests Abydos as the place of origin for this stela.

395 Wb. IV 2, 15.

396 Mond-Myers, Armant, 164, Pl. XCIII 3. For similar inscriptions of his at Armant, see under years 51-A, 54-A, 57-A, 60-A and 66-A.

397 Discussed under years 51-A and 61-C. For the other Armant texts, see year 60-A. Habachi, ZAeS 97 (1971), 65, says it is his thirteenth Jubilee.

398 Černý, Doc. de fouilles 6, 12, Pl. 12 (no. 285). For similar ostraca, see years 35-C, 37-D, 38-B, 40-E, 48-A, 54-C, 59-A, 64-A and 66-B.

399 Weigall, Report, 113, Pl. LXIV 7.

400 Weigall, *op. cit.*, 113.

401 *Ḏḥwty-ms* of Aniba appears to be known only from this inscription, unless the *ḥ3ty-'* whose shabtis were discovered at Aniba is the same *Ḏḥwty-ms*. See Steindorff, Aniba II 1, 220 (SA 14, 7). For a wine jar inscription from this tomb, see year 56-B.

402 For earlier mentions of the Viceroy *St3w*, see years 38-A and 44-B.

403 Sauneron, Doc. de fouilles, 13, 14, Pls. 31-32.

404 For similar ostraca dated to the reign of Ramesses II, yet having no royal name, see years 35-C, 37-D, 38-B, 40-E, 48-A, 54-C, 59-A, 63-B, 64-A and 66-B.

405 Blackman, JEA 23 (1937), 147; Porter-Moss VII 173.

406 A possible reference to a *Ḥb-Sd* of Ramesses at Armant is dated to either years 65, 66 or 67, see under year 66-A.

407 Mond-Myers, Armant, 164, Pl. XCIII 3.

408 For the inscription of *Yw-p3* and *Nfr-rnpt*, see under regnal years 54-A, 57-A and 60-A. That inscription has the earliest regnal date on top with the latest on the bottom.

409 The reading 67 is quite unlikely since the majority of strokes in an uneven number are placed on top in Egyptian numerals.

410 The Jubilee could have been celebrated in either year 65, 66 or even early 67, though the last date is unlikely. Since a general at Sesebi chose to commemorate year 65 of Ramesses II, this might be the date of the Jubilee, but this too is uncertain. Hence the year of his twelfth (or thirteenth?) Jubilee remains questionable. Habachi, ZAeS 97 (1971), 65, opts for year 65 for this inscription but says that the Jubilee was celebrated in regnal year 66, this being only the announcement thereof. On p. 67, he lists fourteen *Ḥb-Sd*'s and gives their years as 30, 34, 37, 40, 43, 46, 49, 52, 55, 58, 61, 62, 64 and 66.

411 Mariette, Catalogue, no. 1497.

412 Daressy, Cairo Cat. no. 25237, pp. 60-61.

413 Spiegelberg, OLZ 5 (1902), 317-318 gives his own copy of the ostracon and restores the year date on the *verso*; however, in places his copy differs from Daressy's.

414 Černý, JEA 15 (1929), 256. Also see Černý, Doc. de fouilles 4, 20, Pl. 49, no. 179, where *Nfr-ḥtp* is mentioned with *Inpw-m-ḥb*, a scribe.

415 It must be the same scribe, *Inpw-m-ḥb*, who is mentioned on Ostracon Deir el-Medineh 179; see previous note.

416 Bouriant, Rec. Trav. 9 (1887), 100 (77); Porter-Moss V 129. Also see Maspero, Struggle of the Nations, 426, with note 3, and Gauthier, Livre des rois III 48. The Cairo Number Reg. is 34507, as I have been kindly informed by Miss Helen Murray on behalf of Dr. Rosalind Moss of the Griffith Institute.

417 What is written 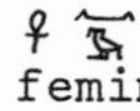 should probably be read 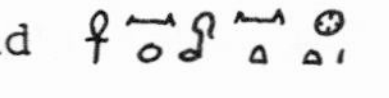, since it precedes a feminine personal name.

418 Even the name *B3k-wr*, according to Ranke, Personennamen II 276 (9), is only attested once, the expected form for the New Kingdom being *B3k-'3* (I 90 [15]).

419 Gardiner, RAD, xii, 30-32. For a similar situation with a text dated to two different kings, see above under year 64-A.

420 The month and its number is not well preserved, though it is restored as 2nd month of *3ḫt*. It is quite certain that Rameses' 67th year was his last, for line 1, 8 reads, "Regnal year 67, which was reported to him as regnal year 1."

421 The second date is usually accepted as given; Hornung, Chronologie, 95; cf. Helck, Analecta Biblica 12 (1959), 120-121.

422 Contra Apionem, i 97; Waddell, Manetho, 102-103; Helck, Untersuchungen zu Manetho und den aegyptischen Koenigslisten, 70.

423 Porter-Moss V 44; Breasted, ARE §§470-471; Kitchen, *op. cit.*, VI 17-20. Now in the Cairo Museum, no. 48876.

424 For the numerous inscriptions which have retrospective dates, see years 1-A, 8-C, 15-A, 16-A, 18-B, 26-A, 30-A, 30-B, 30-C, 33-A, 33-E, 34-A, 34-B, 34-C, 37-A, 37-B, 55-A, 56-A and 66-C.

425 Černý, Doc. de fouilles 5, 11, Pl. 20.

426 Černý, *loc. cit.*, gives one small upright stroke  in his transcription but does not give the hieratic traces; in Cahiers d'Histoire Mondiale 1 (1953-54), 911, he states that it must be 1 but not more than 5 years.

427 Gauthier, Livre des rois III, *passim*.

428 Porter-Moss I² 420-421; Bruyère, FIFAO 7 (Rapport, 1929), 70-77.

429 Hoelscher, Das Grabdenkmal des Koenigs Chephren, 114, Abb. 167; Porter-Moss III 6 (dated to year 20). Gauthier, Livre des rois III 40, completely restores the word *rnpt*, without giving any indication that it is questionable; he also omits the *nb-t3wy* before the prenomen in the second line.

430 ZAeS 62 (1927), 112, followed by Kitchen, *op. cit.*, 338.

431 The entire *r* of the word *prt* is not as Sethe says "ganz deutlich," but its position and rounded shape would just as easily represent the end of the *3ḫt* sign.

432 The same longer prenomen was also used by Siptah and later by Sheshonq III (Gauthier, Sheshonq II) and Pemay (Dyn. XXII), though none of these employed the abbreviated form.

433 Spiegelberg, Aegyptische und andere Graffiti, no. 18, p. 4.

434 There is also an ostracon, Munich 22 a, mentioned by Spiegelberg, Rechnungen, 65, which might be assigned to the reign of Rameses II, but the year is not well preserved in it either, though it might be read as 38.

435 Nagel, Doc. de fouilles 10, 15-16 (1 and 3).

436 *Ibid.*, 14.

437 *Ibid.*, 15 (6).

438 Year 40+ can only be his at this time.

439 For another wine inscription from this same tomb, see year 36-C.

440 For example, the Turin Revenue Papyrus, once dated by Lieblein in Videnskabs--Selskabet i Christiania Forhandlinger, 1875, 269-278, to the reign of Ramesses II, is now correctly dated to Ramesses XI (Gardiner, RAD xiii). These examples need not be multiplied; it was not felt necessary to correct that which has already been set aright.

441 The Toulane stela of the scribe *Ms* published by Varille in Kêmi 3 (1930-35), 39-43, has the regnal date of "year 7" of an unspecified king; it is impossible to date this stela more precisely than to the general "Ramesside period."

442 The statue fragment (no. 298) of regnal year 33 can only be dated to the reign of Ramesses II; other texts can either be dated by the royal name given or by the person who erected the stela, if he is known from dated monuments. Most of the dated material is accompanied by a royal name.

443 Gardiner-Peet-Černý, Inscriptions of Sinai I, Pl. LXXVII; II, 194.

444 For these, see in the previous section under year 2.

445 *Ibid.*, I, Pls. LXXIV and LXXI; II 187-189.

446 *Ibid.*, I, Pl. LXXV; II, 194.

447 See note 444 above and the discussion under year 2-B.

448 *Ibid.*, I, Pl. LXXVIII; II, 195.

449 *Ibid.*, I, Pl. LXXII; II, 193.

450 The wording of nos. 275, 276, 301, 302 and 294 is distinctly different from that on the stelae belonging to the reign of Ramesses II; cf. nos. 250, 252, 254, 260 and 261.

451 For such ostraca, see under years 35-C, 37-D, 38-B, 40-E, 48-B, 54-C, 59-A, 63-B and 66-B; for the jar inscriptions, see years 33-D, 39-A, 44-C, 46-B, 47-A, 48-A, 49-A, 52-B, 56-B, 57-B and 58-A; for papyri dated in a similar way, see years 36-B, 52-A, 54-B, 61-A and 67-A.

452 These are given in the list of abbreviations in Chart I. Scattered material with high regnal dates, such as years 49 and 55 found in a Theban tomb (Davies, Two Ramesside Tombs, Pl. 19), have not been included, likewise Goedicke WZKM 59/60 (1963-64) 5, Pl. XI.

453 An asterisk indicates that the author has given no date whatsoever; in the higher years an attempt has been made to indicate a general date for the inscription.

454 Cairo Ostracon 25603 is an example of the difficulties involved in dating an ostraca to a specific reign; Černý in Cairo Cat., 36, dates it to the second half of the Nineteenth Dynasty, but Helck, Materialien, 852, dates it to Ramesses II. Černý in Cairo Cat., 32, assigns Ostracon 25592 to Ramesses III, but

Helck, Materialien, 409, states that it must belong to Ramesses II; in neither instance is there any sure evidence for a specific date.

455 Spiegelberg, Hieratic Ostraka and Papyri, Pls. XIX-XXXVIII. To maintain a control to show distribution, the material by Spiegelberg, ZAeS 58 (1923), 25-36, has not been included in the Chart.

456 Wiedemann, ZAeS 21 (1883), 33-35; Spiegelberg, *loc. cit.*; Helck, Materialien, 732-735.

457 As the Turin "Strike Papyrus" shows, the Ramesseum was in use at least as late as the 29th regnal year of Ramesses III; Gardiner, RAD 52-53; Edgerton, JNES 10 (1951), 139-142.

458 We do know that the names of Seti I, as well as Siptah and Ramesses VI or X occur among the inscriptions. See Wiedemann, *op. cit.*, and Helck, *op. cit.*

459 These have been treated under years 33-D, 39-A, 57-B and 58-A.

CHAPTER III

ANALYSIS OF DATED MATERIAL

For purposes of analysis the dated material will be divided into two sections, one consisting of the "royal" records and the other of "private" texts. The division has been made for convenience to compare and contrast the two. Royal records may be defined as those produced under royal or official directive and thus may include some inscriptions which contain the names of private individuals; private records are those produced under individual or local directive. This definition and division is arbitrary and does not imply that official inscriptions have more worth for historical interpretation than private ones. The division has been made in order to see how each falls numerically and how each might complement the other. For quick comparison two charts have been included in this section containing only that material securely dated to the reign of Ramesses II; a complete chart of dated material, both royal and private, is given in the Appendix.

Section 1. The Royal Dated Material

All dated records of Ramesses' foreign military activity are limited to his first decade, with the exception of the Beth Shan stela of year 18, which does not refer to a specific campaign. His initial campaign to Asia appears to have been in regnal year 4 and his second in year 5 (Qadesh). A later one was conducted in year 8 and most likely another in year 10.[1] Whether there were any others between years 5 and 10 remains unknown; it is possible that one more was recorded on the now completely defaced North Stela on the Nahr el-Kelb, unless it was inscribed during the campaigns of years 5 or 8.[2]

The entire first decade, however, was not given over to conquest and warfare; prior to year 4 there is no indication of any such activity. On the contrary, the early inscriptions present a very peaceful scene, one filled with domestic matters. The dedicatory inscription at Abydos, though written at a later time, mentions Ramesses' concern for the monuments and endowments of his predecessor(s). The "Hymn to the Nile" at Gebel Silsileh reflects the royal interest in the economic prosperity of the land, a theme which is prominent throughout the reign of Ramesses II. One specific domestic action on the part of Ramesses was the installation of *Nb-wnn.f* as the High Priest of Amun in his first regnal year.

Ramesses' second year is recorded on only one monument, and it is not found in Egypt proper; his stela from the Serabit el-Khadim in Sinai shows Egyptian presence there but does not indicate any military activity on the part of the Egyptians sent out to that inhospitable place. On the contrary, it reflects economic prosperity and political stability; even the names of the royal representatives on the stela are the same as those on the monuments of Seti I. Year 3 is represented by two texts: the Quban stela, concerned with the gold mines of the Wadi Allaqi, specifically its water supply, and the Luxor building inscription. Both reflect peaceful endeavors on the part of Ramesses II.

The first three years of Ramesses' reign form a unit of domestic activity, but regnal year 4 inaugurates a new period when Asia becomes prominent in Egyptian affairs of state. Nothing is known of the activities of year 4, though the mutilated stela on the Nahr el-Kelb, shows that Egypt was present on Asiatic soil. Year 5, however, became one of the most significant in the entire career of Ramesses II, for the battle of Qadesh eventually received more attention through text and picture than any other single campaign and is one of the best known battles of ancient times. The military activity, if any, of the two years following the 5th remains unknown, but in year 8 he conducted another campaign into Asia. The South Stela of the Nahr el-Kelb, dated to year 10, may have recorded an Asiatic campaign, though its text can no longer be read; simultaneously, the Aswan Stela, also dated to year 10, confirms his military activity in general terms, though it does not refer to a particular campaign.

The first decade, then, may be split into slightly uneven parts: the first, consisting of 3 regnal years, is represented by "domestic" inscriptions, while the latter is filled with military activities, primarily in Asia. The second decade is attested by only one royal inscription, the Beisan Stela of regnal year 18, which is military in character although no campaign is mentioned.

The record of the alliance with the Hittite king, Hattushilish III, is the next official document with a regnal year. This is significant, for it and the Mnevis Stela of year 26 are the only royal inscriptions from the third decade. The Alliance has additional significance, for it is the second dated text after year 10 and as such must be examined with regard to the preceding empty period.[3] The Mnevis Stela of year 26 commemorates the completion or restoration by Ramesses II of a tomb for a Mnevis bull which apparently had been buried in the reign of Horemhab. Since there are only two royal dated inscriptions from this period, it is difficult to characterize it on such slim evidence.

Regnal year 30 opens a new era, and in comparison with the preceding decade there is an abundance of dated texts, many of which refer to Ramesses' royal Jubilees; in fact, the second half of Ramesses' reign may be called the "Jubilee period," for that is the most characteristic activity reflected in the royal dated monuments. The first *Ḥb-Sd* occurred in the same year that an Apis was buried in the Serapeum, and both events are well attested by dated material. Ramesses' second *Ḥb-Sd* of year 34 was also paralleled by an important event, a marriage between the royal houses of Hatti and Egypt,[4] as is attested by a number of stelae and also by the "Decree of Ptah" of regnal year 35. Towards the end of this fourth decade, the high official, *St3w*, Viceroy of Kush, is first mentioned in the dated material; as he is responsible for monuments erected in years 38, 44 and 63, his activity in Nubia belongs to the latter half of Ramesses' reign.

The fourth Jubilee was celebrated in year 40, and from that time on most of the royal material with regnal dates pertains to Ramesses' Jubilees. Later, beginning with year 51, the royal Jubilee was regularly celebrated at three-year intervals. It is, however, the stela of another king, Ramesses IV, which records Ramesses II's final regnal year, year 67.

CHART III

49791

The Royal Dated Material

Year	Description		Porter-Moss
1-A	Abydos, Seti Temple, Dedicatory Inscription		VI 3 (34-37)
1-B	Gebel Silsileh, Rock Shrine, Hymn to Nile		V 217
1-C	Giza, Sphinx Stela Fragment, B. M. 440		III 9
1-D	Abu Simbel, Door Thickness		VII 108(92-93)
1-E	Theban Tomb 157, *Nb-wnn.f*		I^2 267 (8)
2-B	Sinai, Serabit el-Khadim, No. 252		VII 349-350
3-A	Quban Stela		VII 83
3-B	Luxor Pylon, East Wall		
4-A	Nahr el-Kelb, Middle Stela		VII 385
5-A	Qadesh: Abu Simbel, dated year 5	(I)	VII 103-4 (41)
	Ramesseum, First Pylon, year 5	(R_1)	II 151 (6-12)
	Ramesseum, Second Court, year 5	(R_2)	II 152
	Luxor, First Pylon, year 5	(L_1)	II 100 (6-9)
	Luxor, South Side, fragmentary	(L_2)	II 110(136-41)
	Luxor, West Side, date lost	(L_3)	II 109(130-31)
	Abydos, date lost	(A)	VI 39-41
7-A	Aniba, Stela Fragment		
8-A	Ramesseum, First Pylon, Asiatic Campaign		II 151
8-C	Heliopolis Stela		IV 62
9-D	Heliopolis Stela		IV 62
10-A	Nahr el-Kelb, South Stela		VII 385
10-B	Aswan Stela		V 245
18-C	Beisan Stela		VII 379
21-A	Thebes, The Hittite Alliance		
	Karnak, with the date, year 21		II 49 (2)
	Ramesseum Fragment, no date		II 152 (14)
26-A	Heliopolis Mnevis Tomb, Stela		IV 59

Year	Description	Porter-Moss
	FIRST *ḤB-SD*	
30-A	Bigeh Inscription, *Ḫ'-m-W3st*	V 256 (5 B)
30-B	Gebel Silsileh, Stelae (Duplicates)	V 212 (42-43)
30-C	Gebel Silsileh, Vizier *Ḫ'y*	V 212 (47)
30-D	Gebel Silsileh, Niche in Facade, *Ḫ'-m-W3st*	V 209 (4)
30-F	Serapeum, Apis Stela, Louvre 3	III 206
30-G	Serapeum, Apis Stela, Louvre 4	III 206
33-B	Sinai, Serabit, el-Khadim, Statue Fragment	VII 365
	SECOND *ḤB-SD*	
34-A	Bigeh Inscription	V 256
34-B	Gebel Silsileh, Stelae (Duplicates)	V 212 (42-43)
34-C	Gebel Silsileh, Vizier *Ḫ'y*	V 212 (47)
34-D	Marriage Stela	
	Karnak	II 59 (54)
	Elephantine	V 225
	Abu Simbel	VII 98(8),VII 106
	Amarah West	VII 159 (3)
	Aksha	
35-A	Decree of Ptah	
	Abu Simbel	VII 106
	Amarah West	VII 159 (2)
	Aksha	
	Karnak	II 59 (55)
35-B	Faiyum, Fragment, Cairo 42783	IV 99
36-A	Bigeh Inscription, *Ḫ'-m-W3st*	V 256 (5 B)
	THIRD *ḤB-SD*	
37-A	Gebel Silsileh, Stelae (Duplicates)	V 212 (42-43)
37-B	Gebel Silsileh, Vizier *Ḫ'y*	V 212 (47)
38-A	Abu Simbel, Stela of *St3w*	VII 118-19(24)
	FOURTH *ḤB-SD*	
40-A	Gebel Silsileh, Stelae (Duplicates)	V 212 (42-43)
40-B	Gebel Silsileh, Vizier *Ḫ'y*	V 212 (47)

Year	Description	Porter-Moss
	(FOURTH *ḤB-SD*)	
40-C	Sehel Inscription, *Ḫ'-m-W3st*	V 251 (137)
40-D	Gebel Silsileh, Great Speos Gallery, *Ḥy*	V 211 (30)
41-A	El-Kab, Temple of Amenophis III	V 188 (1)
	FIFTH *ḤB-SD*	
42-A	Gebel Silsileh, Stela of *Ḫ'y*	V 212 (48)
42-D	Aswan *Ḥb-Sd* Inscription	
	SIXTH *ḤB-SD*	
44-A	Gebel Silsileh, Stela of *Ḫ'y*	V 212 (49)
44-B	Wadi es-Sebua', Stela of *St3w*	VII 55
	ḤB-SD (?)	
51-A	Armant, Temple Pylon, Fragment	
	NINTH *ḤB-SD*	
54-A	Armant, Temple Pylon	
	TENTH *ḤB-SD*	
57-A	Armant, Temple Pylon	
	ELEVENTH *ḤB-SD*	
60-A	Armant, Temple Pylon	
	TWELFTH *ḤB-SD* (?)	
63-A	Armant, Temple Pylon, Fragment	
63-C	Tonqala, Stela of *St3w*	VII 90
	THIRTEENTH *ḤB-SD* (?)	
66-A	Armant, Temple Pylon, Fragment	
67-B	Abydos Stela, Ramesses IV	V 44

Section 2. Analysis of Private Dated Inscriptions

In contrast to the royal dated monuments, the first four years of Ramesses II are not represented by private documents, except for graffiti from the Theban necropolis. The next date which appears in these records is regnal year 5 on the Cairo Ostracon 25671; it is securely dated to Ramesses II, as both his nomen and prenomen appear in the text. In section 1, it was established that the first three years of Ramesses' reign were typified by domestic activities and that it was only with regnal year 4 that military events are first mentioned.

Not only the first four years, but the entire first decade of Ramesses' reign is better attested by royal records than private ones; there are only seven private inscriptions with regnal dates from the first decade. The graffiti of years 1 and 2 might have been written during a visit, which perhaps was connected with the opening of a new royal tomb in the valley. This is only conjecture; the texts do not indicate why the scribes were there. The Cairo ostracon of year 5 and the Turin Papyrus of year 8 are both business documents and give no information concerning the general spectrum of royal activity. A graffito from the Valley of the Queens (5-C) is very brief, having nothing more than regnal year, royal name, and the title and name of the person, *R'-ms*. It might indicate some special activity within the area at that time, but whether it was the burial of some person or the opening of a new tomb remains to be established. The Hathor stela from Deir el-Medineh (9-B) was probably erected as a result of a royal visit by the king to Thebes, at which time he granted certain offerings to the Temple of Hathor. The only reflection of military activity during this time is a copy of the "Poem of Pentawer," which was made in regnal year 9 by the scribe *P3-n-t3-wrt*.

The second decade of Ramesses' reign is not represented by any contemporary private inscription. There are references to it in later documents, but all of these are retrospective dates; there is not one record concurrent with the regnal year to which it refers. Since this period is attested by only one royal inscription (18-A), the lack of private material underlines the emptiness of that time.

The third decade is attested by a private document of regnal year 26. Ostracon 250 from Deir el-Medineh definitely dates to year 26 of Ramesses II, but the Theban jar inscription (26-C) of the same year is not certain, for the prenomen there is more likely a part of a religious establishment than an element of a specific date. Ostracon 250 indicates some activity at Deir el-Medineh in year 26 but otherwise furnishes little historical information. It therefore appears that this part of Ramesses' reign is also not well attested; the two royal inscriptions of years 21 and 26 are substantiated by one private document dated to year 26.

With regnal year 30 the private dated material increases somewhat in proportion to the royal. Ramesses' first *Ḥb-Sd* is lauded in a literary work written upon an ostracon; though the specific year is not given, it does refer to the "first Jubilee." The wine jar inscription of year 33 is the first of several such records which are assigned to Ramesses' reign by paleography combined with the high regnal year. Even though the second half of the reign appears better attested by ostraca, papyri and jar inscriptions than the first, most of these are assigned to Ramesses by default; therefore no historical conclusions may be drawn from the different proportions. The only sound comparison may be made between those ostraca and papyri which have definite regnal dates on them. Since wine jar inscriptions are not normally dated to a specific king, it cannot be ascertained whether any belong to the first half of Ramesses' reign, prior to year 33. None of those listed in chart IV are specifically dated to him; this, however, does not negate their contribution to a chronological structure. Of the ostraca, only those of years 30, 34, 38 and 42 are dated to Ramesses II by name; all the others are simply assigned to him. The papyri of years 33, 52 and 56 are dated to him, while those of years 36, 54-55, 61 and 67 are only attributed to him. Hence it can be seen that there is widespread representation of regnal years by ostraca and papyri dated or assigned to Ramesses II and that they apparently do not form nor follow any pattern.

The royal Jubilees are not well attested in the private inscriptions, which is partially due to the nature of the material. The first one is recorded on an ostracon, as mentioned, and the second is found in a graffito on the island of Sehel, near the First Cataract. These are the only truly non-royal inscriptions which refer to Ramesses' Jubilees; what little information we have of his *Ḥb-Sd*'s comes from the short royal records left by those instructed to proclaim the festivities.

The remaining inscriptions of the second half of the reign are of a varied nature. Building activity is mentioned in Papyrus Anastasi of year 33. The graffito of *N3-šwyw* of year 34 does not indicate the re-use of older material by Ramesses II, as has been assumed; rather, like the graffito found in the tomb of *Ptḥ-špss* belonging to year 50, it reflects the interest in older monuments prevalent at that time.[5] Lawsuits are recorded for years 38 and 54; these are the only ones extant, though others must have occurred during his reign.

Egyptian activity in Nubia is attested by various private records. The Wadi Allaqi graffito of year 40 is the only dated one among many in that valley belonging to the Ramesside period, all of which attest the success reported in the Quban stela of year 3. The wine jar inscription found at Aniba and assigned to Ramesses' 56th year may have arrived at that site during his reign or at a later time, as perhaps did the small faience tablet bearing regnal year 65; neither of these can be used as specific dates for the sites at which they were found, for they are only too easily carried about.[6]

Several private stelae have regnal dates upon them, but their owners are not particularly important and thus contribute little historical information.[7] There are three papyri, however, which are significant: Papyrus Sallier III gives the full titulary of Ramesses II and contains additions to his name which were likely made in that specific year 56; Papyrus Gurob, Fragment N, is dated to regnal year 61 and records the delivery of fish to the royal harim at *Mr-wr*; and Fragment L not only contains year 67 of Ramesses II, it also records year 1, which must refer to his successor though the royal name is not stated.

CHART IV

The Private Dated Material

Year	Description	Porter-Moss
1-F	Theban Graffito, No. 298	
2-E	Theban Graffito, No. 225	
5-B	Cairo Ostracon 25671	
5-C	Thebes, Graffito of *R'-ms*	I^2 771
5-D	Louvre Leather Manuscript	
8-B	Papyrus Turin	
9-A	Papyrus Sallier III, Colophon	
9-B	Deir el-Medineh, Hathor Stela	
26-B	Deir el-Medineh, Ostracon 250	
30-E	Ostracon Gardiner 28, First *Ḥb-Sd*	
33-A	Sehel Inscription, Second *Ḥb-Sd*	V 251 (137)
33-D	Ramesseum, Wine Jar Inscription, No. 275	
33-E	Papyrus Anastasi V 24, 7-8	
34-E	Deir el-Medineh, Ostracon 447	
34-F	Saqqara, Graffito of *N3-šwyw*	
35-C	Ostracon Gardiner 24	
35-D	Theban Necropolis Graffito	
36-B	Papyrus Gardiner 9 (unpublished)	
36-C	Deir el-Medineh, Wine Jar Inscription	
36-D	Saqqara, Step Pyramid Graffito	
37-C	Thebes, Graffito (unpublished)	I^2 590
37-D	Deir el-Medineh, Ostracon 333	
38-B	Ostracon Michaelides 47	
38-C	Cairo Ostracon 25809	
39-A	Ramesseum, Wine Jar Inscription, No. 321	

Year	Description	Porter-Moss
40-E	Ostracon, British Museum 5634	
40-F	Wadi Allaqi, Graffito	VII 318
42-B	Abydos, Stela of *Wn-nfr*	V 70
42-C	Ostracon Louvre 2262	VI 203
44-C	Abydos, Jar Inscription	V 80
45-A	Valley of the Kings Graffito	
46-A	Papyrus Berlin 3047	
46-B	Deir el-Medineh, Wine Jar Inscription	
47-A	Deir el-Medineh, Wine Jar Inscription	
47-B	Saqqara, Step Pyramid Graffito	
48-A	Deir el-Medineh, Wine Jar Inscription	
48-B	Deir el-Medineh, Ostracon 294	
48-C	Saqqara, Step Pyramid Graffito	
49-A	Deir el-Medineh, Jar Inscription	
50-A	Abu Sir, Mastaba of *Ptḥ-špss*, Graffito	III 79
52-A	Papyrus Leiden I 350 *verso*	
52-B	Qantir, Wine Jar Inscription	
53-A	Ostracon Louvre 2261	
54-B	Papyrus British Museum 10447 (also year 55)	
54-C	Deir el-Medineh, Ostracon 351	
55-A	Papyrus British Museum 10447 (also year 54)	
55-B	Serapeum, Graffito	III 204
56-A	Papyrus Sallier IV *verso* 17, 1-4	
56-B	Aniba, Wine Jar Inscription	
56-C	Theban Necropolis Graffito	
57-B	Ramesseum, Jar Inscription No. 323	

Year	Description	Porter-Moss
58-A	Ramesseum, Jar Inscription No. 300	
59-A	Cairo Ostracon 25619	
61-A	Papyrus Gurob, Fragment N	
62-A	Stela, British Museum 163, *Nfr-ḥr*	
63-B	Deir el-Medineh, Ostracon 285	
64-A	Deir el-Medineh, Ostracon 621	
65-A	Sesebi, Votive Tablet	VII 173
66-B	Ostracon Cairo 25237	
66-C	Coptos Stela, *B3k-wr*	V 129
67-A	Papyrus Gurob, Fragment L	

NOTES TO CHAPTER III

AN ANALYSIS OF THE DATED MATERIAL

[1] The examination of these different inscriptions was made in the preceding chapter under the appropriate regnal years, where references may be found; only the results of that examination are incorporated here.

[2] The North Stela was treated under year 10-A in chap. II.

[3] See below, chap. IV.

[4] See above, chap. II, under regnal year 34-D.

[5] Another example is the restoration text of *Ḫ'-m-W3st* at the pyramid of Unis, Drioton-Lauer, ASAE (1937), 201-211.

[6] For wine jar inscriptions assigned to Ramesses II but found in a tomb belonging to the time of Ramesses IV, see years 46-B, 47-A, 48-A and 49-A. In this same tomb a jar inscription which probably dates to Horemhab was also found.

[7] Years 42-B and 62-A.

CHAPTER IV

THE HITTITE ALLIANCE

The text of the Egypto-Hittite Alliance was first published by Burton in his "Excerpta Hieroglyphica" of 1825 and was followed shortly thereafter by Champollion's "Monuments," which included both the Karnak and Ramesseum texts.[1] Though Champollion offered a partial translation of the inscriptions,[2] it fell to his pupil, Rosellini, to grasp its content and to publish the first complete translation.[3] Since then a number of copies of the text have been published;[4] until the recent publication of Kitchen's Ramesside Inscriptions,[5] the best was that of W. M. Mueller,[6] with minor corrections by Sethe.[7] Mueller not only published the text but accompanied it with a translation and commentary. Soon thereafter Breasted included a translation in his "Ancient Records of Egypt,"[8] and Roeder incorporated it in his "Aegypter und Hethiter";[9] Langdon and Gardiner translated and compared the Akkadian and Egyptian copies of the Alliance,[10] but since 1920 the only major translation has been the one by Wilson, in "Ancient Near Eastern Texts,"[11] where it is accompanied by a translation of the Hittite version by Goetze.[12]

The Karnak copy of the Alliance is engraved upon a traverse wall between the Hypostyle Hall and the Seventh Pylon,[13] where the text is situated between a number of battle scenes. On the side nearest the Hypostyle Hall a battle between Ramesses II and some Syrians is depicted;[14] this scene is not well preserved and it is difficult to determine the location of the battle. On the other side of the Alliance there is the storming of Askelon in Palestine.[15] Further along the wall are more battle scenes placed there by Ramesses II.[16] At the Ramesseum the Alliance was placed on the outer face of the second pylon, but so little of this structure is now standing that the fragmentary text of the Alliance itself is all that remains.[17]

As shown in the preceding analysis, the Alliance between Hatti and Egypt is one of the few records belonging to a dark period in the reign of Ramesses II.[18] For many years this inscription has been recognized as an important record from the past; however, because of its particular importance for an understanding of the events of this period in the reign of Ramesses, the text will be examined and both a translation and commentary will be given.

THE HITTITE ALLIANCE, A TRANSLATION

Line

1 Year 21, first (month) of *prt* (second season) day 21,
under the Majesty of:
King User-Ma'at-Re, Chosen-of-Re,
Son of Re, Ramesses, Beloved-of-Amun,
may he live forever and ever,
the beloved of Amun-Re-Harakhty, Ptah-south-of-his-wall
and Lord-of-life-of-the-two-lands, Mut-the-Lady-of-Ishru,
and Khonsu-*nfr-ḥtp*,
who appeared upon the throne of Horus of the living
(citizens) like (his) father Re-Harakhty forever and ever.

2 (2) On this day, his Majesty was at the city of Per-Ramesses,
Beloved-of-Amun, performing the ritual functions of his father
Amun-Re-Harakhty, Atum Lord-of-the-two-lands-of-Heliopolis,
Amun of Ramesses, Beloved-of-Amun, Ptah of Ramesses, Beloved-of-Amun, and [Suth] Great-of-strength the son of Nut--since
they (shall) give him an eternity in festivity and an everlastingness in peaceful years, while all lands and all countries
3 are under his control forever--(3) (at that time) there arrived
the royal envoy and deputy...the envoy...[of Per-Ramesses,
Beloved-of-Amun?] together with [*T3r*]-*tsb*, envoy of the land of
4 Hatti...[bearing the tablet of silver which] (4) the great
chieftain of Hatti, Hattushilish [caused] to be brought to
Court, l.p.h., to request accord [with the Majesty of King
User-Ma'at-Re], Chosen-of-Re, the Son of Re, Ramesses, Beloved-of-Amun, may he be given life forever and ever, like (his)
father Re every day.

Copy of the tablet of silver which the great chieftain of
Hatti, Hattushilish, caused to be brought to Court, l.p.h.,
5 by means of his envoy (5) *T3r-tsb* and (also) his envoy
Ra-mes, to request accord with the Majesty [of King User-Ma'at-Re, Chosen-of-Re] the son of Re, Ramesses, Beloved-of-Amun, Bull-of-rulers who makes his limits that which he
desires in every land.

The terms which the great chieftain of Hatti, Hattushilish, the
6 mighty, the son of Murshilish, (6) the great chieftain of Hatti,
who is mighty, the son of the son of Shuppi[luliumash, the
great chieftain of Hatti, who is] mighty, made upon a tablet of
silver for User-Ma'at-Re, Chosen-of-Re the great ruler of Egypt,
who is mighty, the son of Men-Ma'at-Re (Seti I) the great ruler

of Egypt, who is mighty, and the son of the son of Men-pehty-Re
7 (Ramesses I) (7) the great ruler of Egypt, who is mighty. The
good terms of accord and alliance, may they produce [good]
accord [and good alliance]...unto eternity, from beginning to
end forever. As for the agreement of the great ruler of Egypt
with the great chieftain of Hatti, may God not allow discord to
separate them concerning the terms.
8 Now even though (it was) (8) in the reign of Muwatallish, the
great chieftain of Hatti, my brother, that he fought wi[th]..?.
the great ruler of Egypt. Ever since then, beginning from
that day, Hattushilish, the great chieftain of Hatti, has been
searching [for the] terms which would stabilize the situation
which Pa-Re has made and which Suth of the land of Egypt
9 (9) together with (the god) of the land of Hatti have made,
in order never to allow discord to come between them forever.
Behold, Hattushilish, the great chieftain of Hatti, places himself within the terms with User-Ma'at-Re, Chosen-of-Re, the
great ruler of Egypt, beginning from this day, in order to
cause good accord and good alliance to exist between us forever:

10 (10) "He is in alliance with me and he is in accord with
me forever."
"I am in alliance with him and I am in accord with
him forever."

Now that Muwatallish, the great chieftain of Hatti, my brother,
11 has gone after his fate, Hattushilish sits (11) as the great
chieftain of Hatti upon the throne of his fathers. And I am
looking forward to coexistence with Ramesses, Beloved-of-Amun,
the great ruler of Egypt, that [we] may come [together] for
[our] accord and our alliance. May it be better than any
accord or any alliance which previously existed upon earth.
I shall see to it that the great chieftain of Hatti is with
12 (12) [Ramesses, Beloved-of-Amun], the great ruler of Egypt, in
good accord and in good alliance and that the children of the
children of the great chieftain of Hatti are in alliance and
in accord with the children of the children of [Ra]mes[ses],
Beloved-[of-Amun], the great ruler of Egypt. It is our agree-
13 ment for alliance and our agreement (13) [for accord, that the
land of Egypt] with the land of Hatti be in accord and in
alliance like our design forever, and may no discord (ever)
separate them.

The great chieftain of Hatti shall never trespass against the land of Egypt forever, in order to take even a trifling from it and (likewise) User-Ma'at-Re, Chosen-of-Re, the great ruler of
14 Egypt shall never trespass against the land (14) [of Hatti to take even a trifling] from it forever.

Now with regard to the sworn terms which were (here) in the reign of Shuppiluliumash, the great chieftain of Hatti, and likewise, the sworn terms which were in the reign of Muwatallish, the great chieftain of Hatti, my father (sic), I will observe them and behold Ramesses, Beloved-of-Amun, the great ruler of
15 Egypt shall observe (15) [them and we will act] jointly from this day on; we will observe them and act within this sworn agreement:

If another discord comes against the territories of User-Ma'at-Re, Chosen-of-Re, the great ruler of Egypt,
and he sends to the great ruler of Hatti saying,
"Come with me in a campaign against it,"
16 then the great chieftain of Hatti (16) [shall come]
and the great chieftain of Hatti shall route his (Ramesses') disorder.

However, if it be not the wish of the great chieftain of Hatti to go when he (Ramesses) dispatches [his] infantry and his chariotry,
then he (Ramesses) shall route his (own) disorder.

Or, if Ramesses, Beloved-of-Amun, [the great ruler of
17 Egypt], be incensed (17) against his own subjects since they have committed another crime against him,
and he goes to route them,
then the great chieftain of Hatti shall act with him [to destroy] everyone [against whom he be] incensed.

If, however, another disorder [comes] against the [great] chieftain of [Hatti]
and [he sends to User]-Ma'at-[Re], Chosen-of-Re, [the
18 (18) great ruler of Egypt that he] come to him in a campaign to route his disorder.
If it be the desire of Ramesses, Beloved-of-Amun, the great ruler of Egypt, to come,
19 then he... (19)...
chariotry, while the reply is returned to Hatti.

If, however, subjects of the great chieftain of Hatti trespass against him,
then Rames[ses], Beloved-of-Amun, [the great ruler of

Egypt,]...
the land of Hatti.
The [great chieftain of Hatti]...
20 (20)...[according] to this oath, and shall say:
"When I shall go after [my] fate, then Ramesses, Beloved-of-[Amun], the great ruler of Egypt, may he live forever, [shall come]...."
21 (21)...(which) they have done in order to cause that he be given to them as lord; [never] shall User-Ma'at-Re, Chosen-of-[Re, the] great ruler of Egypt, be silent to his claim forever. And after he [is expelled from] the land of Hatti, then he shall return [it to] the great chieftain of Hatti....
[If...to] the great chieftain of Hatti, or a town
22 (22) [which belong] to the territories of Ramesses, Beloved-of-Amun, the great ruler of Egypt,
and they come to the great chieftain of Hatti--then the great chieftain of Hatti shall not act to receive them, but the great chieftain of Hatti shall cause that they be brought back to User-Ma'at-Re, Chosen-of-Re, the great ruler of Egypt, their lord....
23 Or, if a man or two, and they be unknowns, [flee] (23)...
... and they come to the land of Hatti to change allegiance,
they shall not remain in the land of Hatti, but one shall bring them back to Ramesses, Beloved-of-Amun, the great ruler of Egypt.
Or, if an important person flee from the land of Hatti and [he come to User]-Ma'at-[Re], Chosen-of-Re, the [great]
24 ruler of Egypt, or a town or an area or (24)...which belong to the land of Hatti and they come to Ramesses, Beloved-of-Amun, the great ruler of Egypt,
then User-Ma'at-Re, Chosen-of-Re, the great ruler of Egypt, shall not act to receive them, but Ramesses, Beloved-of-Amun, the great ruler of Egypt, shall cause that they be returned to the great chieftain [of Hatti], and they shall not remain. And likewise,
25 if only one or two people flee (25) [and] they be unknowns, and they come to the land of Egypt in order to change allegiance,
then User-Ma'at-Re, Chosen-of-Re, the great ruler of Egypt, shall not tolerate them but he shall cause that they be brought back to the great chieftain of Hatti.

Concerning the words of the terms which the great chieftain of
Hatti made with Rames[ses, Beloved-of-Amun,] the great ruler
26 (26) [of Egypt, they are] in writing upon this tablet of silver.
Concerning the words, a thousand deities of the male gods and
of the female gods among those of the land of Hatti along with
a thousand deities of the male gods and the female gods among
those of the land of Egypt--they are with me as witnesses.

"[Hear] these words, O Pa-Re, lord of the sky; Pa-Re of the
27 town of Arinna; (27) Suth lord of the sky; Suth of Hatti; Suth
of the town of Arinna; Suth of the town of Zippalanda; Suth of
the town of Pe(tt)iyarik; Suth of the town of Hissas(ha)pa;
Suth of the town of Sarissa; Suth of the town of Halab; Suth of
28 the town of Lihzina; Suth of (28) [the town]...; Suth [of the
town]...Suth of the town of Sahpin; Antaret of the land of
Hatti; the god of Zithari(as); the god of Karzis; the god of
29 Hapantaliyas; (29) the goddess of the town of Karahna; the
goddess of...(?) and the Queen of heaven and of the gods and
Lady of the oath; the goddess--the Mistress of the earth and
30 the Mistress of the oath, Ishara; the Mistress [of?] (30) the
mountains and the rivers of the land of Hatti; the gods of the
land of Kizzuwadna; (and) Amun; Pa-Re; Suth; the male gods; the
female gods; the mountains and the rivers of the land of Egypt;
the sky, the earth, our (sic) great sea, the air and the storm
wind."

31 Concerning the words (31) which are upon this tablet of silver
for the land of Hatti and for the land of Egypt,
as for him who shall not observe them--
a thousand deities of the land of Hatti together
with a thousand deities of the land of Egypt shall
destroy his house, his land and his subjects.
However, as for the person who shall observe these words
which are upon this tablet of silver, be they Hittites or
32 Egyptians, (32) and they do not act in ignorance against
them,
then a thousand deities of the land of Hatti
together with a thousand deities of the land of Egypt
shall give him health and give him life, together
with his house(hold), together with his [land] and
together with his subjects.
If a man, or two or three, flee from the land of Egypt and

33 (33) come to the great chieftain of Hatti,
the great chieftain of Hatti shall lay hold of them and
he shall cause that they be brought back to User-Ma'at-Re,
Chosen-of-Re, the great ruler of Egypt.

However, concerning the person whom one shall cause that he be brought (back) to Ramesses, Beloved-of-Amun, the great ruler of Egypt,
do not allow one to arraign his crime against him and do
34 not allow one (34) to destroy his house, his women or
his children....
And do not allow one to trespass against his eyes, his
ears, his mouth, or his legs,
And do not allow one to arraign any crime against him.
And likewise,

If people flee from the land of Hatti, whether he (sic) comes
as one, two or three, and they (sic) come to User-Ma'at-Re,
35 Chosen-of-Re, (35) the great ruler of Egypt,
then Ramesses, Beloved-of-Amun, the [great ruler of Egypt,
shall lay hold of them and he shall] cause that they be
brought back to the great chieftain of Hatti,
And the great chieftain of Hatti shall not [arraign their]
crime against them and one shall not destroy his [house],
his women or his children,
And one shall not slay him nor shall one trespass
36 against his ears, (36) against his eyes, his mouth, or his
legs--and one shall not arraign any crime against him.

That which is in the middle of the tablet of silver on its front side:

An engraving in the likeness of Suth embracing an image of the
great chieftain of Hatti, bordered by the legend saying, "The
sealing of Suth the ruler of the sky (is) the seal of the terms
37 which Hattushilish, the great chieftain of (37) Hatti, who is
valiant, made, the son of Murshilish, the great chieftain of
Hatti, who is valiant." That which is within the border of the
engraving, "The seal of Suth [lord of the sky.]"

That which is in the middle, upon its other side:

An engraving of a female image of the goddess of Hatti embracing
a female image of the Great One of Hatti, bordered by the
38 legend saying, "The seal of Pa- (38) Re of the town of Arinna,
lord of the land; the seal of Puduhepa, the Great One of the
land of Hatti, the daughter of the land of Kizzuwadna, the...

[of the town of] Arinna, the Mistress of the land, the servant of the goddess." [That which is] within the border of the engraving, "The seal of Pa-Re of Arinna, the lord of every land."

Hittite Alliance Commentary

1 The date given, "Regnal year 21, 1st month of *prt* day 21," is the *hrw pn* mentioned below, that is, the day when the messengers arrived from Hatti; on that day Ramesses was in the city of Per-Ramesses, Beloved-of-Amun. The "first month of *prt*" is also that time when Ramesses announced his Jubilees later in his reign.[19] For a discussion of royal documents bearing regnal dates, see Goedicke, JARCE 3 (1964), 31-41. The location of Per-Ramesses, Beloved-of-Amun, a city in the eastern Delta, is still disputed; both Tanis and Qantir have been proposed as possible sites.[20]

The compound *st-Ḥr*, referring to the royal throne, was in use since the Middle Kingdom, cf. Wb IV 7, 21-23; it has also been compounded with *'nḫw* since the same period, Wb IV 7, 23. In the Quban stela (line 2) there is a similar phrase, *ḫ'w ḥr st Ḥr nt 'nḫw mỉ ỉt.f R' r' nb*, and in line 8, *ỉst ḥm.f ḥms ḥr bḥdw n ḏ'mw ḫ'w m sšd m3'ty*. The phrase occurs earlier in the Eighteenth Dynasty, cf. Urk. IV 103, 3 (Tuthmosis I), and also a number of times during the Nineteenth Dynasty, Ramesses I, Buhen Stela, line 3;[21] Merneptah, Hermopolis Stela, line 26.[22] In Urk. IV 563, 15, the verb *ḫ'ỉ* is followed by *ḥr nst R' ḥr st Ḥr*. In these examples, the verb *ḫ'ỉ* refers to the royal accession and its further manifestations by the king upon the royal throne;[23] for the reference to the Hittite king's coronation, see line 11 below.

2 *Hrw pn*, as mentioned above, refers to the preceding date and introduces the specific activities of that day; this compound is commonly found in business documents, especially on ostraca.[24] For a similar use of *hrw pn* to introduce an historical narration after the royal titulary, see the Beth Shan Stela (no. 2) of Seti I, line 9.[25]

The formulation, *ỉst ḥm.f (r dmỉ)...ḥr ỉrt ḥss(t) ỉt.f NN*,

2 is a standard form used to introduce royal activity; though found earlier, it became common in the Nineteenth Dynasty.[26] A specific date or, as here, the words *hrw pn* precede the phrase; the place mentioned may change as may the deity, but the basic structure remains the same. In this text it is used to define the activity of Ramesses II at the time when the messengers arrived at Per-Ramesses, Beloved-of-Amun: his Majesty was performing the ritual functions when the royal envoy arrived. This literary form was already in use in the Eighteenth Dynasty, for the Konosso stela of Tuthmosis IV reads, "Regnal year 7, 3rd month of *prt* day 2, lo his Majesty was in the Southern City at the city of Karnak, his hands purified...."[27] The phrase occurs a number of times in the inscriptions of Seti I: the dedicatory inscription of the Speos Artemidos, line 3;[28] the Nauri Decree, line 2;[29] a Silsileh stela of year 6, lines 4-5;[30] and at the Wadi Miah (Text B, line 1).[31] It also occurs in the Buhen stela of Ramesses I, line 3,[32] and in Ramesses II's own Quban stela, line 7.[33]

The compound *r-dmỉ* has been understood by Fairman and Grdseloff, JEA 33 (1947), 26, note 3 and 29, as referring to a "quarter" or a "district" within a city. Caminos, on the other hand, in The Chronicle of Prince Osorkon, 29, retains the meaning of "town" for *dmỉ*.[34]

The epithet of Atum, *nb t3wy Ỉwnw*, "Lord-of-the-two-lands-of-Heliopolis," is probably a unit and *Ỉwnw* not a nisbe meaning the "Heliopolitan," as it is usually understood; for which, cf. Wb I 54, 8, to which one may add for this period, Seti I's dedicatory inscription of the Speos Artemidos, line 3[35] and Nauri Decree, line 2.[36] This epithet of Atum brings Heliopolis into the fore with regard to the "two lands," that is, Egypt, and was a popular formulation of the Nineteenth Dynasty.

In lines 2 and 3 a number of deities are mentioned; those in line 2 are the Theban triad, with one extra member, the god Ptah. One would expect to find Amun, Mut and Khonsu listed here since the text was set up at Thebes within the confines of Karnak. The god Ptah did have a chapel at Karnak but his inclusion here can only be seen as personal favoritism towards this god, who was a very important deity in the reign of Ramesses II. In line 2, the gods listed differ from those in line 1 and appear to be the personal gods of Ramesses II, whom he venerated in his city of Per-Ramesses, Beloved-of-Amun.[37]

The preposition *mỉ* used to introduce a condition dependent

2 upon a previous statement, as here, is found in this period to state a *quid pro quo* condition between the king and the gods, "King *NN* does such for the gods, as they give him...." For this preposition in a comparable construction, see, for example, Quban stela, line 7; Speos Artemidos, Seti I dedicatory inscription, line 5; Nauri Decree, line 3; for Ramesses I, Sinai Stela (no. 244), line 6, and Buhen Stela, line 4.[38]

Towards the end of the line, the phrase *ḏt m rnpwt ḥtpw* is a peculiar formulation, and its counterpart *nḥḥ m Ḥbw-Sd* appears to be equally unusual.[39] The nearest one may approach the wording *ḏt m rnpwt ḥtpw* is the phrase *rnpwt nḥḥ* (Wb II 300, 9), which is certainly not the same; for the shorter formulation of *rnpwt ḥtpw*, cf. Wb III 190, 5 and 193, 8. This particular formulation, the *nḥḥ*-eternity of Jubilees with the *ḏt*-eternity of "peaceful years," is different than most combinations of these words and appears to have been a particular predelection of Ramesses II. Another inscription of Ramesses, from Beit el-Wali, has *dỉ.n(.ỉ) n.k nḥḥ m Ḥbw-Sd ḏt m 'nḫ w3s.*[40] One of the closest parallels to the statement of Ramesses II in the Alliance is found on a stela of Seti I dated to his regnal year 1: *nḥḥ m Ḥbw-Sd ḏt m 'nḫw ḥfnw m rnpwt ḥtpw*;[41] similar phrases occur in the Nauri decree: *m rnpwt ḥfnw m rnpwt ḥtpw* (line 3) and *ỉmỉ n.f nḥḥ m Ḥbw-Sd* (line 12). An inscription of Seti I at Karnak has *nḥḥ m ḥbw mỉ R'*,[42] while the Abydos stela of Ramesses IV has the formulation *ḥḥ n Ḥbw-Sd ḏt ḥr st-Ḥr* (line 2).[43] The phrase, as given in the Alliance, appears to have been a wish to stress the hope for longevity to celebrate many Jubilees, but especially a hope for peaceful years upon earth.

The clause *ỉw t3w nbw ḫ3swt nbw ḫtb ḫr ṯbwty.f ḏt* must grammatically be contingent upon *mỉ dỉ.sn*; for a comparable phraseology, see the stela of year 1 of Seti I, line 14,[44] and his Gebel Silsileh stela of year 6, line 13.[45] The verb *ḫtb/ḫdb* occurs again in line 16 below, where it is translated differently; here the phrase *ḫ(t/d)b ḫr ṯbwty.f ḏt* has been paraphrased to fit the context.

3 Restorations for the beginning of line 3 have been recently proposed by Edel in Orientalia 38 (1969), 177-186, where he suggests the reading *ỉdnw 'nty n tnt-ḥtrw*. This suggestion contains several difficulties; the name *'nty*, as Edel recognizes, is not typical of this period,[46] and at the same time, the insertion of a name within a title is unusual.[47] The read-

3 ing of *tnt-ḥtrw* is feasible, except that in line 16 it is written 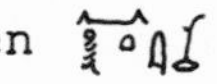 and not 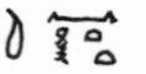 ; since the orthography is rather consistent throughout the text, this restoration can only remain conjecture. In spite of attempts at a restoration, this part is still uncertain.

In the same article, Edel discussed the names of the messengers, *T3r-tsb* and *R'-ms*, both of whom are known from letters found in the archives of Boghazköy.[48] The name *T3r-tsb* is also found at Ugarit, where he is described as a "messager que (le Soleil) a envoyé en Égypte."[49] However, there appears to be no reasonable evidence of a third messenger accompanying these two men; as will be seen below, they apparently represented their respective kings during the negotiations.[50]

The end of line 3 might be restored as *rdỉ.n.*, as later in line 4, though it is not certain that the *'nw n ḥḏ* is the object of the action, as in that later sentence; either the messengers or the silver tablet was "caused to come" to the Egyptian court. In line 4, the seeming parallel reads, "Copy of the tablet of silver which the great chieftain of Hatti, Hattushilish, caused to be brought to Court in the hand of his envoy...." Recently, Kitchen has suggested reading *ẖr(w) p3 'nw n ḥḏ rdỉ n* for the last part of this line.[51]

4 This line contains the first direct reference to Hattushilish III with whom Ramesses II entered the alliance. As we know from his "Apology," Hattushilish deposed his nephew Urkhi-Teshub and installed himself as king upon the throne of Hatti.[52] According to the same source, Urkhi-Teshub reigned for seven years before being deposed; as discussed in chapter I above, the most reasonable dates for the accession of Urkhi-Teshub is regnal year 10 of Ramesses II and regnal year 17 for Hattushilish III.[53] Assuming that these dates are as accurate as can be achieved by means of comparative chronology, then Hattushilish had been great king in Hatti for three to four years before the date given in this text.[54] How long negotiations were conducted remains an unknown factor, though a certain amount of time would have been required simply for communications.[55]

The kingly epithets employed throughout this text vary slightly; the main epithet of Hattushilish is "The great chieftain of Hatti," which is used not only as an epithet but also as a substitute for his personal name (lines 11ff). Ramesses epithet is "The great ruler of Egypt," which is used only once

4 in this text in place of his name (line 7). In the Hittite version, the personal names of both rulers are employed throughout; therefore, the change in the Egyptian version appears to have been one of local preference rather than an indication of some legal situation. In lines 4 and 5 the epithet "The great chieftain of Hatti" precedes the name of Hattushilish (in two instances); thereafter it follows his name whenever the two are found in conjunction, as it also follows the names of other Hittite rulers.[56] One further epithet is the word *ṯnr* "mighty"; only once does it have the article *p3* (line 5, after the name of Hattushilish); otherwise it is used as a participle after the royal name. It is only found in lines 5 to 7 and disappears thereafter,[57] except for line 37 (description of the seal).

The various usages of the royal names and epithets indicate the origins of these different sections of the text. Lines 1 through 4 (down to the word *mỉtt*) are of Egyptian origin, wherein the name of Ramesses II is accompanied by special epithets, and in which the one (extant) mention of the name of Hattushilish is preceded by "The great chieftain of Hatti."[58] Another section (from *mỉtt* in line 4 to *p3 nt-'* in line 5) must also be of Egyptian origin, as indicated by the lengthy epithet appended to the name of Ramesses II; here again the name of Hattushilish is preceded by "The great chieftain of Hatti," but no epithet follows it.

In line 5, the words *p3 nt-'* open a third part, which must have been drafted under the auspices of the Hittite king, for not only is it the place where the Hittite version begins, it is also the first time that the word *ṯnr* appears and the first time that the name of Ramesses is followed by "The great ruler of Egypt," which becomes standard throughout. It appears then that the first introduction (lines 1 to 4) was added to the inscription when it was to be publically announced upon the temple walls, while the second introduction, beginning with the word *mỉtt* in line 4 was the "official" heading given to the text (or translation thereof) probably at the time when it was placed in the royal archives. The actual communication from the king of Hatti then commences in line 5 with the words "The terms...."

The words *r dbḥ ḥtpw* were translated "Frieden zu erbitten von der Majestaet..." by W. M. Mueller[59] and "To beg peace from the Majesty..." by Gardiner,[60] followed in like manner by Wilson;[61] this understanding led Gardiner to see this as "a common-

4 place of Egyptian style...that every Egyptian scribe would naturally represent the foreigner as suing for peace,"[62] even though he thought it "may in this case have corresponded roughly to the actual political situation."[63] W. M. Mueller, on the other hand, disregarding the "Egyptian introduction" ("ohne die aegyptische Einleitung"), saw this as a "Buendnisabschluss" or "Buendnisvertrag."[64] The word *dbḥ* does not mean to "beg" or to "supplicate" but rather to "request/require"; cf. Wb V 439-40.[65] The silver tablet was sent in order to "request peace" or to "request accord with the Majesty...." The word *ḥtp* reflects the proper condition which should exist rather than just the cessation of warfare, and therefore the word has been rendered "accord" throughout.[66]

The Tablet of Silver (*'nw n ḥḏ*) upon which the "terms" were inscribed is mentioned in both versions;[67] it would appear that each party received a copy of the alliance contained upon a tablet of silver which was then placed before the gods who were witnesses to the oaths the kings had sworn.[68]

4/5 At the end of line 4 and the beginning of line 5 the word *ỉpwty* occurs twice, each time with the third masculine singular suffix (*.f*): "Copy of the tablet of silver...brought to court ...by means of his envoy *T3r-tsb* and (also) his envoy Ra-mes...." This ambiguous use of the suffix has caused some confusion; Gardiner[69] assumed that both of these men were in the employ of Hattushilish, an interpretation which was also followed by Edel.[70] There is no need, however, to posit an Egyptian in the service of the Hittite king; the first suffix "his" before the name *T3r-tsb* must refer to Hattushilish, while the second, before the name Ra-mes, relates to Ramesses II. For a similar use of the suffix, see line 16 below. The envoy Ra-mes, most appropriately, represented Ramesses II in the negotiations, while *T3r-tsb* served Hattushilish; both came to Egypt for the ratification of the alliance.

5 The word *ṯnr* with the article is found only in line 5, and there only once, in reference to the ruler of Hatti; the word *ṯnr* itself is only used in lines 5 and 6. After the genealogical reference, it is dropped and does not appear again until line 37.

The compound *nt-'* was translated by W. M. Mueller as "Vertrag"[71] and was followed by Gardiner when he chose the word

5 "treaty";[72] Wilson, however, used "regulations" instead,[73] a translation which better fits the Egyptian than does the word "treaty." The word *nt-'* literally means "according to the book" and can refer to the regulations of a particular office or directions for a specific activity.[74] In this case it may be seen as the directions or regulations which were to govern the relationship between the two lands, that is, the "terms" of their agreement or of their intentions (*sḫr*) which were codified and placed upon silver tablets.

5/6 Hattushilish's genealogy is correct as given in lines 5-6,[75] but in this way he is able to omit his two immediate predecessors: his brother Muwatallish and his nephew whom he deposed, Urkhi-Teshub. Though Muwatallish is later mentioned in the text (lines 8, 10 and 14), the seven year reign of Urkhi-Teshub is completely ignored.[76]

The word *snsn* has been translated "alliance" rather than the usual "brotherhood"[77] in order to convey the more technical meaning which the word connotes in this context; for this, see Wb IV 172-173 and also 174, 1. The word *ḥtp* has been discussed above in line 3.

6 As in the Hittite genealogy mentioned above, so also here: three generations are given for Ramesses II.[78] Since genealogies are not a necessary element of treaties, it would seem that these rulers felt the need to stress their legitimacy.

7 The phrase *ỉr r ḥ3t n ḏr nḥḥ* has in the past been translated as a part of the following sentence beginning with *ỉr p3 sḫr*; Gardiner, "Now aforetime, since eternity, as regards the policy...," and Wilson, "Now from the beginning of the limits of eternity, as for the situation...."[79] The preceding *lacuna* has prompted translators to attach *ỉr r ḥ3t n ḏr nḥḥ* to the following instead of the preceding, but the difficulty in doing so is evident in the resultant translations. It therefore seems better to understand this phrase as a part of the preceding thought and begin a new sentence with *ỉr p3 sḫr*.

The word *sḫr* is used throughout this text as a parallel to *nt-'*; *sḫr* actually refers to the negotiations and thereby to the intention of the two kings, while the *nt-'* refers to the result of such, that is, the codified agreement. The word *sḫr* is used in line 8 to indicate the intentions of the gods for

7 the two lands; here, as also in line 12, it is employed to show that the two kings have now brought themselves into conformity with the intent of the gods, who are later called upon to witness the alliance. The sentence beginning with *bw dỉ p3 nṯr* has here been translated in hortatory form, even though it has been understood as referring to the past: "The god did not permit...."[80] For the use of *bw* in this way, see line 13 below and Edgerton, AJSL 48 (1931), 34 (23), with references to Gunn, Studies in Egyptian Syntax, 113, and Gardiner, Grammar[3] §418; one may also compare the examples given in Hintze, Untersuchungen zu Stil und Sprache neuaegyptischer Erzaehlungen, 250-252, and see Gardiner, JNES 12 (1953), 148.

P3 nṯr has simply been translated "God," as indicated by the form which appears in Coptic (ⲡⲛⲟⲩⲧⲉ); this may be seen as a reference to "God" in general and not to any particular manifestation.[81]

The word *ḫrwy* occurs several times in this text, always written the same way; here it can best be translated as "discord," for it seems to represent disharmony in general. The word is related to "battle" in that it also is a "disturbance," especially when one considers the melee which accompanies a battle.[82] W. M. Mueller translated the word as "Feindschaft,"[83] and Gardiner chose the word "hostilities"[84] but Wilson left it in the abstract singular, "hostility."[85]

The compound *r ỉwd*, meaning to "come between, separate, divide,"[86] is used in a negative sense here and also in line 9; however, in the phrase *rdỉt ḫpr ḥtp nfr snsn nfr r ỉwd.n r nḥḥ*, in line 9, it is construed in a positive way. Such usage indicates that the term itself is neutral in meaning. Since it is employed with abstracts in line 9, such is likely its use here; in line 9 the "concord" and "alliance" are the counterparts of the *ḫrwy*, the "discord," of line 7.

8 The last two words of line 7, *ḫr ỉr*, begin a new thought, though one contingent upon the preceding idea; for such use of *ḫr ỉr* in this text, see lines 16, 17 and 31 and also Erman, Neuaegyptische Grammatik[2] §805 and §807, and Hintze, Untersuchungen zu Stil und Sprache neuaegyptischer Erzaehlungen, 7-31 and 212-213.

The sentence referring to the reign of Muwatallish is not found in the Hittite version of the Alliance. This reference to Muwatallish and that in line 10 below are both omitted from

8 the Hittite copy, as is the reference to the "sworn terms" in line 14. The two versions are certainly not exact parallels, as has been recognized.[87] There are only general references to the past in the Hittite version, such as Hattushilish's genealogy in lines 5-6; specific historical statements such as occur in the Egyptian version are missing from the Hittite altogether.[88]

For the word *h3w* with reference to the "reign" of a particular king, see the heading of Papyrus Rhind (Mathematical), Westcar 6, 24, and also Wb II 478, 2 and 7. The reference to the reign of Muwatallish is introduced by the form *ḫr ỉr*, which contrasts the proposed time of concord with the past time of fighting; this is the only direct reference to warfare in the entire inscription. Hattushilish continues in line 8 to use another *ḫr ỉr* construction, this time the longer form of *ḫr ỉr ḥr s3* (cf. Hintze, *loc. cit.*) to contrast his pacific activity with that of his warring brother. Hattushilish does not directly state that there has been no warfare between Egypt and Hatti during his lifetime; he only states that "ever since that day" he has been searching for some solution to stabilize the situation.

In this sentence Hattushilish chooses to use the word *hrw* "day" rather than repeating *h3w* "reign." "Even though it was in the reign of Muwatallish...that he (Muwatallish) fought with the king of Egypt, ever since that day, Hattushilish...has been searching for some 'type of settlement.'"[89] The use of the more restricted temporal term *hrw* "day" strongly reminds one of that specific "day" at Qadesh.[90]

The missing cartouche in line 8 may be reasonably restored as containing "Ramesses, Beloved-of-Amun" (see line 9, for the prenomen); since after line 8 there is a regular alternation of Ramesses' nomen and prenomen, one may restore it here, assuming that it was Muwatallish with whom Ramesses fought. Nowhere in the records of the battle of Qadesh is the name of Ramesses' Hittite opponent ever given,[91] but it may be reasonably assumed that it was Muwatallish who opposd Ramesses II at Qadesh.

After *ḫr ỉr ḥr s3 š3' m p3 hrw*, the word *ptr*, according to Professor Goedicke's suggestion, is taken as a verbal form rather than the particle introducing a noun clause; for such, cf. Wb I 564, 17-19.[92] Further in the line in the *lacuna* just prior to *nt-'* the words *n p3* have been restored.[93]

The phrase *n dỉt mn p3 sḫr* literally means "of causing to make permanent the plan" or, as Wilson translates it, "for mak-

8 ing permanent the situation" which Pa-Re has made; beginning with the second *ỉrw*, the sentence becomes more involved. The Akkadian copy of the Alliance has two deities listed here, but there is some difficulty in considering this arrangement for the Egyptian version because of the two verbs *ỉrw* and their relationship to the preposition *ỉrm* at the beginning of line 9.[94] The translation given assumes that a reference to a Hittite deity,[95] perhaps another Suth, has been omitted near the beginning of line 9 just after the preposition *ỉrm*. One would therefore have, "The plans which Pa-Re made and which Suth-of-the-land-of-Egypt made together with (the god or Suth)-of-the-land-of-Hatti"; Pa-Re is then supreme rather than representing the god of Egypt, while the two Suths represent the specific countries of Hatti and Egypt.[96]

9 The negative *tm* is here used in contrast to the *bw* in line 7 above,[97] which reads, "may God never allow..."; this then is the assertory counterpart of that construction. The use of the plural suffix *.sn* (*r ỉwd.sn*) in the phrase "in order never to allow discord to come between <u>them</u> forever" indicates that this is an indirect quote of a statement by the gods placed in the mouth of Hattushilish; instead of the word "them" one would expect to find "us" (*.n*), as in line 9 below. It may be understood that the gods have decreed, "never let discord separate them forever"; as earlier in line 7, the wish is "may God never allow discord to separate them." In line 7, the kings, as stated by Hattushilish, pray that the will of the gods be done, by causing peace and concord to exist between them forever.

Beginning with *ptr ỉr.sw*, the indirect quote of the gods changes to a direct statement on the part of Hattushilish; even though he refers to himself in the third person, the first plural suffix *.n* after *r ỉwd* shows that it is the Hittite king who is speaking and not the deities. After the reference to the gods, Hattushilish asserts that he is in accord and alliance with Ramesses, the great ruler of Egypt; line 10 contains the actual oath which must have been taken by each king.[98]

The phrase *š3ʿ m p3 hrw*, as in line 8 above, denotes a specific day. Here it refers to that day when the king of Hatti swore to uphold the "arrangements" (*sḫrw*) (as they are written in the "terms" (*nt-ʿ*) of the Alliance) in order to cause good accord and good alliance to exist between the two rulers. At that time Hattushilish committed himself to the

9 terms which were recorded upon the silver tablet.

The verb *ḫpr* is here used in a similar manner to that in the preceding sentence; there it was in the negative clause *r tm ḫpr ḫrwy r ỉwd.sn*, but here it is employed in a positive statement. The verb *ḫpr* was also used in a similar way in line 7 above.

10 The declaratory statement of line 10 contains the oath taken by each king when he ratified the alliance in the presence of his local gods;[99] this statement is found in both the Egyptian and Hittite versions. Here, contrary to the usual formulation in this text, the word *snsn*, an Old Perfective, precedes the word *ḥtp*; the same order is found in the Akkadian of the Hittite version.

As above in line 8, so also here, the historical reference to Muwatallish is missing in the Hittite copy. The formulation *ḥnn NN m s3 p3y.f š3yt* is apparently a translation of the Akkadian *ki-i-me-e*...[*a-na*] *ši-im-ti-šu*[100] and is one way to refer to a person's death; the concept is apparently Mesopotamian. For Hittite references to death, see Apology I 22 and III 38. For a comparable Egyptian term, *sbỉ n k3.f*, cf. Wb III 430, 1-3.[101]

Hattushilish's statement is historically inaccurate, as he did not succeed to the throne of Hatti upon the death of his brother Muwatallish;[102] the seven-year reign of his nephew, Urkhi-Teshub, intervened (Apology III 38-45). The present situation of alliance and accord is contrasted to that "fighting" during the reign of Muwatallish (line 8 above), but this alone does not explain the complete absence of Urkhi-Teshub.[103]

11 In contrast to the Egyptian throne in line 1, the *st-Ḥr nt ʿnḫw*, the Hittite throne upon which Hattushilish sits is referred to as the "throne (*ỉsbt*) of his fathers";[104] both men were apparently concerned with their coronation, as evidence of their legitimate kingship, since they stressed it within the context of the Alliance.[105] The point of reference here is, now that Hattushilish sits upon the Hittite throne, instead of Muwatallish, the two lands can reach some type of concord.[106]

Again the verb *ḫpr* is used, and the phrase *ḥr ḫpr ỉrm* has been translated as "coexistence with," to use modern terminology. So far the verb *ḫpr* has been used four times: twice in the sense of not allowing some discord to come between these two

11 kings, once in the positive counterpart of the two preceding negatives (line 9), and finally here where the two kings have "come about" with each other and are now in one accord. The sentence is missing in the Hittite version, which moves from the swearing of brotherhood and alliance into the narrative statement of the same, which is the middle of line 11 of the Egyptian version.

In the middle of line 11 read: *ỉw [.n ỉỉ ỉrm n] p3y[.n] ḥtp p3y.n snsn.*[107] The words *p3 t3* here must simply mean "the earth" (cf. Hebrew הָאָרֶץ); there is no need to assume with Gardiner that "some words have been omitted here: 'which was in the land of Hatti with the land of Egypt.'"[108]

The next sentence, beginning with *ptr.ỉ m* (cf. Wb I 564, 17)[109] is another declaratory statement by the Hittite king, stressing his responsibility for seeing that the alliance succeed and that the children and the grandchildren also observe it. In the Hittite version, Ramesses II swears the same to the Hittite king, but only the sons of Ramesses are mentioned, not his grandchildren.[110]

12 In this line the word *sḫr* again denotes the intent of these two rulers, which manifests itself in the *nt-'*, the codified form written upon the tablet of silver. The word *sḫr* as the intent of these kings first appeared in line 7 above, where it was hoped that God would allow no discord to separate the two with regard to their plans or intentions (*sḫrw*). The word is repeated towards the end of line 8, referring to the plan of God for the two countries. It is here formulated in line 12, with the words *ḥtp* and *snsn*, where it is hoped that their agreements--that is, their intentions for alliance and their intentions for accord--may result in accord and alliance forever, according to their design for such.[111]

13 The clause *ỉw bw ḫpr.n ḫrwy r ỉwd.sn r nḥḥ* is a repeat of line 9, except that here *ỉw bw* is used instead of *r tm dỉt*.[112] The *n* after *ḫpr* should be understood as a mistake for *r*; for a discussion of *ḫpr n*, see Edgerton, AJSL 48 (1931), 34, and also line 7 above. This *ỉw bw ḫpr* formation is similar to the *ỉw bw dỉ* of line 7, which was also understood in an hortatory sense. The suffix *.sn* after *r ỉwd* seems to refer to the two countries and is thus distinguished from the third plural suffix of line 9, after *r ỉwd*.[113]

13 What may be considered the first "term" of the Alliance appears in line 13, with the words *ỉw bw ỉr p3 wr '3 n Ḫtt3...,* "The great chieftain of Hatti shall never trespass against the land of Egypt to take even a trifling from it," and the same is said for Ramesses II in the succeeding clause.[114] The negative construction employed here is similar to the preceding *ỉw bw ḫpr ḫrwy*, which could be translated in similar fashion: "May the great chieftain of Hatti never trespass against the land of Egypt."[115] In this line the negative *bw* is used for the last time[116] (later in the text whenever a negative is needed, the element *bn* is employed); it therefore seems that the construction of this "term" is different from those which are found in lines 15ff.[117] For the use of *bw* in a similar manner, see Erman, *op. cit.*, §529 and §773. This part may then be classified as belonging to the general terms of agreement rather than the specific terms, which begin in line 15. This general agreement is followed by one more historical reference by the Hittite ruler in the Egyptian version only; the Hittite version does not refer to the "sworn terms" which existed aforetime in earlier reigns.

For the word *thỉ*, cf. Wb V 319, 5-12. For *nkt* meaning "profit" or "advantage," see Gardiner, Papyrus Wilbour II 85, note 5; this meaning might be indicated here, even though the sense is conveyed by the word "trifling."[118]

14 The "sworn terms" which existed in the reign of Shuppiluliumash and in the reign of Muwatallish are to be included in and act as a foundation for the present alliance. Again the word *h3w* is used to indicate a king's reign, as above in line 8. For the compound *wn dy*, cf. Wb I 308, 6.[119] For a use of *mḥ ỉm* similar to that found here and dating to approximately the same time, see Papyrus Boulaq 3.[120]

We are uninformed concerning these "sworn terms," whether or not they were actual treaties or some other agreements cannot be ascertained from the information given in the text. If there were an agreement in the time of Shuppiluliumash, then it was broken during the reign of Muwatallish, as shown by the battle of Qadesh.[121] The agreement reached with Muwatallish most likely dates after Qadesh in regnal year 5; again, nothing is said about the reign of Urkhi-Teshub.[122]

15 At the beginning of line 15, the phrase *š3' m p3 hrw* is

15 found again and relates back to line 9, where Hattushilish said, "Beginning from this day (when he swore the oath) to cause good accord and good alliance to be between them (the two kings) forever...." Here in line 15, these two kings swear to carry out the "sworn agreement (*sḫr*)" which they have formulated in this *nt-ʿ*. For the previous use of *sḫr*, see above in lines 7, 8 and 12.[123]

In line 15, the first clause of the "terms" begins with the words *ỉr ỉw ky ḫrwy*. Here the word *ḫrwy* is written the same way as in lines 7, 9 and 13.[124] In this instance W. M. Mueller chose to translate the word as "Feind"[125] and was followed by both Gardiner and Wilson in their translations.[126] However, there is no reason at this point to change the translation of the word *ḫrwy* to one different from that in lines 7, 9 and 13 above. Instead of mentioning a specific "enemy," the text employs the more general term "discord" to cover any type of disturbance which might occur.[127] The use of the qualifying *ky*, "another," is unexpected, for within this text no previous disturbance has been mentioned as having arisen against either ruler;[128] the word "another" is found not only in the Egyptian version but in the Hittite also (Akkadian, *ša-nu-u*).[129]

16 The beginning word or words of this line are lost. The suggested restoration, as reflected in the translation, is *ỉỉ(t) m.tw*, though this might not fill the entire *lacuna*. Kitchen, Ramesside Inscriptions II 228, proposes *ỉrm.f m.tw*.

For a discussion of *ẖtb/ẖdb* as a reaction against political disorder, see Fairman and Grdseloff, JEA 33 (1947), 27; and Wb III 402, 12-15 and 403, 3-13.[130] For *ḫr ỉr*, see Erman, *op. cit.*, §§668, 673 and 807, and for *ỉw bn*, §§758 and 766; here the negative particle *bn* is used instead of the earlier *bw* of lines 7 and 13. The negative expression is missing in the Hittite version.[131] Here this sentence is translated, "if it be not the desire of the great chieftain of Hatti to come when he (Ramesses II) dispatches his troops," because of the combination *ḫr dỉt* instead of the expected *r dỉt*.[132] The phraseology of this section is awkward; it is similar to the situation mentioned above in lines 4-5, where the antecedents to the suffixes were not clear. An alternative could be that *ỉw.f ḫr dỉt* introduces a concomitant fact: "If it be not the desire of the great chieftain of Hatti to come and to send his troops...."[133] However, the translation "But if it be not the desire of the

16 great chief of Hatti to come, he shall send his troops..."[134] does not agree with the grammatical construction *ỉw.f ḥr dỉt.*[135]

The use of the compound *r3-pw* to coordinate these two "terms" shows that they are contingent upon each other. For the use of *r3-pw* between sentences, see Wb II 396, 18. It is interesting to note that the *r3-pw* is not employed in line 19, in the parallel which refers to the Hittite ruler. The word *ḳnd* indicates anger, but it is more "righteous indignation" (Wb V 57, 2-6) than fury without cause. It is used in the Qadesh inscriptions (P 330) in a similar way.[136]

17 The word *b3kw* denotes a king's subjects but does not refer to any specific social class; cf. Wb I 429, 15-17. For the emphatic suffix, see Gardiner, ZAeS 50 (1912), 114-117.[137] Again the word *ky* appears in this text, this time defining the word "crime" instead of "disorder," as in line 15 above. The word "other" is not found in the Hittite version,[138] neither with reference to Hattushilish nor to Ramesses; it is also not found in the Egyptian version referring to Hattushilish in line 19 below. The three uses of *ky* in this text cannot be termed a literary device, for the text is precise in its formulation. Apparently, as the record indicates, the subjects of Ramesses II had once committed a crime against him, a situation against which he is to be protected in the future by Hittite aid.[139] For the combination *ỉr ṯ3y r,* cf. Wb V 349, 1-2, to which add Papyrus Anastasi II 10, 7 and Papyrus Boulaq 3, 6-7. The word *ẖdb/ẖtb* is used again, in the sense of disbanding or routing those who have committed the second crime against the Egyptian king.[140]

In the latter part of this line the words *ky ḫrwy* are reasonably certain in the part pertaining to the Hittite king; the same terminology is also found in the Akkadian.[141] The words "another disorder" have been discussed above in line 15; that which follows is in bad condition but enough remains of the phrase "against the great chieftain of Hatti" for this to be reasonably certain.[142] In the *lacuna* following, read *m.tw.f h3b n*, as in line 15 above.[143]

18 There is a slight change here from the preceding parallel, which contained a quote by Ramesses II, "Come with me in a campaign against it." In this part, referring to Hattushilish, the narrative continues and simply refers to Ramesses' coming

18 in a campaign against Hattushilish's disorder; it does not give the quotation, as in line 15 of the previous section.[144] There is one more variation in this part; here the negative is missing before the word *ỉb*. In the previous section it was said, "If it be not the wish of the great chieftain of Hatti to go..." but here it is stated positively, "If it be the desire of Ramesses...to come...." There is no need to restore a presumed missing negative in line 18, as Gardiner proposed to do;[145] the positive form should be kept, since the Hittite version does not contain a negative either with reference to Hattushilish or to Ramesses.[146]

The end of line 18 is too badly destroyed to attempt any restoration with accuracy.[147]

19 The first signs of line 19 form the ending of the word "chariotry" (*nt-ḥtrw*). Following this, a new clause begins with the words *m dỉ 'nn wšb*.[148] This part differs from its parallel section in line 16. It seems that Ramesses was expected to send his troops to the aid of the Hittite king, whenever that king sent word for help, though no alternative was allowed him, as it was for the Hittite ruler in line 16. Unfortunately, the words preceding the phrase "While the reply is returned to Hatti" are lost, and its connection to the obligations which Ramesses had to the Hittite king remains unknown.[149]

The verb *thỉ* is used here, but in the parallel section referring to Ramesses in line 17 above, the phrase *ỉr ky ṯ3y r*, "to commit <u>another</u> crime against him," was employed. It would seem that this text only gives a variant reading when a specific point is to be made (cf. lines 22ff) therefore the choice of words in this section should be indicative of the historical situation, especially with regard to Ramesses II, against whom a previous "crime" must have been committed by his subjects (for this, see the discussion of line 17 above). The word *thỉ* was used earlier in line 13 to refer to the transgression against either land which was disavowed by the two kings. The Hittite version, in this instance, is similar to the Egyptian.

Much of the end of line 19 is badly destroyed and any restorations must remain conjectural.[150]

20 It appears that line 20 is concerned with an oath, as shown by the words *p3 'nḫ* followed by *k3 ḏd*. The oath itself contains references to the dynastic succession in Hatti only;

20 the end of the oath in line 21 is too badly damaged to ascertain whether there was a reference to a reciprocal action with regard to Egypt or not.[151]

For the word "fate," signifying a person's death, see line 10 above where it referred to Muwatallish. Here one would expect Hattushilish to say "my fate," but there is no indication, or place, for the seated person of the first person, singular, suffix. There is possibly room for the third person, singular, suffix under the two reed leaves in *p3y*, but this would be inconsistent with the first person which introduces the sentence. If *p3y.f š3y* is to be read, perhaps one should understand it as a circumlocution for the expected "my fate."[152] Later in the line, after the words *'nḫ r nḥḥ*, one might restore *m ỉwt*, but the rest is questionable until the beginning of line 21.[153]

21 What remains of this line appears to read *ỉrw.sn r dỉt.f n.sn r nb [m] dỉt gr...*, "(which) they have done in order to cause that he be given to them as lord; [never] shall (Ramesses) be silent...."[154] Since Hattushilish refers to his death in the preceding line, what follows should refer to his successor; considering the dynastic struggles which had only recently affected Hatti, this concern is understandable.[155] The next phrase might be read as *ỉr m-ḫt [ỉw].f...p3 t3 n Ḫtt3 m.tw.f 'n [.f r] p3 wr '3 n Ḫtt3...*, but the rest of the sentence is too badly damaged to suggest any restorations.[156] In the Hittite version this section is also in poor condition,[157] and therefore does not offer much help except for general content. It, too, like the Egyptian text, is concerned with Hattushilish and the land of Hatti, and with a possible rebellion against Hattushilish's heir and successor upon the death of the present king. In neither version is there any reference to a reciprocal action on the part of the Hittite king in case of Ramesses' death, even though such reciprocity was common even in treaties formed with vassals.[158]

Towards the end of line 21 a new section begins, which is concerned with fugitives; the previous part treated the possibility of future discord and internal rebellion in addition to the Hittite throne succession.[159] With the terms pertaining to national security settled, the text of the Alliance now turns to other matters.

The parallel sections in this part are more uniform and contain less variation than the preceding ones.[160] Taking a

21 clue from line 23, this section should read, "If an important person flee from the land of Egypt and he come to the great chieftain of Hatti...."

22 The beginning of line 22 is difficult to restore. The parallel (line 23) which refers to Egypt contains one element more than can be reasonably inserted here in the *lacuna* of line 22; therefore it is unsound to speculate upon the missing word(s).[161]

Other than the missing part at the beginning of line 22, the rest contains few difficulties though there is a short *lacuna* after *p3y.sn nb*.[162] *R-pw ỉr w['r w'] rmṯ* can be safely read when it is compared with line 23 below.[163] The short phrase *ỉw bw rḫ.tw.w*, "and they be unknown(s)," signifies that the people under discussion are common folk in contrast to the *rmṯ '3*, "nobleman."[164] The use of *ỉw bw* is similar to that above in lines 7 and 13.

23 From the parallel below in line 25, there does not appear to be anything missing from the beginning of line 23, even though W. M. Mueller indicates that at least one sign is lost.[165] The words *ỉr b3kw n ky* imply the changing of one's allegiance and may therefore be considered "treason"; for this, cf. Wb I 428, 4-5. It is peculiar that in the section referring to Ramesses II the parallel word appears in the plural *ktḫw* (Wb V 145, but see pages 114-115, and Erman, *op. cit.*, §§326-327). In line 23 the word *ky* must refer to the Hittite king, to whom the Egyptian subjects could change their allegiance; however, in line 25, the plural "others" is very difficult to explain, for there was theoretically only one king in Egypt and at this period it should be Ramesses II.[166]

24 The beginning of line 24, like that of line 23, is difficult to restore; regarding the second *lacuna*, following *dỉt ỉn.tw.w n p3 wr '3 [n Ḫtt3]*, the words *n Ḫtt3* would fit the space available.[167]

The use of the epistolary form *m-mỉtt* is not common in this text but does not appear to have great significance.[168]

25 Towards the end of line 25, the section listing the divine witnesses begins with "Concerning the words of the terms which the great chieftain of Hatti made with Ramesses...in writing

25 upon this tablet of silver...." First a reference to gods in general is made, both of Hatti and of Egypt, and then in the following lines the specific manifestations are enumerated.[169]

26 After *mtrw* restore the verb *sḏm*, here used as an imperative followed by the vocative, "Hear these words, O Pa-Re...."[170]

30 Lines 26-30 comprise the longer list of Hittite deities. In line 30 only three Egyptian gods are mentioned by name, Amun, Pa-Re and Suth; the rest are simply assumed under the words, "the male and female gods." At the end of line 30 when "Our great sea" is listed among the witnesses of the alliance, the statement reminds one of the later *mare nostra*.[171]

31 Here begin the "curses and blessings" of the alliance;[172] for the formulation *bn ỉw.f r s3w*, cf. Erman, *op. cit.*, §§763-764, with future reference. The following verb *ỉr* may be taken as optative in meaning, rather than the simple future used by Gardiner and Wilson, and consequently translated, "May a thousand gods of the land of Hatti together with a thousand gods of the land of Egypt destroy...." For the construction *ỉr...r*, cf. Erman, *op. cit.*, §559.

The contrasting formulation *ḫr ỉr* has been used before, especially in lines 7 and 8 above, where Hattushilish wanted to make his position clear. The reference to "Hittites or Egyptians" at the end of the line shows that not only were the respective kings held responsible for keeping the terms of the Alliance but apparently their subjects were also.[173]

32 Reading the first part of line 32 as *m.tw.w tm ỉr ḫm (sp sn) r.sn*, this clause can only refer to ignorance as a violation of the terms of the Alliance, not that ignorance may be offered as an excuse when a violation is committed. The phrase may then be seen as a negative way of saying, "If a person hears the words of this alliance and acts in accord with them ...."[174]

Suddenly in line 32, beginning with the words *ỉr w'r w' rmṯ*, the text of the Alliance appears to repeat itself; this "addendum," like lines 22-25 above, refers to potential fugitives. The stress in this section, however, is not on the person who might flee but the punishment which they might receive once they have been returned to their native land. No fugitive

32 who has been deported and returned to his own country is to have charges brought against him.[175]

33 There are structural differences between this section and that in lines 22-25; instead of the negative construction *bn ỉr ...r šsp.w* found in the section above, this has the positive, *ỉr...mḥ ỉm.sn.*[176] The words *'n n* are added in line 33 after the formulation *m.tw.f dỉt ỉn.tw.w*, but they are missing in the parallel of line 35.

There is one significant grammatical element which differs within the addendum itself and which throws light upon the origin of this section. Near the end of line 33, in that part referring to Egypt, the verbal form is *m dỉ ỉr.tw*; the same construction is also found at the beginning of line 34. This *m dỉ* can only be the negative imperative; cf. Gardiner, Grammar[3], §§340-341, especially §340, 3, and Erman, *op. cit.*, §§292 and 790-791. However, in line 35, which refers to Hattushilish, there is an entirely different construction, *m.tw tm* or *m.tw.tw tm* (for this see Erman, *op. cit.*, §576 for *m.tw* and §§793-795 for *tm*, particularily §794 for this very construction). In the first part, which refers to Ramesses II, the verbal form is a negative imperative; Ramesses is commanded not to allow one to raise any crime against a fugitive. On the other hand, in the section pertaining to Hattushilish, it simply states that the Hittite king will not allow any harm come to a fugitive. The distinction is clear but cannot be explained as a stylistic variant, for the text is too careful in its terminology suddenly to become literary at such a crucial point.[177] Further, the use of *ỉmỉ mḥ* in line 35, with respect to Ramesses, stands in contrast to *ỉrỉ...mḥ* in line 33, which refers to Hattushilish. The imperative (*ỉmỉ*) is, again, only directed to Ramesses II.[178] Grammatically, then, this appendage can only have had Hattushilish as its author since Ramesses could not address himself in this manner.

In this section the same word *fẖ*, to "destroy/disband" something, is found just as it was in the "curses" in line 31 above. The combination *s'ḥ' bt3...r.f* is normally found within a legal context and can mean "to arraign a crime against someone"; cf. Wb I 484, 10 (which only refers to this text). For similar constructions, see Papyrus Mayer A 4, 14; 8, 18-19, 8, 24; 9, 25; Amenophis, son of Kanakhte 4, 19; Anastasi IV 11, 7; Book of the Dead, chap. 163; and Gardiner, Papyrus Wilbour II

33 57, with note 3.

36 The final part of the Alliance gives a description of the seals placed upon the silver tablet. On the front side was the engraving of the royal seal of Hattushilish, and on the back side, the seal of his queen Puduhepa.[179] Sealings belonging to this royal couple have been discovered in excavations, though none exactly fit the description given here; according to these examples, the sealing was placed in the center of the tablet, as described in the Alliance.[180] Lines 36-38, then, were not an integral part of the Alliance text, which ended in line 36 with the addendum, but must have been an explanation which accompanied the text, was included in the official translation, and thereby came to be inscribed upon the temple walls.

The Egyptian text of the Alliance between Hattushilish III and Ramesses II consists of different elements, not all of which belong to the original document. The basic structure of the text is:

I. Egyptian Introductions.
- A. Introduction A, the date with its historical background, lines 1-4.
- B. Introduction B, the "copy of the silver tablet" giving origin and names of the envoys, lines 4-5.

II. Hittite Introduction.
- A. Preamble, lines 5-7.
- B. Historical background and royal intent, lines 7-9.
- C. Announcement and acceptance of the present alliance, lines 9-13.

III. Minor Preamble, with general renunciation of aggression and historical references to former agreements, lines 13-15.

IV. The Terms of the Alliance.
- A. Mutual assistance clauses, lines 15-19.
- B. The problem of succession, lines 19-21.
- C. Extradition of fugitives, lines 21-25.

V. Invocation of the Gods as Witnesses.
- A. Hittite deities, lines 25-30.
- B. Egyptian deities, line 30.

VI. Curses and Blessings, lines 30-32.

VII. Addendum, amnesty for extradited fugitives, lines 32-36.

VIII. Explanation and Description of the Silver Tablet, lines 36-38.

This document, which formed the basis of an alliance between the kings of Egypt and of Hatti during the time of Ramesses II, exists in two versions, the Akkadian and the Egyptian. The cuneiform text does not parallel the Egyptian exactly but omits certain parts, especially the historical references; this difference is not due to the fragmentary nature of the Akkadian version, but is just characteristic of it. Other differences are also apparent and cannot be dismissed as carelessness on the part of scribes.

The Egyptian introductions (I A and I B) are, of course, not a part of the text of the Alliance but were added subsequent to the final ratification.[181] The first introduction, containing the date, seems to have been composed as a heading for the text when it was prepared for public announcement. The second Egyptian introduction (I B) appears to have been a notation or "docket" placed upon the translation when it was filed in the Egyptian archives.[182]

The Hittite introduction, beginning with line 5, contains a preamble with an historical statement, giving the Hittite background to the alliance and also proclaiming the Hittite king's intent. At the end of this introduction, there is the announcement that the Hittite king accepts the present text and that he considers himself in accord with Ramesses II. In the Hittite version, similar though not identical action is taken by Ramesses II (lines 1-21), though he gives no historical background as Hattushilish does.

Lines 13-15 consist of a minor preamble which has a general renunciation of aggression; the structure of this section shows that it is not truly one of the "terms" of the Alliance, for it is not formulated in the same manner as those in lines 15ff. The general renunciation of aggression is followed by further historical references; the Hittite version does not closely parallel the Egyptian in this part, for the reference to former "sworn terms" is not found in the cuneiform text.

The main terms of agreement begin in line 15, where the first clause concerns mutual aid against aggression; here the difference in the sections may be seen. The section referring to Egypt is not exactly the same as that pertaining to Hatti; it appears that individual needs were taken into consideration when the document was composed. The "terms" concerning mutual aid first deal with a possible discord in general and then speak specifically of rebellion by either king's subjects. In this part there are two "terms" which refer to Ramesses and two which refer to Hattushilish; in the next part, however, (lines 19-21), the problem of succession which appears in both the Hittite and Egyptian versions, refers to Hattushilish only. This "term" therefore seems to have been inserted because of the Hittite king's concern for such matters, understandable in view of his background.

The second half of the Alliance (lines 21-25) is structurally more regular; the sections pertaining to Hatti more closely parallel the Egyptian ones and there is less variation. Following that, the gods are invoked as witnesses to the alliance and to the wording of the text; significantly, in the Egyptian version, most of the deities invoked belong to Hatti. After the invocation, the curses and blessings are given, with the negative curses placed first, followed by the statement of good fortune which would accrue to any who kept the alliance.

Lines 32-36 are an addendum which stresses amnesty for extradited fugitives. This part was apparently a later development of the negotiations, after the major part of the Alliance had already been concluded; it must have been added to the text by Hattushilish III, as the grammatical structure indicates.

At the very end, there is a description of the tablet and the seals which it contained; this was either an explanation written in Akkadian which accompanied the silver tablet or one composed to accompany the text when it was placed before the god for safekeeping.

The text is written in an epistolary style, as Gardiner has noted, but to criticize it because of this is unjust.[183] The alliance was concluded between two supposedly honorable heads of state and not between suzerain and vassal. In the text, individual clauses were reciprocal but were adapted to the needs of either king; therefore the wording could vary according to the historical situation, but this does not mean that the text was not carefully drawn up or that it was inaccurately copied by scribes. Since it is a unique document from ancient times, of itself it is invaluable; coming at the time when it does, in the reign of Ramesses II, it also has particular value for the political developments during this part of his reign.

NOTES TO CHAPTER IV
THE HITTITE ALLIANCE

1 Monuments de l'Égypte et de la Nubie. Notices descriptives conformes aux manuscrits autographes rédigés sur les lieux par Champollion le jeune, Paris, 1844.

2 See his Lettres écrites de l'Égypte, 426.

3 Monumenti Storici III, part II, 116 and 268-282.

4 Both W. M. Mueller, MVAG 1902/5, 1-7, and Breasted, ARE III §367, with note a, give references to former publications.

5 Kitchen's work also contains references to earlier publications and major studies of both the Karnak and Ramesseum texts. Through the courtesy of Professor Charles Nims, I was able to use a photograph of the Karnak text made by the Epigraphic Survey of the Oriental Institute (Karnak 0-30, Neg. no. 5218).

6 *Op. cit.*, 1-48, with plates.

7 Published in Langdon and Gardiner, JEA 6 (1920), Pl. XVIII.

8 ARE III §§370-391.

9 Pp. 36-45.

10 *Op. cit.*, 179-205.

11 Edited by Pritchard, 199-201.

12 *Ibid.*, 201-203.

13 Porter-Moss II 49 (2).

14 *Ibid.*, 47; cf. Wreszinski, Atlas II 57.

15 Porter-Moss II 49 (3); Wreszinski, Atlas II 58.

16 Cf. Porter-Moss II 49.

17 *Ibid.*, II 152 (14); Bouriant, Rec. Trav. 13 (1891), 153-160.

18 See above, chap. II, section 1.

19 For this date, see chap. II above, years 42-A, 44-A, 51-A, 54-A, 57-A, 60-A, 63-A, 66-A.

20 In a major work in JEA 5 (1918), 127-138, 179-200, 242-271, Gardiner collected references to Per-Ramesses-Beloved-of-Amun and concluded that it should be located in or near Pelusium, a view which was challenged by Montet, Revue biblique 39 (1930), 5-28. Later in JEA 19 (1933), 122-128, Gardiner retracted his earlier view and agreed with Montet that Per-Ramesses-Beloved-of-Amun, should be identified with Tanis (San el-Hagar), as Brugsch had done much earlier, ZAeS 10 (1872), 18. In the meantime, however, Hamza in ASAE 30 (1930), 31-68, proposed Qantir as the site of Per-Ramesses-Beloved-of-Amun and was later supported by Habachi, ASAE 52 (1954), 443-562. Consequently, there are two reasonable locations for this city,

Tanis or Qantir, and no conclusive evidence for either site has yet been produced.

The discussion continues; see Redford, Vetus Testamentum 13 (1963), 401-418, with a reply by Helck, Vetus Testamentum 15 (1965), 35-48; and Uphill, JNES 27 (1968), 291-316. Further references may be found in von Beckerath, Tanis und Theben, 31-33; Drioton et Vandier, L'Égypte, 367; Gardiner, Egypt of the Pharaohs, 258.

21 Louvre C 57, Porter-Moss VII 130 (4); Kitchen, Ramesside Inscriptions I 2.

22 Roeder, ASAE 52 (1954), 346; Kitchen, Ramesside Inscriptions IV 30.

23 For a recent discussion of the verb *ḫ'ỉ*, see Redford, History and Chronology, 3-27; for other examples of the term *st-Ḥr nt 'nḫw*, see *ibid.*, 8-10.

24 Cf. Wb II 499, 9-10; and Černý, Doc. de fouilles, 3-7 *passim*.

25 Porter-Moss VII 380, and Kitchen, Ramesside Inscriptions I 15-16, with references. In this text, *hrw pn* precedes *ỉst...ḥm.f....*

26 Most of the examples of this formulation from the Nineteenth Dynasty belong to the reigns of Seti I and Ramesses II; see the examples listed above.

27 Urk. IV 1545, 7-8.

28 Fairman and Grdseloff, JEA 33 (1947), Pl. VII.

29 Griffith, JEA 13 (1927), Pl. XL; Porter-Moss VII 174.

30 Porter-Moss V 220.

31 Schott, Kanais, Der Tempel Sethos I. im Wadi Mia, Taf. 19.

32 See note 3 above.

33 Tresson, Bibl. d'étude 9; Porter-Moss VII 83.

34 The compound *r-dmỉ* may also occur as *m-dmỉ*; cf. Fairman and Grdseloff, *op. cit.*, 26. For a possible interchange in the Late Period between *r-dmỉ* and *m-ḫnw*, see Legrain, Rec. Trav. 22 (1900), 55, and 31 (1909), 6. The words appear to be used more in the manner of compound prepositions consisting of preposition plus noun (Gardiner, Grammar[3] §178).

35 See note 28 above.

36 See note 29 above.

37 See Goedicke, CdE 41 (1966), 23-39.

38 For the Sinai Stela of Ramesses I see Gardiner-Peet-Černý, The Inscriptions of Sinai, I, Pl. LXVIII; II 174.

39 For various formulations of the word *Ḥbw-Sd* after the verb *rdỉ*, cf. Wb III 60, 4. For the discussion of *ḏt* and *nḥḥ*, see Thausing, Mélanges Maspero I 35-42; Bakir, JEA 39 (1952), 110-111; Iversen, Rivista degli Studi Orientali 38 (1963), 177-186. For the various used of these words in the inscriptions of Seti I,

see Sethe, ZAeS 66 (1931), 1-7.

40 Roeder, Der Felsentempel von Bet el-Wali, 126.

41 Sander-Hansen, Historische Inschriften der 19. Dynastie, 2, line 14.

42 Kitchen, Ramesside Inscriptions I, 20.

43 Porter-Moss V 44; Kitchen, *op. cit.*, VI 17, line 2.

44 See note 41 above.

45 Sander-Hansen, *op. cit.*, 3.

46 Ranke, Personennamen I 69 (16).

47 Schulman, Military Rank, Title and Organization in the Egyptian New Kingdom, 34-35.

48 Edel, JNES 7 (1948), 17-18, and JNES 8 (1949), 44-45.

49 Schaeffer, Le Palais royal d'Ugarit IV 106, no. 17.137; and also Ugaritica III 37.

50 Edel, in Orientalia, N. S. 38 (1969), 177-182, wishes to see the name of a third messenger in the fragmentary part at the beginning of line 3. Kitchen, in Ramesside Inscriptions II 226 is uncertain as to how many messengers there might have been. This line is in such bad condition that further restorations concerning these envoys must remain conjecture; for the suggestions by Edel and Kitchen, see p. 226 in the Ramesside Inscriptions.

51 Kitchen, *op. cit.*, 226. Neither Gardiner nor W. M. Mueller ventured a restoration of this part; since this is not found in the Hittite version, no comparison between the two texts may be made.

52 Goetze, MVAG 29/3 (1925), III 63 - IV 33.

53 Chap. I with notes 41-43.

54 Rowton, JNES 25 (1966), 245.

55 For a contemporary reference to communications with Hatti, though not without a certain bias, see the Marriage Stela of Ramesses II (34-D). A slightly different example of Egyptian negotiations with Asiatics is recorded in the tale of Wen-Amun.

56 This formulation of the titulary indicates the origins of the different sections. The proper Egyptian form would have the title precede the royal name, while Akkadian normally places such titles after the name.

57 For the use of *ṯnr* as an epithet, see Wb V 382, 12-15; it seems that this word was not just a Ramesside term but one particularly favored by Ramesses II. For a possible Ugaritic cognate, see Gordon, Ugaritic Textbook, no. 2754; and Brugsch, Revue égyptologique 1 (1880), 23. The origin of the word is still obscure, but it is interesting to note the similarity in spelling between the "-tallish" in the name Muwatallish (line 8) and *ṯnr*.

58 In this first section, the name of Hattushilish is written in a manner slightly different from the standard form found in the rest of the text. This could indicate a chronological difference between this and the rest of the text, or perhaps a different scribal tradition.

59 W. M. Mueller, *op. cit.*, 10.

60 Gardiner, *op. cit.*, 186.

61 Wilson, *op. cit.*, 199.

62 *Loc. cit.*

63 *Ibid.*

64 *Op. cit.*, 23-24; the word "Buendnisvertrag" is the term he used in the title of his study of this text.

65 One might wish to note the use of Hebrew בקש.

66 The word "peace" could be retained as the translation for *ḥtp* but for the unfortunate association with the cessation of warfare, which has beguiled translators into viewing this text as a peace treaty.

67 In the Hittite version it is mentioned in line 14.

68 For a specific reference of a treaty being deposited before a god, see KBo I 1, 35; an English translation is provided by Goetze in ANET³ 205.

69 *Op. cit.*, 186, but see note 4.

70 JNES 7 (1948), 17.

71 *Op. cit.*, 10.

72 *Op. cit.*, 186, and in note 5 says, "This Egyptian word means something like 'ordinance,' 'prescription,' 'arrangement.'"

73 *Op. cit.*, 199, and says in note 4, "The 'prescribed form,' used throughout this inscription for the treaty."

74 For *nt-'* as "duty" or "regulation," see Faulkner, Dictionary, 142; translated as "contracts" by Breasted, ARE IV §1022. Also see Gardiner, JEA 24 (1938), 165 (27).

75 Goetze, MVAG 29/3 (1924), I 1-11; Otten, Die hethitischen historischen Quellen und die altorientalische Chronologie; Gueterbock, JNES 29 (1970), 73-77.

76 The deposed nephew of Hattushilish is never mentioned in this text; for a possible reference to Urkhi-Teshub in Egypt, see Helck, JCS 17 (1963), 87-97.

77 Both Breasted and Gardiner translate *snsn* as "brotherhood"; Roeder, in Aegypter und Hethiter, 38, used "Verbruederung," while W. M. Mueller, *op. cit.*, 12, chose "Buendnis," which is followed here.

Edel, in Phraesologie §37, has shown that this was a legal term, already in use in Old Egyptian, meaning "'die beiden, die sich (zu einem Rechtsstreit) zusammengetan haben', d.h. 'die beiden

Prozeszparteien'."

78 For a discussion of the "400 year Stela," see Goedicke, CdE 41 (1966), 23-39, *contra* Stadelmann, CdE 40 (1965), 46-60. For a publication of the text with photograph, see Montet, Kêmi 4 (1931), 191-215; and the text only, Kitchen, *op. cit.*, 287-288. For further discussions of Ramesses' genealogy, see Gaballa and Kitchen, CdE 43 (1968), 259-263, and Habachi, Revue d'égyptologie 21 (1969), 27-47.

79 W. M. Mueller, Roeder and Breasted attach this phrase to the following sentence.

80 Gardiner, *op. cit.*, 187; the translations by W. M. Mueller and Roeder are similar to Gardiner's, but Breasted has "...the god prevented hostilities between them" (§374).

81 For a Ramesside reference to "God" in general, see the Qadesh inscriptions, Poem (P97), with Gardiner's translation, Ḳadesh Inscriptions, 9, of "What careth thy heart, O Amun, for these Asiatics so vile and ignorant of god?"

82 Compare the use in Papyrus Anastasi III 5, 12 (Caminos, LEM 94) and especially Papyrus Lansing 10, 2; in Papyrus Sallier III 8, 9 (the Battle of Qadesh--Poem), this very spelling is observed with similar meaning. Also see Wente, Late Ramesside Letters, 26 (q).

83 *Op. cit.*, 10.

84 *Op. cit.*, 187, who follows Breasted (§374) in his choice.

85 *Op. cit.*, 199.

86 Wb I 59, 1, and Faulkner, Dictionary, 14.

87 For convenience, see Gardiner and Langdon, *op. cit.*, 185-199, with a discussion on 'The relations between the Two Versions' on pp. 199-201.

88 It should be noted that the cuneiform tablets from Boghazköy (KBo I 7 + KUB III 121 and KBo I 25 and KUB III 11 + [fragment]) are also copies of the original, copies in which perhaps the historical allusions were omitted. Since both the Hittite and the Egyptian versions are copies, neither has more weight historically than the other.

89 The phrase [*n p3*] *nt-' n dỉt mn p3 sẖr* may be liberally translated as a "settlement," even though it is envisioned as being that plan which Pa-Re, together with the god of Egypt and the god of Hatti, has established for the two countries; see note 94 below.

90 The most recent translation of the Qadesh inscriptions is by Gardiner, The Ḳadesh Inscriptions of Ramesses II.

91 Kuentz, MIFAO 55.

92 For the verb *ptr* meaning "look for," see Wente, Late Ramesside Letters, 44 (a), 64 (al) and 74 (d); for the use of *ptr* as "behold," see line 9 below.

93 Kitchen, *op. cit.*, 227, suggests other possible restorations but understands *ptr* as "behold" rather than the verbal form.

94 Since the verb *ỉrw* is repeated after Pa-Re instead of inserting the preposition *ỉrm* (which coordinates equals), it is difficult to follow the accepted translation here, "...which Pre' made and Setekh made for the land of Egypt (9) with the land of Hatti..." (Gardiner, *op. cit.*, 187).

95 As perceived by Professor Goedicke.

96 For the use of Pa-Re and Suth with regard to both Hatti and Egypt, see the Divine Invocation (lines 26-30) below.

97 For the negative *tm* construed with the preposition *r* to refer to future events, see Erman, *op. cit.*, §795. For the reference to *bw* see under line 7 above.

98 For references to oaths within specific treaties, see the treaty between Murshilish and Duppi-Tessub, Friedrich, Staatsvertraege, 1-48, and an English translation by Goetze in ANET[3] 203-205.

99 See note 68 above.

100 As mentioned above, this historical reference is not found in the Hittite version; however, a very similar phrase is found in KBo I 8, line 16, "Now when (Muwatallish)...went to his fate, I, Hattushilish, sat on the throne of my father...." For the Egyptian, see Wb IV 403, 8.

101 The concept of "fate" is also found in Egyptian; for a discussion of this, see Goedicke, JNES 22 (1963), 187-190, and Morenz, Untersuchungen zur Rolle des Schicksals in der aegyptischen Religion, and in particular p. 19. However, the phrase "to go to one's fate" as a statement of death is not used in Egyptian. It is a foreign term.

102 For his own statements in his "Apology," see Goetze, MVAG 29/3 (1924); MVAG 34/2 (1930), III 40-51.

103 See note 76 above.

104 The word *ỉsbt*, according to Wb I 132, is only attested in Egyptian since the Amarna Period; it can refer either to the royal throne or to the base of a statue.

105 We know that Hattushilish was a usurper and not the proper heir to the throne, according to the "Edict of Telepinush"; cf. Korošec, Hethitische Staatsvertraege, 38. That is, if the Edict had any force or validity at this time.

106 There is some difficulty in the text at this point. Hattushilish implies that Muwatallish was a source of trouble for Ramesses II (cf. line 8, where fighting is mentioned), but he later in line 14 refers to "sworn terms" which were in existence at the time of Shuppiluliumash and also at the time of Muwatallish; he further states that these "sworn terms" were to serve as a part of the present alliance. Therefore for Hattushilish to state that he has been looking for some way to "stabilize the situation" appears to contradict the statement that there had been some type of agreement after the battle of Qadesh, unless Muwatallish had come to terms with Seti I. This, however, seems unlikely.

107 The *ỉw* is very clear, but the suffix is uncertain; there might be room for an *.n* beneath. The top of a sign belonging to the

next word is visible, and it could represent a reed leaf, hence the reading *ỉỉ*. Of the word *ỉrm* there is no trace. There are possible traces of the *n* above *p3* (as seen by W. M. Mueller). It is, however, not certain that all this might be placed in the *lacuna*. One might wish to read *ỉw.ỉ ỉrm.f n p3y.n...*, but the traces after *ỉw* do not fit the first person, singular, suffix.

108 *Op. cit.*, 188, note 3.

109 Gardiner, *op. cit.*, 188, note 4.

110 Line 19.

111 For the word *sḫr*, cf. Wb IV 258-260; it is the equivalent of the Akkadian *ṭe-ma* of line 9 of the Hittite version.

112 In line 9, the *r tm dỉt* expresses future purpose (Erman, *op. cit.*, §795), while *ỉw bw* is here understood as hortatory; cf. Edgerton, AJSL 48 (1931), 34, and Hintze, *op. cit.*, 250-251.

113 In line 9, the suffix *.sn* referred to the two kings; here it is either the descendents of those kings or, more likely, the two countries which are indicated.

114 The Hittite version, lines 22-24, is very similar to the Egyptian version in this section.

115 See above note 112.

116 There are occurrences in lines 22 and 25, but in a different setting; there the negative is used in similar fashion as here: "and they be not known," i.e., "and they be unknowns."

117 This preliminary "term" appears to be in the form of an oath; for such see Wilson, JNES 7 (1948), 129-156.

118 For *nkt* as a small (insignificant?) amount, see Černý, Late Ramesside Letters, 8, 3, and Wente, Late Ramesside Letters, 25 (j). For the relationship between *nkt* and *kt*, see Wente, *op. cit.*, 65 (au), with references.

119 The compound *wn dy* appears to differ little from the shorter *wn*, which is used above in line 11 as well as later in the same line. Cf. Wb I 308, 6, and also Černý, *op. cit.*, 45, 9, and Wente, *op. cit.*, 62 (j).

120 Maspero, ZAeS 19 (1881), 119.

121 There does not seem to be any evidence beyond this reference for a treaty during the reign of Shuppiluliumash; cf. Kitchen, Suppiluliuma and the Amarna Pharaohs, *passim*. For the renewal of former "sworn statements" by kings of Egypt, see Goedicke, Koenigliche Dokumente aus dem Alten Reich, 115.

122 There is no direct evidence for any agreement between Ramesses II and Muwatallish, though there is a reference to such an oath sworn by Ramesses to the king of Mira concerning Urkhi-Teshub (KBo I 24). See note 106 above.

123 The *sḫr mtry* are the sworn intentions in contrast to the *nt-ʿ mtry* in line 14 above, which must refer to some written form.

124 See above note 80. For *ky*, see discussion of line 17.

125 *Op. cit.*, 13. But he questioned in note 3 whether this could be a correct translation of the Akkadian, the text of which had not then been discovered.

126 Gardiner, *loc. cit.*, has "enemy" as does Wilson, *op. cit.*, 200. Both Roeder, *op. cit.*, 40, and Breasted, *op. cit.*, §378, agree with W. M. Mueller.

127 Discussed above under note 80. For *ḫrwy(w)* as "conflict" or "rebellion" see Wente, *op. cit.*, 26 (q), with references.

128 For the word *ky*, cf. Wb V 110-114; Gardiner, Grammar³ p. 30. The word can mean only "other" or "another" and it cannot be viewed as treaty style, for it does not occur elsewhere.

129 Line 27, also see the discussion under the parallel of line 18 below.

130 The verb was used in line 2; see note 45 above.

131 The entire clause, "However, if it be not the wish of the great chieftain of Hatti to go when he (Ramesses) dispatches his infantry and his chariotry, then he (Ramesses) shall route his (own) disorder," is omitted in the Hittite version.

132 Gardiner, Grammar³ §323 and particularly §332.

133 *Ibid.*, §323.

134 Gardiner, JEA 6 (1920), 190.

135 If the King of Hatti were required to send his troops and chariotry, one might expect to find *m.tw.sn* introducing the next clause instead of *m.tw.f* (Kitchen, *op. cit.*, 228, has neither *.f* or *.sn*; W. M. Mueller, *op. cit.*, Taf. VII, shows the *.f* which is still visible in the original). Since the text has "and he shall slay his enemy" instead of "and they shall slay his enemy," the translation given seems the most reasonable according to grammar and structure.

136 Gardiner, Ḳadesh Inscriptions, 14, translates it, "...for who shall withstand(?) thee on the day of thy wrath?"

137 See also Erman, *op. cit.*, §109.

138 Cf. lines 31-32 and 37 of the Akkadian.

139 In the Hittite version, Hattushilish is also to be protected against any rebellious citizens, but it is only stated "If they sin (trespass) against him"; the word "another" is not found there.

140 See line 16 above.

141 Cf. lines 27-28 of the Hittite version.

142 The signs for *r p3 wr* may still be seen so that *'3 n Ḫtt3* may be restored after them.

143 Kitchen, *op. cit.*, 228, suggests "(R.II) shall act and come...." But the first traces there need not represent a reed leaf; it

seems better to follow line 15 and read *m.tw.f h3b n*, which would just fit the space.

144 This section is partially destroyed, but enough remains to indicate the dissimilarity of the two sections. Here Kitchen, *op. cit.*, 228, suggests *m.tw.f* before *ỉỉt*, which would fit with his earlier restoration at the end of line 17. This suggestion is feasible, as is the reading *ỉw.f r ỉỉt*.

145 *Op. cit.*, 191, with comment, "The word 'not' is carelessly omitted in the hieroglyphs," in note 4.

146 Lines 29-30 and 35-36 of the Hittite version.

147 Since this part is not found in the Hittite version, restoration is very difficult. W. M. Mueller translated, "Wenn es (aber) [nicht] der Wunsch Ramses Meiamun's, des Grosskoenigs von Aegypten, ist, zu kommen, so [schickt] er [seine Soldaten und seine Wagentruppen, und] sie [sind mit denen des Grossfuersten von Chet(t)e. Er sendet sie (gleich) mit den Boten, und er laesst den Grossfuersten von Chet(t)?] sie sehen, (noch) waehrend er Antwort zuruecksendet zum Chet(t)e-Land" (*op. cit.*, 14).

Gardiner, *op. cit.*, 191, though more cautious, also attempted to restore this section according to the parallel above; Wilson, *op. cit.*, 200, follows Gardiner.

148 The context is too broken for this phrase to be properly understood, though it might have a negative connotation; for such see Wb I 189, 4.

149 See note 147 for suggested restorations.

150 For the proposed restorations for the first part of line 19, see note 147 above. For the latter part of the line, W. M. Mueller, *op. cit.*, 15, has "...und Ramses Meiamun [hoert davon, so soll er gleichfalls seine Fusssoldaten und Wagentruppen schicken, und] das Land Chet(t)e und das Land Aegypten [werden so zusammenstehen]...." Gardiner, *op. cit.*, 191, did not attempt a translation.

Kitchen, *loc. cit.*, suggests reading *p3 t3 n Kmt* after *p3 t3 n Ḫtt3*, since he believes there are traces of a *t3*-sign under the *p3*; W. M. Mueller, *op. cit.*, Pl. VIII, recorded a trace of a horizontal line but put a question mark beneath it. The traces do not seem to fit the land-sign and hence the restored *n Kmt* is very uncertain. Since Hattushilish is being quoted at the beginning of line 20, it is possible that "great chieftain of Hatti" belongs here.

151 One would assume a statement of reciprocal action on behalf of both countries, as in the rest of the Alliance; however, in both versions this section is given over to the Hatti throne succession.

152 Below the two reed leaves in *š3y* there is possibly room for another sign; this could be a ⌓ (*t*) or, more likely, a book roll as determinative. A similar problem is encountered with the next word, *ḫr*; there appears to be room below the *r* for another sign.

153 After *'nḫ r nḥḥ* one might be able to read *ỉw.f...ỉỉ r(?) p3 t3 n Ḫtt3*.... There are other traces following that, but not enough remains for a translation.

[154] W. M. Mueller, in his copy, *op. cit.*, Taf. IX, proposed to restore an *r* but questions it; in his notes to his translation he remarks, "Alles sehr schwierig!" concerning this part. Gardiner, *op. cit.*, 192, translated, "...to make him for themselves to lord, so as to cause Usima're' setpen [re'], the great ruler of Egypt, to be silent with his mouth forever," and in note 3 says, "No Babylonian equivalent for this striking phrase appears to be forthcoming." Since Mueller indicates that there is a deep hole here one might conjecture that originally an *r* was carved by mistake, then deepened in order to be filled with plaster; this has since fallen out and with the plaster has gone the *m* which had replaced the *r*. Thus one would have the negative *m-dỉt* (Erman, *op. cit.*, §791).

The words "to his claim forever" depend upon a reading of *r r3.f r nḥḥ*. W. M. Mueller, *op. cit.*, Taf. IX, shows traces of what looks like an *m* but notes "*r* nach Abkl." Kitchen, *op. cit.*, 229, records traces of an *m*. There still seem to be traces of an *r* without relying upon the Berlin "Abklatsch." Above *nḥḥ* there are definite traces of an *r*.

[155] In his "Apology" Hattushilish states that he finally declared open war against his nephew Urkhi-Teshub (III 63-IV 23), after there had been some earlier strife.

[156] The *ỉr m-ḫt* is still preferable to Kitchen's reading (*loc. cit.*) of  instead of *ḫt*; see lines 15, 18 and 21 for the different forms of the  . The next group might be read *ỉw.f*. It appears to be written 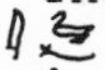 ; for such see lines 8 and 16 above. In the next group there is probably an  as the bottom sign, but the portion above is obscure. Following that, there are traces of *fḫ*(?) (as indicated by W. M. Mueller, *loc. cit.*, and followed by Kitchen, *loc. cit.*), and there is possibly room above *p3 t3* for an  . Hence one might read *ỉr m-ḫt* [*ỉw*].*f* ...*f(?) fḫ(?)* [*m*] *p3 t3* [*n*] *Ḫtt3*.

[157] Lines 40-44 of the Hittite version, though concerned with the same matter, are not similar in wording nor construction.

[158] See the treaty between Murshilish and Duppi-Teshub, line 8*; Friedrich, MVAG 31/1 (1926), 1-48, and Weidner, Boghazköi Studien 8 (1923) 76-79, with an English translation by Goetze, ANET^3 202.

There are traces of an *(m?)-mỉtt* after the "great chieftain of Hatti" (discussed above). This could introduce a reciprocal "term" but since the *lacuna* is so short and the next "term" begins in it, there does not appear to be enough space for the statement of reciprocal action.

[159] For a more detailed discussion of the composition and structure of the text, see below.

[160] The Hittite version is slightly different here and also not well preserved.

[161] Gardiner, *op. cit.*, 192, in note 6, summarized the difficulty well, "The words *r-pw-w' k'ḥ r-pw...* found in the parallel section 1. 23 should perhaps be restored here, but there is no room for them in the lacuna."

[162] There are traces of the seated determinative to "lord" followed by a small space and then an *s*. Kitchen, *op. cit.*, 229, suggests [*'nḫ wḏ3*] *snb*, but even if there were room for this it would not be in character with the rest of the text.

163 In lines 23 and 34 below, where the phrase *ỉr w'r w' rmṯ* occurs, there is slightly more space allowed than is here; however, there is still enough room here for this phrase. I do not understand how Kitchen, *op. cit.* (note 5c), saw a possible *w'* sign after *rmṯ*.

164 For *bw rḫ*, see Wb II 444, 2-6; the compound, used in contradistinction to "nobleman," signifies a "commoner." For *rmṯ '3* as "influential man" or even perhaps as "rich man" see Wente, *op. cit.*, 61 (ai) and 64 (ai).

165 Mueller, *op. cit.*, 16, restored "aus dem Land Aegypten," but this is too long for the space given; Gardiner, *op. cit.*, 193, with note 2, leaves it blank. More recently Kitchen, *op. cit.*, 229, has followed Mueller's suggestion.

166 Regnal year 21 of Ramesses II is certainly too late to be considered a part of the coregency with his father Seti I; for this see chap. V below.

167 As suggested by Kitchen, *op. cit.*, 229. W. M. Mueller, *op. cit.*, Taf. X, did not allow sufficient space.

168 For *m-mỉtt*, cf. Wb II 40, 17-18 and 41, 1-4; Faulkner, Dictionary, 104; Gardiner, Grammar[3] §205, 3.

169 The treaty between Shuppiluliumash and Mattiwaza (KBo I 1) contains a long list of deities also, as well as a stipulation that the treaty tablet was to be deposited before the god Teshub; if the treaty text happened to be damaged, the gods were to be called to assembly to restore the missing parts. For this treaty, see Weidner, Boghazköi Studien 8 (1923), 27-33, and an English translation by Goetze, ANET[3] 205-206. For Kurtiwaza instead of Mattiwaza, see Goeterbock, JCS 10 (1956), 121, note 18.

170 Gardiner, Grammar[3] §87. Edel, in ZAeS 90 (1963), 31ff, and Orientalia 37 (1968), 417-420, offered some restorations for line 29; Edel restores "Ishtar of Nineveh" and also "the god Ninatta and the god Kulitta" as well as the "god Hebat." The text is still very difficult to read. For a discussion of Hittite mythology, see Dussaud, Les Religions des Hittites et des Hourrites, des Phéniciens et des Syriens and Otten, Die Religionen des alten Kleinasien in Handbuch der Orientalistik 8, part 1, 1964, pp. 92-121.

171 Most translators ignore the *p3y.n* (possessive, first person, plural), but it is unlikely that it is a "mistake."

172 Hillers, Treaty-Curses and the Old Testament Prophets, 12-29.

173 For the word "Hittites," cf. Wb III 349, 17, and for "Egyptians," cf. Wb V 127, 20, and 128, 1.

174 For a use of *ḫm* in this way, see Wb III 279, 1-4.

175 This section has been understood as "an afterthought or addition to the finished treaty" (Gardiner, *op. cit.*, 197). As Professor Goedicke has suggested, it probably could not be accepted by the Egyptian envoy, Ra-mes, during the negotiations in Hatti but had to be ratified by Ramesses himself and therefore did not become an integral part of the Alliance itself.

[176] For *bn ỉr*, cf. Erman, *op. cit.*, §547, and Hintze, *op. cit.*, 248. For *ỉr...mḥ*, cf. Hintze, *op. cit.*, 270.

[177] For this see above, note 128.

[178] For this use of *ỉmỉ*, see Erman, *op. cit.*, §356.

[179] For the supposed importance of the Queen in Hatti, see Edel, Indogerman. Forsch. 60 (1950), 72-85.

[180] For seals and sealings of Hittite kings found in excavations, see Gueterbock, MDOG 75 (1937), 54, Abb. 34 (Hattushilish and Puduhepa), and Abb. 35, p. 57, which depicts a deity embracing a Hittite king, such as is mentioned in the Alliance; and Otten, MDOG 87 (1955), 18 (Urkhi-Teshub). For examples of sealings impressed into the centers of texts, cf. Laroche, in Ugaritica III, Pls. I-V, and pp. 105, 109 and 125. For other examples of Hittite seals of this period, see Alkim, Anatolia I, Pls. 137-138 (Urkhi-Teshub and Muwatallish); L'art au pays des Hittites, Pls. 202-203 (Hattushilish III and Urkhi-Teshub); Akurgal, The Art of the Hittites, Pl. 45 (Urkhi-Teshub and Queen Puduhepa). For a discussion of the name Urkhi-Teshub, see Gueterbock in Urgaritica III, 161-163; also see Bittel, Jahrbuch fuer kleinasiatische Forschung I (1950-51), 164-173.

[181] For this literary form, see Hermann, Die aegyptische Koenigsnovelle, especially pp. 53-56, where he discusses the Heliopolis stela of years 8 and 9 of Ramesses II. This introduction acts as the frame for the following document.

[182] It is quite clear that the Egyptian text as we have it was not the "official" version from which the Akkadian was translated. There are too many grammatical peculiarities in this text which cannot be explained unless it is understood as a translation from another language. It does not seem unreasonable to assume that the Egyptian version is a translation of an Akkadian (or Hittite ?) original and that the Akkadian was translated from an Egyptian.

[183] Gardiner, *op. cit.*, 200.

CHAPTER V

THE COREGENCY

The major evidence for a coregency between Seti I and his son Ramesses II comes from the dedicatory inscription of Ramesses in the temple of Seti I at Abydos.[1] In this text Ramesses relates, "When my father appeared to the people ("masses" *kyw/k3yw*,) and I was a youth (*sfy*) within his embrace, then he said concerning me, 'Crown him as king that I may see his goodness while I am alive.'" Therewith the diadem was placed upon his brow, this being done while Seti was yet on earth that Ramesses might organize (*ṯs*) the land and administer (*nwy*) Egypt. Though he was a youth (*sfy*) he was given a royal harim, filled with wives and concubines. He was "Re over the common folk (*rḫyt*)"; he who had once been installed as hereditary prince on the throne of Geb, now set to work administering the land as coregent with his father.[2] This, then, is Ramesses' only direct statement about the coregency; there are other indications but none so specific as this.

The Quban stela[3] of year 3 alludes to the coregency, when the courtiers fawning before the splendor of his Majesty address him, saying, "You made plans while you were in the egg (cf. Abydos line 44) in your office of child-crown prince (*ẖrd r3-p't*); the affairs of the two lands were told you while you were a youth (*sfy*) (still) wearing the side-lock of youth...you were a spokesman (*r3-ḥry*) of the army while you were a young man (*ḥwn*) of ten years."[4] In this manner Ramesses is lauded by his followers in the court at Memphis. The text makes no explicit reference to Ramesses as coregent, but it does indicate that he held certain high positions as a part of his royal training.

It can be seen that the major document supporting a coregency is the dedicatory inscription at Abydos; the information obtained from the Quban stela does not directly mention a coregency, but it does indicate that Ramesses was involved in the royal administration prior to his sole rule. The composition of the Abydos text, as pointed out in chapter II (I-A), must postdate regnal year 1, for it only refers to that year in the past.[5] This should be stressed, for in discussions of the coregency, this text has sometimes been considered contemporaneous with the date it records and thus some historical interpretations have been based on a misunderstanding.[6] It is interesting that Ramesses' major statement of a coregency comes from a later time, for one would expect a new king to stress the coregency which he presumably enjoyed with his father, especially if there were some doubt as to his legitimacy. However, after the ruler has become established upon his throne, there should be less need for such to be propounded. Therefore, since there seems to be no reason to regard these statements by Ramesses in the Abydos text as fabrications, they may be accepted as representing the historical situation.

There is also pictorial evidence for a coregency both at Abydos and at Thebes. As a part of the scene in the Seti temple at Abydos representing the royal forebearers of the Nineteenth Dynasty, Seti I and his son, Ramesses II, present offerings before the gods and before the lists containing the cartouches of these ancestors.[7] Here Ramesses is depicted as a crown prince. His name is not placed within a cartouche, except for one instance; in the scene before the list of the gods, Ramesses II is shown wearing a garment which has his royal cartouches upon it.[8] Also on a wall of the staircase (Y'), Ramesses stands alongside his father, and it appears that they are meant to be depicted as both living and as kings of Egypt.[9]

There is further indication of a coregency in the Temple of Seti I at Qurneh, where Ramesses is depicted receiving a crown from the Theban Triad in the presence of his father;[10] the crown which he receives is given at the direction of Seti I, with the benison of the local gods.[11] There is no doubt that this is a coronation scene and that Seti is specifically directing the activity as carried out by the local Theban triad; the scene is executed in bas-relief, which was typical for the reign of Seti I.[12] Thus far the major evidence for a coregency.

This relationship between two rulers is not always easy to establish, for unless there is a direct reference to it by either one coregent or the other, joint rule may be concluded only from the material evidence, no matter how slim. Questionable coregencies, such as that between Amenophis III and Amenophis IV, still plague Egyptian chronology.[13] During the Middle Kingdom some records were dated according to regnal years of each coregent;[14] but even then when a coregency was the rule rather than the exception, most official inscriptions recorded the name of either junior or senior partner and not of both men.[15]

The coregency of Ramesses II with his father Seti I was questioned by Breasted,[16] who based his arguments upon some scenes of Seti I at Karnak; his interpretation has been rejected,[17] but his influence and attitude are still felt. The reliefs in question are on the north wall of the great Hypostyle Hall at Karnak, where Ramesses is shown as a young prince, accompanying his father in a Syrian campaign.[18] These reliefs had been interpreted as support for Ramesses' statement that he acted as a coregent with his father,[19] but Breasted reinterpreted them and introduced them as evidence against a coregency.

In answer to this, Seele remarked, "Professor Breasted has somewhat beclouded the way to an understanding of the relationship of Ramses II to his father and of his right to the throne, but his contention that Ramses II only shortly before his accession removed an elder brother who was the legitimate crown prince, and that Ramses misrepresented the facts by inserting his figure in Seti's war reliefs in order to indicate a participation in those wars which never took place, appears to me to have been properly denied."[20] Gardiner, after quoting those lines of the Abydos text which pertain to the coregency, said, "The accuracy of this statement has been impugned, but wrongly, since scenes at Karnak and at Kurna confirm Ramesses's co-regency with his father. Probably, however, he was less young when the co-regency began than this passage suggests, because there is evidence that he accompanied Sethos on his military campaigns whilst he was still only the heir-apparent...."[21] Thus the interpretation has turned full round and again some historians agree with Maspero that the Karnak scenes do support the coregency.[22]

The development of the royal prenomen has played an important role in the question of a coregency, and for Seele, the "short form of Ramses II's prenomen comes so near to being the keystone on which the entire structure of the coregency is supported that any discussion of the problem must begin with it."[23] Sethe, in his article on "Die Jahresrechnung unter Ramses II. und der Namenswechsel dieses Koenigs,"[24] attempted to arrange the various writings of Ramesses' prenomen in a chronological order. A common form, called the "short" form, consists of the basic element, *Wsr-M3't-R'*, to which could be added other elements such as *Iw'w-R'*, *Mry-R'* or *Ḥḳ3-W3st*, as well as the standard form of *Stp-n-R'*. Sethe attempted to show that the variants were used for only a short time until Ramesses decided upon *Wsr-M3't-R' Stp-n-R'* as the official form of his royal prenomen; for Sethe all this occurred during the first regnal year.

Seele, in his work "The Coregency of Ramses II with Seti I," accepted Sethe's arguments for the development of the royal prenomen but applied them to the period of coregency and used them in support of such a relationship.[25] He took Sethe's proposed development of Ramesses' prenomen, combined it with Roeder's interpretation of the stylistic changes found at the temple of Beit el-Wali,[26] and said, "in his publication Roeder has shown that the temple reveals four distinct periods of execution. The first period is marked by the fact that the scenes were carved in bas-relief, while in the second period the reliefs were all incised. In the reliefs of both these periods Ramses' short prenomen *Wsr-m3'.t-R'* is characteristic. In the third period...they were cut in incised hieroglyphs, and Ramses' prenomen occurs with the additional epithet *Stp-n-R'*."[27] Even though the different sytles of sculptured decorations have no date, Seele accepted "Roeder's somewhat detailed description of the different styles of relief and his consequent assignment of them to successive periods"[28] and applied them to the question of a coregency.

Seele's basic arguments for a coregency between Seti I and Ramesses II are therefore founded upon Sethe's proposed development of the royal prenomen and upon Roeder's interpretation of the decorations at Beit el-Wali; these served as a foundation for the interpretation of other reliefs which possibly indicate a coregency. There are, however, difficulties involved in both Sethe's proposal and Roeder's interpretation.

The only "dated" monument which Sethe could muster in support of his theory was the fragment found in the Chephren mortuary complex by Hoelscher, who read the date as "year 20." Sethe saw in the traces not a year number but a day number and interpreted the few remaining lines "? month of *prt* day 20."[29] He then assigned the fragment to Ramesses' first year. The other inscriptions used are also questionable: the door thickness from Abu Simbel is probably a retrospective date, and might even belong to a later king,[30] while the dedicatory inscription from Abydos is not contemporary with the year it records,[31] nor is the text from the tomb of *Nb-wnn.f.*[32] The only remaining monument, aside from the Sphinx stela which has only the regnal year (the prenomen has been destroyed),[33] is the Silsileh stela containing the "Hymn to the Nile" and it employs the various different forms of the royal prenomen.[34] Therefore Sethe's arguments for the development of the royal prenomen within the first regnal year of Ramesses II can no longer be maintained.

Beit el-Wali is also questionable as evidence for the development of the royal prenomen, for there the shorter form of *Wsr-M3't-R'* is found in the same inscription with a later form of the Horus name of Ramesses II.[35] This longer Horus name, *nb Ḥbw-Sd mỉ ỉt.(f) T3-tnn*, occurs only in dated inscriptions after Ramesses' second Jubilee in year 34.[36] Therefore it appears that some of the decorations of Beit el-Wali were carved after the second Jubilee, and consequently Roeder's interpretation should not be applied to the coregency.

Since Seele's main argument for the coregency rested upon the presumed development of the royal prenomen, combined with the stylistic changes supposed to develop along the same lines, it would appear that one is again forced to rely mainly upon the statements of Ramesses II to substantiate the coregency, except that one or two more pieces of evidence may be introduced.

On a door jamb of the temple of Seti I at Qurneh, the names of Ramesses II occur parallel to those of Seti I.[37] As one approaches the doorway, the royal names on the door jamb to the right belong to Ramesses II while those to the left belong to Seti I. On the lintel, both names occur; beginning with the word *'nḫ* in the center, the Horus names, the *nswt*-names and the *s3-R'*-names of Ramesses and Seti extend to the right and to the left. As this doorway stands before the sanctuary of Ramesses I, there is no reason to assume that this was inscribed after the death of Seti I, for Ramesses II's prenomen, in one instance, contains the phrase, *Iw'w-R'*, an epithet which is only attested in one dated monument and that belongs to year 1 (Gebel Silsileh, "Hymn to the Nile").[38] It would seem that the entrance to the sanctuary of their common royal ancestor would be a natural place to proclaim the joint rule of these two descendants.

In addition to the material presented above, records from Sinai substantiate the coregency between Seti I and Ramesses II. There is one fragmentary stela from the temple of Hathor at the Serabit el-Khadim which contains the names of both father and son in cartouches. The text reads, "Giving praise to the ka of the Lord [of the lands] ...many...powerful chariotry...[*Mn-M3't-R'*] the son of Re, *Sty*, Beloved-of-Ptah, and his royal son, *Wsr-M3't-R'*...Hathor, the Lord of appearances, *R'-ms.sw*, Beloved-of-Amun, may he live like Re [forever]."[39] At one side there is a person with raised hands adoring the royal pair; the accompanying inscription reads, "...and royal butler, *'š3-m-ḥbw-sd*." It is clear that the name of Seti I is not a part of a compound phrase referring to a location or one used within a title, for it is preceded by the usual nomen introduction of *s3-R'* and we may therefore safely assume that his prenomen is to be restored in the missing section. The prenomen of Ramesses II is introduced in a most unusual manner by "his royal son"; this phrase may introduce the names of princes, but for it to precede a cartouche in this manner would seem to indicate a coregency.[40]

Both Seti I and Ramesses II each left one dated stela at the Serabit el-Khadim; Seti's is dated to his 8th regnal year while Ramesses' belongs to his 2nd.[41] The *'ȝ3-m-ḥbw-sd* who erected the stela containing the names of both rulers in the temple of Hathor also erected these two dated stelae. *'ȝ3-m-ḥbw-sd* had a companion at Sinai named *Imn-m-Ipt*, for these two men appear in the same inscriptions (Nos. 252, 260 and most likely 247),[42] and one may assume that they were active on Sinai at the same time.

Seti I apparently did not leave many records at Sinai; at least only three are preserved.[43] Besides the one bearing the royal names of both Seti I and Ramesses II, there is one fragment depicting him offering to the god Ptah.[44] In addition to these two, there is the huge monolith which he erected on the hill overlooking the temple of Hathor and which can be viewed from a considerable distance.[45] This plinth is engraved on both sides, and though most of the inscription is now illegible, the regnal years remain on either side; both record his 8th year. The north face has "Regnal year 8, 1st month of *prt*, day 2"; it also has the name of *'ȝ3-m-ḥbw-sd*, with the title "Royal envoy in every land and valiant (?) commander of troops." The south face is badly weathered so that most of the text is obliterated, but beyond the regnal year enough traces of the titulary remain to show that it belongs to Seti I.

Since this monolith is thicker than most stelae, it can easily accommodate inscriptions on its edges. One inscription on the west edge contains the name of *Imn-m-Ipt*, who has the title "Commander of bowmen of the Well-of-Ramesses--Beloved-of-Amun." It is impossible to say whether this is a later addition to the stela or whether it was placed there when the texts on either face were inscribed.[46] Since the two men were contemporaries, one might reasonably assume that this record of *Imn-m-Ipt* was placed there at the same time as the text of *'ȝ3-m-ḥbw-sd*. If it is contemporary with the main texts on the north and south faces, then Ramesses must have been coregent in year 8 of Seti I.

There is another indication that this stela is directly related to the coregency between Ramesses II and his father; the month given in *'ȝ3-m-ḥbw-sd*'s inscription is the "first of *prt*" and the day is "day 2".[47] We know from a number of Ramesses' Jubilee inscriptions that there was a close relationship between the "first of *prt*" and the celebration of his Jubilee;[48] also, in most of the inscriptions, the day given is "day 1" (though it may be "day 17").[49] If Ramesses were crowned on the first of *prt* (since it seems that the royal Jubilees were a reflection of the king's coronation),[50] a distinct possibility exists that on day 2 there was a decree issued, a copy of which was placed upon the stela at Sinai by the royal representative. This would explain why a huge monolith was erected in such a conspicuous place: it was intended to proclaim the coregency. Therefore, if this stela of Seti I may be seen as a proclamation of the coregency, then the stela of Ramesses II at Sinai, dated to his year 2, would fall within the coregency period, for we do know that Seti ruled into his 11th year (Gebel Barkal stela).[51]

Reisner, in his study of "The Viceroys of Ethiopia,"[52] was confronted with a unique situation, for according to the inscriptions Amenemopet, son of Paser I, and Yuni both served as viceroys under Seti I and Ramesses II. Reisner acknowledged that "the inscriptions cited for Amenemopet and Yuni might be considered evidence that these two viceroys held office at the same time during the close of the reign of Sethos I and the beginning of the reign of Ramesses II,"[53] except for the fact that there was "no other case of a divided vice-royalty during the whole four centuries."[54] He therefore suggested that sometime during the coregency Amenemopet was succeeded by Yuni as Viceroy of Kush and that though Yuni might have been the choice of Seti I he "may have found no great favour with his son";[55] he therefore assumed that "Yuni was replaced by another viceroy (Hekanakht?) as soon as Sethos was dead."[56] Reisner further stated that he knew "of no evidence for ascertaining the length of the co-regency of Sethos I and Ramesses II, but even if it lasted only two or three years, its length would have been sufficient for the events suggested above."[57]

There are other indications that the coregency lasted at least three years; in chapter III it was shown that there are no private documents which belong to the first four years of Ramesses II,[58] which indicates that all private transactions were dated according to the regnal years of the senior partner of the coregency. Further, this would explain why Ramesses waited until his fourth year to make a royal tour of the Asiatic territories.[59] Returning to Sinai, the stela there bearing "year 2" of Ramesses has an unusual formulation of his royal titulary, which seems to have been used while he was coregent.

Taking all the evidence into consideration, a 3-year-plus coregency between Ramesses II and his father seems most reasonable.[60] The first day of the first month of *prt* may be postulated as Ramesses' coronation day,[61] which occurred in Seti's 8th regnal year;

sometime in his 11th year Seti died and Ramesses assumed the full position of kingship. Within this structure one could assume that Ramesses might have been about 10 years old when his father became king, as reflected in the Quban stela where it states that Ramesses was a *r3-ḥry* of the army at age ten;[62] he would then have been approximately 21 years old when he became sole ruler in Egypt and nearly 88 years old when he died.[63]

There appears, therefore, no reason to assume, as has been done, that Ramesses began dating inscriptions to his own rule only after the death of Seti I,[64] but immediately upon coronation followed the known examples of earlier times and dated monuments to his reign. This, then, is a chronological factor which might be taken into consideration, not only for the reign of Ramesses II but Egyptian history in general.

NOTES TO CHAPTER V

THE COREGENCY

1 Gauthier, Bibl. d'étude 4, with a translation by him in ZAeS 48 (1910), 52-66; Breasted, ARE III §§251-281; Porter-Moss VI 3 (34-37); Kitchen, Ramesside Inscriptions II 323-326.
This chapter formed the basis of a paper delivered in Toronto on November 14, 1970, at the Annual Meeting of the American Research Center in Egypt.

2 Dedicatory inscription at Abydos, lines 44-49; this is said to have taken place "in the first year of my appearing" (*m rnpt tpyt n[t] ḫ''.i*). For the word *sfy*, see Quban, line 16, and for the courtiers bowing to the ground before him, see Quban, line 12, and note 3 below.

3 Tresson, Bibl. d'étude 9; Sander-Hansen, Bibl. Aeg. IV 30-32; Porter-Moss VII 83; and a translation by Breasted, ARE III §§282-293.

4 Quban stela, lines 16-17.

5 It is difficult to determine just how much later the composition of this text really is; only a thorough literary-critical examination could help determine the date more precisely. It seems, as will be seen below, that much of Ramesses' building activity was conducted in the latter half of his reign.

6 Sethe, ZAeS 62 (1927), 110-114; Seele, The Coregency of Ramesses II with Seti I, 81.

7 Porter-Moss VI 25 (223-225 and 228-230); Seele, *op. cit.*, 47-48.

8 Porter-Moss VI 25 (229-230).

9 Porter-Moss VI 26 (239-242); Seele, *op. cit.*, 48.

10 Porter-Moss II 143 (13); Seele, *op. cit.*, 27-29, especially fig. 9. Also see Matthiew, JEA 16 (1930), 31-32; Shorter, JEA 20 (1934), 18-19; Gardiner, JEA 39 (1952), 22, with note 9, and 26.

11 For the Atef-crown and its relation to kingship, see Abubakr, Untersuchungen ueber die aegyptischen Kronen, 18-24.

12 The attempt to date certain scenes solely upon the criterion of incised versus bas-relief, such as was done by Roeder, Der Felsentempel von Bet el-Wali, 154-166, and followed by Seele, *op. cit.*, *passim*, is seriously open to question; see below.

13 See the discussion in chapter I above, with note 22.

14 For example, see Cairo stela 20516 (Lange and Schaefer, Grab- und Denksteine des Mittlern Reichs II 108, and IV, Taf. XXXV) where year 30 of Amenemhat I corresponds to year 10 of Sesostris I.

15 Simpson, JNES 15 (1956), 214-219. For the Old Kingdom, see Goedicke, JAOS 75 (1955), 180-183. On January 13, 1972, a paper was delivered by the author to the Society for the Study of Egyptian Antiquities in Toronto on the "Repeating of Births," in which the theory was postulated that the *wḥm mswt* was used

during the coregency, during the time of Seti I and Ramesses II as well as Ramesses XI and Herihor. It is intended that this be published in the near future.

16 ZAeS 37 (1899), 130-139.

17 Meyer, Geschichte des Altertums II 1, 455, with note 1, and 456, with note 2; Seele, *op. cit.*, 24-25; Drioton and Vandier, L'Égypte, 387. But Edgerton, in his work, The Thutmoside Succession, 31, follows Breasted's interpretation and assumes that Ramesses' claim of a miraculous birth indicates that at his birth he was not regarded as heir to the throne. The reference to Ptah as the divine father of Ramesses II is made in the "Decree of Ptah" dated to his 35th regnal year, a late time to be propounding a fiction which supposedly occurred many years earlier. For a much later tradition of Hephaestus (Ptah) as the father of Ramesses/Sesoösis, see Diodorus Siculus I 53, 9.

18 Porter-Moss II 21 (57).

19 Maspero, Struggle of the Nations, 387, with note 5.

20 *Op. cit.*, 23-25.

21 Egypt of the Pharaohs, 257.

22 Others like Otto, Aegypten, 174, and Helck, Geschichte 184, give a passing reference to the coregency, while Wilson, Burden of Egypt, does not mention it; Faulkner in CAH[2] II xxiii, 11, states that "he was co-regent with his father for an uncertain period," but agrees with Gardiner, *loc. cit.*, when he further says, "The dates on his monuments, however, refer to his sole rule and do not include the years of the co-regency." Hornung in his Chronologie, 41, note 91, also assumes that the coregency does not affect Egyptian chronology because he, too, believes that Ramesses only began reckoning his regnal years after Seti's death. Hayes, in The Scepter of Egypt, 334, states that Ramesses II "shared with him (Seti I) the administration of the country and the leadership of its armed forces" but does not specifically mention a coregency. Only Drioton and Vandier in L'Égypte, 353-354 and 388, consider a possible overlap in the regnal dates of Seti I and Ramesses II.

23 *Op. cit.*, 27.

24 ZAeS 62 (1927), 110-114.

25 *Op. cit.*, 75-82.

26 *Op. cit.*, 154-166.

27 *Op. cit.*, 33.

28 *Op. cit.*, 34.

29 ZAeS 62 (1927), 112; Seele, *op. cit.*, 32 and 81.

30 See year 1-D.

31 Year 1-A.

32 Year 1-E.

[33] Year 1-C, British Museum No. 440.

[34] Year 1-B.

[35] Roeder, *op. cit.*, 32, Taf. 30; Budge, A History of Ethiopia, I, plate between pp. 24 and 25; Porter-Moss VII 23 (6-7); and most recently, Ricke, Hughes and Wente, The Beit el-Wali Temple of Ramesses II, Pls. 7 and 8.

[36] Discussed below in chapter VI; also see years 34-D and 35-A.

[37] L. D. III 132 f; Porter-Moss II 145 (49). Also see Seele, *op. cit.*, 31, fig. 10.

[38] Year 1-B.

[39] Gardiner-Peet-Černý, Inscriptions of Sinai I, Pl. LXVIII, and II 175-176 (no. 247).

[40] Wb III 409, 6-7.

[41] Gardiner-Peet-Černý, *op. cit.*, I, Pl. LXVIII, and II 175-176 (no. 247) for Seti I; and I, Pl. LXX, and II 177-178 (no. 252) for Ramesses II.

[42] Gardiner-Peet-Černý, *op. cit.*, no. 252 = I, Pl. LXX, and II 177-178; no. 260 = I, Pl. LXXI, and II 180; no. 247 = I, Pl. LXVIII, and II 175-176.

[43] Gardiner-Peet-Černý, nos. 247, 249 and 250.

[44] Gardiner-Peet-Černý, no. 249.

[45] Gardiner-Peet-Černý, *op. cit.*, no. 247. Also see Petrie, Researches in Sinai, Pl. 85.

[46] Gardiner-Peet-Černý, *op. cit.*, II 176.

[47] Gardiner-Peet-Černý, *op. cit.*, I, Pl. LXX, and II 177-178.

[48] See in chapter II, section 1, years 42-A, 51-A, 54-A and 63-A.

[49] Day 17 at Armant, Mond-Myers, Armant, Pl. XCIII, years 57 and 60.

[50] See Borchardt, ZAeS 72 (1936), 52-59; Parker, Calendars, 61-62; Helck, Analecta Biblica 12 (1959), 118-120; Goedicke, MDAIK 21 (1966), 1-71; and especially von Beckerath, ZAeS 81 (1956), 1-3, where he says the coronation day should fall between the 3rd month of *3ḫt* day 24 and the 1st month of *prt* day 1; finally, Hornung, Chronologie, 57, with note 11.

[51] Reisner, ZAeS 69 (1933), 74, and Pl. VIII, where the date is "Regnal year 11, 4th month of *šmw* day 13." Also see Drioton and Vandier, L'Égypte, 388, and Redford, History and Chronology, 208-215, who opts for a 10-year reign and is questioned by Kitchen, CdE 43 (1968), 322-323.

[52] JEA 6 (1920), 28-55 and 73-88.

[53] *Ibid.*, 39.

[54] *Ibid.*, 40.

[55] *Ibid.*, 40 (e).

[56] *Ibid.*

[57] *Ibid.*

[58] The graffiti of years 1 and 2 do not seem to contradict this interpretation, for they are not of the same nature as a court record or a funerary stela. If they were the result of the beginning activity on Ramesses' tomb, it would not seem unusual for a person to use that king's regnal years.

[59] As perhaps reflected in the Nahr el-Kelb stela (4-A).

[60] Assuming that Ramesses' coronation was the "1st of *prt* day 1," then according to the Gebel Barkal stela of Seti I, which has the date "Regnal year 11, 4th month of *šmw* day 13," the coregency lasted almost four years. It actually could have lasted into the fourth year since the date on Ramesses' Nahr el-Kelb stela (Middle Stela) is "Regnal year 4, 4th month of *3ḫt* day 2."
Professor Goedicke, in an unpublished paper, has concluded that the Quban stela represents the transition period from the coregency to the sole rule of Ramesses II. Since the royal nomen of Seti I lacks both *m3' ḫrw* or *dỉ 'nḫ*, he surmises that the activity recorded there began in regnal year 3, which was still part of the coregency period; but by the time water was found, the report returned to the royal court and an order given for the stela to be erected in commemoration of the event, Seti had died and because of the changeover, no epithet was affixed to his name (Quban stela, 21). This study is reflected in Goedicke, JEA 52 (1966), 71.

[61] This day falls at the very end of the limit set by von Beckerath, ZAeS 81 (1956), 3; see note 50 above.
Redford's objection to an accession date in the month of *prt* (JEA 57 [1971], 110, note 3) is based upon the assumption that each inscription with a regnal year attests the king's presence at the site where each is found, but this need not be the case. His statement "But any date in *proyet* would make the visit to Silsileh...antedate the visit to Thebes..." assumes that Ramesses visited Silsileh, though this is not indicated by the Silsileh text (1-B). The inscription confirms (or reconfirms) offerings and is probably a copy of an official decree issued at court.

[62] Line 17.

[63] The age of 88 would be a reasonable one for his death from what we know of his mummy (Smith and Dawson, Egyptian Mummies, 99).

[64] Most historians do not reckon a chronological overlap in regnal years between Seti I and Ramesses II; see note 22 above. An exception is found in Drioton and Vandier, L'Égypte, 354.

CHAPTER VI

AN INTERPRETATION

Ramesses II began his reign as coregent with his father Seti I, a period which seems to have lasted somewhat more than three years[1] and during which there was apparently a division of responsibilities in the empire. Pharaonic affairs of Asia were under the direction of Seti I, who conducted the military campaigns in that area; internal affairs of both Egypt and Nubia were left in the hands of the young king, Ramesses II.[2] The Quban stela is an important source for the activities of Ramesses during the coregency; this text records his concern for the gold mines of the Wadi Allaqi.[3] The royal court was assembled in Memphis to discuss the problem of a water supply; the Viceroy of Kush gave a report to the coregent and his courtiers in which he stated that even Seti I had attempted a solution but had failed. The fragmented dedicatory text at Luxor is another example of Ramesses' supervision of internal matters, for the pylon was completed in the 4th month of *3ḫt*, near the end of his third regnal year.

Other texts which belong to the time of the coregency are not quite as explicit about Ramesses' activities and responsibilities, but they are informative. According to the "Dedicatory Inscription" at Abydos, Ramesses erected a statue of his father in regnal year 1, while in the same year it seems he stopped at Abydos to inspect the building progress there. Not only was he responsible for royal construction,[4] but his concern for the economic well-being of the land is reflected in texts such as the Silsileh "hymn." The Sinai inscription indicates that the area, like the Nubian gold mines, was under his jurisdiction. His nomination of *Nb-wnn.f* as High Priest of Amun in Thebes in his first year of office, like the Silsileh stela, shows that even in the sphere of religious administration the coregent performed the necessary functions of kingship.

The Royal Titulary

In the first year of his coregency, Ramesses assumed a full royal titulary and throughout his reign retained the basic form instituted at that time, with certain additions. Some of the changes in his titulary can be established by means of the dated records, and thereby approximate dates may be given for those changes; these in turn help indicate dates for other inscriptions which bear no regnal year.

Ramesses' full five-fold titulary appears in records of year 1. As found on the Gebel Silsileh stela[5] it is:

Ḥr:	*K3-nḫt Mry-M3't*
Nbty:	*Mk-Kmt W'f-ḫ3swt*
Ḥr-nbw:	*Wsr-rnpwt '3-nḫwt*
Nswt-bỉt:	*Nb-t3wy, Wsr-M3't-R' Stp-n-R'*
	var. *Wsr-M3't-R' Ḥḳ3-W3st*
	Wsr-M3't-R' Iw'w-R'
	Wsr-M3't-R' Mry-R'
S3-R':	*Nb-ḫ'w, R'-ms.sw Mry-Imn.*

His titles may be translated as "The Horus: Victorious Bull, Beloved of Ma'at; the Two Ladies: Protector of Egypt, Subduer of Foreign Lands; the Golden Horus: Rich in Years, Great of Victory; the King: Lord of the Two Lands, User-Ma'at-Re, Chosen-of-Re; the Son of Re: Lord of Appearances, Ramesses, Beloved-of-Amun."

As royal names were carefully chosen, they often indicate political intent as well as reflect the condition of the times.[6] Though Ramesses to our knowledge did not conduct military operations during his coregency, the government must have been oriented in that direction, for some of his epithets are military in nature.[7] The phrase "Victorious Bull"[8] had already become standard, but his *Nbty*-name is an explicit statement of intent to conquer.[9] This name is balanced between internal and foreign affairs; he is, first of all, "Protector of Egypt" and, second, the "Subduer of Foreign Lands (Foreigners)."[10] Even though he was not yet involved in these matters when the name was adopted, he apparently anticipated this as a part of his royal program. When he chose his Golden Horus name, he could not have foreseen that his wish "Rich in Years" would be amply fulfilled; the concept of plentiful years is compounded with "Great of Victory,"[11] which again stresses concern for his military career. Both his nomen and prenomen emphasize the god Re, but the god Ptah is not mentioned, though he was particularly popular in the Nineteenth Dynasty; for example, Ramesses' father's full nomen was Seti, Beloved-of-Ptah.[12]

During the coregency, Ramesses' titulary remained unchanged. Both the Sinai Inscription of year 2 and the Quban stela of year 3 follow the form of the Silsileh stela of regnal year 1.

The first major change appears in year 10, when some phrases are prefixed to the nomen and prenomen as recorded on the Aswan stela:

Nswt-bỉt: Ḥḳ3-pḏtyw-sẖr-bšt Nb-t3wy, Wsr-M3't-R' Stp-n-R'

S3-R': n ẖt.f, Nb-ḫpš, R'-ms.sw Mry-Ỉmn

var. *n ẖt.f mry.f, Nb-ẖ'w, R'-ms.sw Mry-Ỉmn.*

This inscription, which belongs to the time of Ramesses' foreign campaigns, reflects his interest in these matters. His *Nswt-bỉt*-name may be translated, "Ruler of the Bowmen Who Overthrew the Rebellious" and is quite likely an indication of the role of mercenaries in Ramesses' military operations.[13] The word "rebellious" could refer to those Asiatic lands which changed allegiance and became vassals of the Hittite king.[14] The use of the phrase "Possessor of the *ḫpš*-sword" in both the nomen and prenomen bespeaks the royal concern for military might at that time.[15]

In regnal year 18, the titulary on the Beisan stela is the same as the Gebel Silsileh stela of year 1, except as shown:

Nswt-bỉt: Iṯỉ-t3w-nbw, Wsr-M3't-R' Stp-n-R'

S3-R': n ẖt.f Nb-ẖ'w, R'-ms.sw Mry-Ỉmn.

The epithet "Seizer of All Lands" is similar to the Middle Kingdom phrase *Iṯỉ-T3wy*[16] and might represent an attempt or wish to control not only Egypt but also the Asiatic territories; this title again reflects Ramesses' preoccupation with military matters.

The text of the Alliance of year 21 contains only the nomen and prenomen of Ramesses II, and they are identical to those found on the Gebel Silsileh stela; likewise the Mnevis stela of year 26 has the same titulary as the Silsileh stela, with no additions. The records of his first Jubilee of year 30 have no changes, but in year 34, the year of his second Jubilee, a new phrase is added to his Horus-name:[17]

Ḥr: K3-nḫt Mry-M3't Nb-Ḥbw-Sd-mỉ-ỉt.f-Ptḥ-T3-tnn.

After Ramesses celebrated his second Jubilee, he commemorated it by adding "Possessor of Jubilees like his Father Ptah-Ta-tenen" to his Horus-name.

This same epithet occurs on the stela of year 35, the "Decree of Ptah," which also has other additions:

Ḥr: K3-nḫt Mry-M3't Nb-Ḥbw-Sd-mỉ-ỉt.f-Ptḥ-T3-tnn

Nbty: Mk-Kmt W'f-ẖ3swt R'-ms-nṯrw Grg-t3wy

Ḥr-nbw: Wsr-rnpwt '3-nḫwt

Nswt-bỉt: Nb-t3wy, Wsr-M3't-R' Stp-n-R'

S3-R': Pr-m-T3-tnn Ms-ḥm-n-ḥnwt-wrt, R'-ms.sw Mry-Ỉmn.

Here in the *Nbty*-name, there are new important developments; he now proclaims that he is "Re, Born of the Gods"[18] and the one "Who Set

in Order the Two Lands."[19]   The title preceding his nomen, stressing
his divine birth, is a reflection of the statements made within the
decree itself, a development which, as noted above, should have occurred earlier in his reign, since divine births are normally connected with the question of legitimate kingship.[20]

The stela of the Viceroy *St3w* of year 38 has the same reading
of Ramesses' Horus and *Nbty*-names as does the stela of year 35:

Ḥr: K3-nḫt Mry-M3't Nb-Ḥbw-Sd-mỉ-ỉt.f-Ptḥ-T3-tnn

Nbty: Mk-Kmt W'f-ḫ3swt R'-ms-nṯrw Grg-t3wy.

These epithets were still in use and appear to have become permanent
elements of his titulary.

In regnal year 42, the Louvre Ostracon, No. 2262,[21] shows a
change in his nomen:

S3-R':   R'-ms.sw Mry-Ỉmn Ḥk3-Ỉwnw,

while his prenomen remains the same.   This addition is also found on
Louvre Ostracon No. 2261, dated to regnal year 53:

S3-R':   R'-ms.sw Mry-Ỉmn Ḥk3-Ỉwnw.

In year 56, a further change in the nomen appears:

S3-R':   R'-ms.sw Mry-Ỉmn Nṯr, Ḥk3-Ỉwnw.

Approximately in year 42, Ramesses took the title "Ruler of Heliopolis," a concept similar to the epithet of Atum, "Lord of the Two
Lands of Heliopolis," which was popular in the Nineteenth Dynasty.[22]
It further appears that sometime between years 53 and 56, the new
element *Nṯr*, became a part of his nomen, reflecting the deification
of Ramesses II and relating it to Heliopolis.[23]

The full titulary of year 56, as found in Papyrus Sallier IV is:

Ḥr: K3-nḫt Mry-M3't Nb-Ḥbw-Sd-mỉ-ỉt.f-Ptḥ-T3-tnn

Nbty: Mk-Kmt W'f-Ḫ3swt R'-ms-nṯrw Grg-T3wy

Ḥr-nbw: Wsr-rnpwt '3-nḫwt

Nswt-bỉt: Nb-t3wy, Ḥk3-pḏtyw, R'-ms.sw Mry-Ỉmn

S3-R':   Nb-ḫ'w-mỉ-Ỉtm-Nb-t3wy-Ỉwnw, R'-Ḥr-3ḫty, R'-ms.sw
           Mry-Ỉmn Nṯr, Ḥk3-Ỉwnw.

This is the final development of the royal titulary which can be
specifically dated; most of the elements which it contains have been
found in earlier formulations.   The only noteworthy items are the
phrases "Ruler of the Bowmen" and "Lord of Appearances like Atum,
Lord of the Two lands of Heliopolis, Re-Harakhty."   The "Ruler of
Bowmen" occurred earlier, where it seems to have reflected Ramesses'
relationship with the mercenaries, which formed an important part of
his army.   The title "Lord of Appearances like Atum, Lord of the Two
Lands of Heliopolis, Re-Harakhty," like the addition to the nomen
"God, Ruler of Heliopolis," demonstrates royal association with the

city of Heliopolis, as a particular center of his kingship.[24]

There are distinct trends and patterns visible in the development of Ramesses' titulary. These developments form a part of a chronological structure and can be an aid in more closely dating other texts which contain no regnal years. Early in his reign, while he was coregent, he primarily employed the basic form, which indicates his professed royal program as king of Egypt at that time. By year 10, military epithets were added, which reflect his preoccupation with campaigns in Asia; these military epithets are found as late as year 18. By the time the second half of his reign is reached, the military phrases become less important and peaceful elements rise to the fore. In those years, he stressed his Jubilees and the fact that he was the one "Who set in Order the Two Lands."[25] This latter phrase hints that some disorder had plagued Egypt, but matters had been set aright and by year 35 all was back in order. Later in the reign elements of deification enter into his titulary. In general it might be said that there was a change from a concern for warfare and turmoil in his early years to statements of peace and concord in the latter ones.

General Developments

After the death of Seti I, Ramesses' attention was primarily directed towards Asia, though Egypt was not neglected. But for his second decade there is no evidence of Ramesses' activities in Egypt; there is nothing in the dated material which gives any indication of what transpired in the country at that time.[26] For the third decade there is slightly more evidence, though sparce indeed. The Mnevis stela of year 26 reflects an attempt by Ramesses to restore what had been neglected in earlier times.[27] The concern for "another disorder" as stated in the Alliance (line 15) is an indication that the possibility of disorder during the third decade (or even later?) was feared. A statement that "Upper Egypt has returned to its proper place" in a document composed for the first Jubilee reflects some "discord" during the third decade, or earlier.[28]

With year 30 and the first Jubilee, a time of peace and tranquility seems to have descended upon Egypt; from that year onward, there is no reference to warfare or strife. Building activity appears to have become Ramesses' primary public concern, and as far as one can tell, the economy of the land prospered.

In year 30, according to the dated material, Ramesses not only celebrated his first *Ḥb-Sd*, but he also restored more monuments of the past. The Apis stela (Louvre 3), which records the death and burial of an Apis bull in year 30, also refers to a previous death of one in year 16. This concern for the past extended to the buildings of his predecessors; his son, *Ḫ'-m-W3st*, restored a number of earlier monuments,[29] an activity which seems to have largely taken place in the second half of Ramesses' reign, for there is no evidence of *Ḫ'-m-W3st* public activities prior to year 30.[30]

The second half of Ramesses' reign was indeed the "Jubilee Period" and eventually he must have celebrated a total of 13 such festivals.[31] During this thirty-six-year (plus) period, Ramesses erected monuments for his "fathers," the gods of Egypt and Nubia; Thebes, in particular, benefited from this large-scale building activity.

It is difficult to ascertain the exact time when specific buildings were erected during the reign of Ramesses II, but some approximate dates may be given by means of the royal titulary found upon them. Quite often there is only the "standard" form, which could be used at any time during his reign.[32] At other times, however, the modifications and additions are also employed; it is these which are essential for a chronological estimate.

Egypt

Throughout Egypt there are indications that much of his building activity belongs to the second half of his reign.[33] The temple of Hathor at Deir el-Medineh benefited greatly from his beneficence;[34] the construction south of the great temple at Karnak must have been erected towards the end of his reign,[35] while other parts of the immense complex built by Ramesses most likely belong to this period also.[36] At Armant, the temple pylon was probably built shortly before year 51,[37] and at Hermopolis, his constructions appear to belong after year 34.[38] Much of the work on the temple of Ptah at Mit Rahineh, dates to the period after the second Jubilee,[39] as does the temple at Herakleopolis Magna.[40] In the Delta, too, it seems that building was encouraged in the latter half of his reign;[41] even the famous "400 year stela" must date after year 34 and most likely after year 35, when the epithets *R'-ms-nṯrw Grg-t3wy* first appear as a part of his *Nbty*-name.[42] Though there is no explicit statement that many of the buildings for which Ramesses II is famous were constructed in the second half of his reign, there are good indications that his attention was fully turned towards internal affairs of Egypt at that time and he was able again to erect monuments for the gods.

Nubia

During the coregency, Ramesses was apparently in charge of Nubian affairs; as stated above, our major source for his relationship with Nubia during this period is the Quban stela. The young king seems to have been responsible for royal affairs in that land for it was to Ramesses that the Viceroy of Kush made his report and it was from him that he received official orders.[43]

Building activity in Nubia must also have been under the direction of Ramesses in his office of coregent. The temple at Beit el-Wali, though completed later, was probably begun during the coregency since the name of the Viceroy *Imn-m-Ipt* is in one of the scenes.[44] Relations between Egypt and Nubia appear to have been peaceful throughout Ramesses' reign. There is no explicit statement of military activity in that area during his entire sixty-seven years. The few scenes which depict the Pharaoh slaying the wretched Nubian have been recognized as conventional and are not considered representative of actual fact.[45]

Excluding the Quban stela, the dated evidence from Nubia belongs to the second half of Ramesses' reign. Three inscriptions of the Viceroy *St3w* belong to years 38, 44 and 63. Though these three texts of *St3w* are not directly connected with any known event, they do indicate the approximate time when this Viceroy held office and thereby also date various buildings.

Ramesses constructed a number of temples throughout Nubia: beginning in the north, there is one at Beit el-Wali[46] and another nearby at Gerf Husein;[47] further south is the Temple of Amun and Re-Harakhty at Wadi es-Sebua'[48] and beyond that the temple at Quban.[49] He built the temple of Re-Harakhty at Derr[50] and, not least of all, the one at Abu Simbel,[51] which is accompanied by the smaller temple of Queen Nefertari.[52] At Faras he rebuilt a temple of Hathor of Abeshek, which was begun by Hatshepsut,[53] while at Aksha (Serra West) a temple was erected to a statue of Ramesses II.[54] There is also a temple at Amara West,[55] and finally much further to the south there are the remains of one at Gebel Barkal.[56]

Ramesses not only built new temples during his reign, he also added to or embellished others already in existence. The Eighteenth Dynasty temple of Amada,[57] the temple of Horus at Aniba,[58] the rock temple of Ellesiya,[59] the south temple at Buhen[60] and the Triple Temple at Sesebi,[61] all have various additions or alterations for which Ramesses was responsible. Yet even though he conducted all this building activity, not one temple in Nubia contains a regnal date to indicate the exact time of its construction.

Since we are able to give approximate dates for the Viceroy *St3w*, one may attempt to give reasonable dates for the other viceroys also.[62] Besides *St3w*, there are five other viceroys which are assigned to Ramesses' reign: *Imn-m-Ipt*, *Iwny*, *Ḥḳ3-nḫt*, *P3-sr* (II) and *Ḥy*. *Imn-m-Ipt* and *Iwny* both served during the period of the coregency; it seems that *Imn-m-Ipt* was appointed during the reign of Seti I and was succeeded by *Iwny* in the coregency period.[63] Shortly after Seti's death, *Iwny* was probably replaced by *Ḥḳ3-nḫt*, who was followed by *Ḥy* and *P3-sr* (II), though the exact order is not known.[64]

The period of tenure for the three viceroys *Ḥḳ3-nḫt*, *Ḥy* and *P3-sr* (II) is vague; *Ḥḳ3-nḫt* is believed to have served during the early years of Ramesses reign, since he is shown in the presence of Queen Neferteri at Abu Simbel.[65] The Viceroy *Ḥy* is not well attested and is of little value for chronological purposes;[66] the Viceroy *P3-sr* left a few inscriptions, all in the vicinity of Abu Simbel, but there is no way to give even an approximate date for him.[67] Since none of these men can be dated precisely, for chronological purposes the Viceroy *St3w* may be considered as holding office during the latter half of Ramesses' reign and the other three during the first, with *Imn-m-Ipt* and *Iwny* assigned to the coregency or thereabouts.

Asia

Immediately upon his father's death, Ramesses became involved with Asia. No longer was he responsible only for matters pertaining to Egypt; he now had to assume the burden of the Asiatic territories as well. We know from inscriptions at Karnak that Seti I conducted military campaigns into Asia, but the only dates given are his first regnal year and a reference to the first year of the "Repeating of Births."[68] Even though it is unlikely that all the events depicted on the walls of Karnak belong to a single year, we cannot be certain how many there were or when all were conducted. Since it appears that Seti attended to Asiatic affairs, it is not surprising that the first evidence of a military campaign on the part of Ramesses II belongs to his fourth regnal year.

The Middle stela on the Nahr el-Kelb no longer retains anything more than date, royal name and a few epithets; all historical information has been lost, yet this stela is the first indication that the young ruler was involved in Asia.[69] What might have begun as a "royal tour" in year 4 developed into a more serious situation in regnal year 5. The first and, as far as we know, the only direct confrontation between Ramesses II and Muwatallish, king of Hatti, occurred at the battle of Qadesh, which was long remembered.[70]

Ramesses' foreign policy towards Asia was strongly influenced by the developments of year 5, not so much a result of personal planning, but because of the political changes brought about by the battle at Qadesh. During the time of Seti I, the city of Qadesh had been under Egyptian sovereignty, for a stela fragment discovered there during excavations shows that Seti was lord in that place.[71] Ramesses, too, must have considered Qadesh an Egyptian vassal for it is unlikely that he would have marched his army so complacently to that city had it been considered rebellious. We do not know what prompted this campaign, though apparently Ramesses did intend to encounter with the Hittite forces further to the north.[72] The Hittite "cowardice" and ambush of the Egyptian army brought Ramesses into direct confrontation with the northern enemy sooner than he expected.

The battle of Qadesh has been described as having "ended in a tactical victory for the Egyptians, in that they remained in possession of the field and it was their opponent who called off the fight, strategically no result had been attained, and the victory was a barren one, for Ḳadesh did not fall and the *status quo ante bellum* remained unaltered."[73] Actually the Asiatic situation did change, and it appears that Amurru became a vassal of Hatti;[74] because of this Ramesses apparently directed his attention towards the coastal plains instead of the hinterland.

This political change is seen in the campaign of year 8, when Ramesses led his army up the coastal area, possibly as far north as Tripolis.[75] A reference to this campaign might be found in a letter discovered at Ugarit, in which an encounter with the Egyptian army in the vicinity of Tripolis is recorded.[76]

Sometime between the campaign of year 8 and approximately year 10, an agreement seems to have been reached between Ramesses II and Muwatallish, since the text of the Alliance between Hattushilish and Ramesses mentions "sworn terms" which had been drawn up in the reign of Muwatallish.[77] These "agreements" were probably the result of a truce between the two parties.

The years immediately following Ramesses' year 10 are unattested in dated inscriptions; yet in regnal year 21 he formed an alliance with Hattushilish III, great king of Hatti. It has been assumed that this alliance was concluded between the two countries after they had been at war for some time,[78] but there is no evidence for such and the reference in KBo I 10 is vague.[79] It has also been postulated that the alliance was the result of a stalemate between the two lands; since neither side was able to gain military advantage over the other, a "peace treaty" was supposedly signed to acknowledge the existing situation.[80] However, the document drawn up between the two countries was not a "peace treaty" but an alliance for mutual aid; therefore these assumptions alone do not fully explain the situation.

The document concentrates upon mutual aid and protection. If "another" discord should arise against either party, one was to come to the other's assistance. It is significant that it is not just discord in general which is mentioned, but specifically another discord which might arise against either the king of Hatti or the king of Egypt.[81] This word "another" is not required by either Akkadian or Egyptian style, and thus should be taken literally.

Politically, there was only one major power at that time strong enough to pose a threat to either Hatti or possibly Egypt, and that was Assyria. However, even though Assyria was a threat to Hatti, particularly after it had conquered Mitanni and thus approached the very borders of the Hittite Kingdom, it was not a menace to the Pharaonic territories in Asia.[82] In spite of the attempt by Rowton to see this move on the part of Ramesses II as having been very far sighted,[83] Assyria does not seem to have been capable at that time of expanding so far west and south.

Instead of fearing Assyrian expansion, Ramesses should have welcomed it as a matter of political advantage, for Assyria's interest was directed west and northward and was at the expense of Ramesses traditional rival, Hatti. Indeed the most likely countries to have formed an alliance would have been Assyria and Egypt in order to make common cause against Hatti and thereby eliminate their mutual foe.[84]

Assyria thus could not have been the reason why Ramesses entered an alliance with the country which had been the political opponent of the Pharaoh. Yet in order to explain why Ramesses would welcome such an alliance, one must establish the advantage it offered him.

It is not sufficient to assume that both parties were simply tired of warfare, decided to call a truce, and thereby settle the matter for the length of their respective reigns. In the over-all scene Egypt was a prosperous country, not in danger of any economic collapse at that time; there is no indication that the country had been so drained by foreign wars that its economy had been severely curtailed.[85] Hattushilish, on the other hand, does record strife in Anatolia[86] and tense relations with Assyria;[87] but this only explains why Hatti would wish such an alliance, it does not account for such a move on the part of Ramesses II.

The historical situation in Hatti during the "empty" decade of Ramesses' reign is known primarily from the "Apology" of Hattushilish III, in which he gives the background of his accession to the Hittite throne.[88] Muwatallish, the great king of Hatti who fought against Ramesses II at Qadesh, was the older brother and a predecessor of Hattushilish III. In his "Apology" Hattushilish does not hesitate to relate the troubles which beset the land during the reign of Muwatallish, troubles which he himself helped to correct, though he was still a young man (II 16-30). Most of the references to the reign of Muwatallish concern the military exploits of Hattushilish himself (II 35ff), who, we are told, was finally made king in Hakpissa by his brother Muwatallish, ostensibly in gratitude for service rendered the king of Hatti.

At the death of Muwatallish, Hattushilish claims to have personally supported Urkhi-Teshub as great king of Hatti (III 41-43) and even states that he himself placed Urkhi-Teshub upon the throne, though he remained king in Hakpissa (III 45). Hattushilish continues to relate that he rebuilt Nerik and enlarged his own personal kingdom (III 45-54), but as time went on Urkhi-Teshub began to take away those territories which Hattushilish had added to his kingdom (III 54-61). For seven long years he tolerated these demeaning actions until Urkhi-Teshub finally took away Hakpissa and Nerik, at which time the king's uncle revolted and declared open warfare upon Urkhi-Teshub (III 69-71).

Since this is an "apology" on the part of Hattushilish III in which he justifies his seizure of the throne of Hatti, we have only a biased report which must be critically examined. It appears that Hattushilish was jealous of his brother Muwatallish, as the first part of the "Apology" indicates, and considered himself an equally viable cadidate for the kingship (I 9-22), even though he stresses that he supported his brother faithfully. When Muwatallish died, apparently Hattushilish was forced to accept Urkhi-Teshub as great king in Hatti, as prescribed by the "Edict of Telepinush" which governed Hittite throne succession.[89] Hattushilish relates that he placed Urkhi-Teshub upon the throne, but that he remained king in Hakpissa and even added more territory to his kingdom. It is unlikely that Hattushilish was as patient during those seven years as he would lead us to believe; from the very start there seems to have been disagreement, if not outright strife, between the two leaders. Urkhi-Teshub continued to take away territory from Hattushilish until he was reduced to one major fortification. Then an unexpected turn of events took place and Hattushilish overcame Urkhi-Teshub and forced him to Nuhasse (IV 32-33).[90]

We do not know what tipped the scales in favor of Hattushilish, for he was reduced in his holdings and apparently making a last stand against his nephew when suddenly he began a victorious campaign against him. This might have been the result of a treaty concluded with Kadashman-Turgu of Babylon, to which reference is made in the letter which Hattushilish wrote to Kadashman-Enlil.[91] But Egypt, not Urkhi-Teshub, is mentioned as the opponent of Hattushilish in that letter; therefore Babylon may or may not have been the source of Hattushilish's help.[92] It is unlikely that Assyria came to the aid of Hattushilish, for in the same letter to Kadashman-Enlil, Assyria is still viewed as a threat to the peace of Hatti. All this activity seems to have occurred after Ramesses' 10th year. As stated earlier, Rowton has suggested that Urkhi-Teshub ascended the throne of Hatti in regnal year 10 of Ramesses II and that Hattushilish finally became great king in regnal year 17;[93] these dates are only approximates and one cannot be certain how long the struggle between Urkhi-Teshub and Hattushilish continued.

The reign of Urkhi-Teshub roughly corresponds to the "empty years" of Ramesses' second decade.[94] One might conjecture that Ramesses left Egypt in year 10 at the head of an army, perhaps intending to take advantage of the new political situation in Hatti, though at some time he did pledge support for Urkhi-Teshub as great king in Hatti, as evidenced by his letter to the king of Mira.[95] The South Stela on the Nahr el-Kelb might have been carved at that time.[96] What happened then remains unknown, and Ramesses II disappeared from recorded history.

Taking a clue from the words of the Alliance, "If the sujects of Ramesses commit another crime against him,"[97] it appears that there had been a rebellion in Egypt proper. This would help explain why "another disorder" and "another crime" are mentioned within the text of the Alliance with regard to Ramesses II but only "another disorder" (and not "another crime") is mentioned with reference to Hattushilish III.[98] It would seem that at sometime prior to regnal 21, the subjects of Ramesses had rebelled against him. The logical time for this to have occurred would be when he disappeared from recorded history during his second decade. Apparently not only had the subjects rebelled, but there had also been "another disorder." For Hattushilish, one might see Urkhi-Teshub as his (first) "disorder," but for Ramesses one may only conjecture that someone led the country in creating disorder against him. This, then, may be the reason why an alliance was formed between Hatti and Egypt; having been gone from his country for a lengthy period and fearing for his own kingdom, Ramesses might have needed all the support he could get in order to restore his control over Egypt. At the same time one may see the benefits which Ramesses would enjoy from such an alliance and why he would be indebted to Hattushilish.[99]

The date given for the final ratification of the alliance is regnal year 21 of Ramesses II, but that represents the concluding date and not the time when negotiations began. If one allows sufficient time for these negotiations, which were conducted by royal envoys from the respective kings, a lapse of several years would not be unreasonable and one could assume that they began shortly after Hattushilish became great king in Hatti.[100]

Whatever transpired during Ramesses' "empty years" is not entirely clear, but year 18 is commemorated on a stela from Beisan in Palestine.[101] Though the stela does not specifically refer to a military venture by the Egyptian king, it is totally concerned with military matters and some of its phrases are peculiar. It should also be noted that Ramesses is shown in the lunette clad in battle dress and clutching bow in hand; this is an unusual, if not unique, representation of an Egyptian king. The military aspect of the stela cannot be doubted since the king appears in battle dress while he receives the *ḫpš*-sword from the god Amun-Re.

The words accredited the god are also uncommon; he says, "I have given you your boundaries according to that which you have desired, to the limits of the supports of heaven. Receive...for yourself the *ḫpš* against every country, that you might cut off the heads of those which have rebelled against you, since you are Horus, in charge of the Two Lands."[102] The explicit statement which Amun-Re makes about cutting off the heads of those who have rebelled against the king is not typical and reflects the severity of the matter at hand.[103] The rebellion is linked to Egypt by the assurance: "since you are Horus in charge of the Two Lands" (*iw.k m Ḥr ḥry-tp t3wy*), which is a definite reference to Ramesses legitimate rights over Egypt.[104]

The main text of the stela first speaks of the mighty acts of Ramesses as warrior, with phraseology similar to that used by Tuthmosis III, "who reached the limits of the land (earth) seeking battle, without finding anyone who would face him."[105] He is also the one "who rescued his infantry and saved his chariotry," when all lands were in furor.[106] The text then turns to Ramesses' benevolence and he is described as "one who plans, whose [plans] do not fail...

who saves the shipwrecked (stranded), a husband to the widow and protector of the orphan...a valiant shepherd who sustains mankind."[107] The text continues with a significant phrase in line 16: "He has rescued Egypt when it was brought to its knees (*ḥf3*)."[108] It ends by saying that "Ramesses, Beloved-of-Amun, is an excellent place (of refuge) for his soldiers on the day of battle (discord!)."[109]

This stela sheds some light on an otherwise dark period. The military character is undeniable, especially since Ramesses is depicted ready for battle. The royal intent is indicated by the words of the god as he grants the *ḫpš*-sword: "To cut off the heads of those who have rebelled against you," not "among the foreign lands" as one might expect, but apparently in Egypt itself, since Ramesses is described as "Horus, in charge of the Two Lands." Egypt is also mentioned later in the text as having "been brought to its knees," a phrase which hints at some discord within the land.

Since the *ḫpš*-sword was given to destroy the rebellious in Egypt, it might be reasonable to surmise that this stela marks Ramesses' return to Egypt after a prolonged absence. The statements recorded on the stela probably represent the general promises and words of encouragement given to his army, which most likely was composed of mercenaries, who had either remained loyal to him or had joined him in hopes of receiving rewards in Egypt once the land had been returned to its rightful ruler.[110]

Ramesses did, in fact, reward the men of his army with land in Egypt, an act which was remembered even in Greek times;[111] the stelae from Horbeit reflect such a military colony,[112] as do similar memorials found in Nubia, at Derr, which were erected later when *St3w* was Viceroy.[113] The use of mercenaries was already an established practice in regnal year 5, when the battle of Qadesh was fought.[114] A reference to Sherden, who came from the midst of the sea and who "changed their minds," is an indication that this military group formed a part of his army.[115] A mention of the various people composing an army in Papyrus Anastasi I (xviii 3-5) shows that it consisted primarily of foreigners. If, as it seems, Ramesses had to reconquer Egypt, the most likely source of manpower would have been mercenaries.

There is one more possible reference to Ramesses' return to Egypt and that is the "capture of Askelon," which is the scene just to the right of the Alliance inscription on the walls of Karnak.[116] The proximity of these two would lead one to believe there might be some connection between them and that they were not just placed upon the wall haphazardly.

The inscription accompanying the storming of the city reads: "The wretched town which his Majesty plundered (carried off) because it was wicked, Askelon...."[117] The town of Askelon might have withstood the advance of Ramesses on his march southward to Egypt; it has otherwise been difficult to explain how a city so deep in Pharaonic territory could have had the audacity to rebel with any hope of success.[118]

Previously the rebellion of Askelon has been placed in the first decade of Ramesses' reign, during the disturbance associated with the campaign in regnal year 8;[119] yet even then this revolt does not fit into the general geographical pattern of events, and as a result it has sometimes been seen as an isolated rebellion, although one so close to Egypt proper is unlikely. If, however, Askelon might have resisted Ramesses on his return to Egypt, then its "rebellion" would fit into the chronological picture.

Thus far it appears that the chronological structure of Ramesses' reign is more complicated than has been assumed. The royal activities of the empty period which began after regnal year 10 still remain conjectural, but a general pattern may be reconstructed from the available records. Sometime in regnal year 10, or shortly thereafter, Ramesses II appears to have left Egypt; perhaps at this time he conducted the campaigns into Trans-Jordan which are represented on the walls of Luxor, since they do not fit into any of his earlier campaigns.[120] Then something unknown happened to the Egyptian ruler, and he disappeared from recorded history for a number of years; during this period the struggle for the throne of Hatti continued between Urkhi-Teshub and Hattushilish III. Towards the end of the decade, Hattushilish was able to evict Urkhi-Teshub and send him into exile; at approximately the same time, Ramesses again entered the historical picture, with an inscription at Beisan in Palestine.

The ascendancy of Hattushilish and the reappearance of Ramesses, after an eight-year silence, could be related, especially since Ramesses entered an alliance with Hattushilish in year 21. One may conclude that Ramesses was in need of peace in the north, not only peace, but assurance from that area in order to return to Egypt and place that country under his control again. The "first crime," which is alluded to in the text of the Alliance, was apparently a rebellion by Ramesses' subjects. And it was by means of the alliance that he was to be protected against the reoccurrence of "another crime" or "disorder." Here, then, is the reason why Ramesses not only willingly made an alliance with Hattushilish but why he was in need of such an alliance with his traditional enemy.

NOTES TO CHAPTER VI
AN INTERPRETATION

1 The coregency, as proposed in chap. V, lasted into Ramesses' fourth year.

2 There is no evidence that Ramesses conducted a military campaign while he was coregent; it appears that Seti I needed a co-ruler to handle the affairs of Egypt so that he might pursue the affairs of Asia without concern for domestic matters; cf. Faulkner JEA 33 (1947), 34-39.

3 For the gold mines of the Wadi Allaqi, see Saeve-Soederbergh, Aegypten und Nubien, especially pp. 210-212; and Černý, JEA 33 (1947), 52-57. Also see Lieblein ZAeS 4 (1866), 101-102; and Vercoutter, Kush 7 (1959), 130.

4 It is also quite likely that the temple at Beit el-Wali was begun during the coregency, since the Viceroy *Imn-m-Ipt*, who held office during the coregency, is mentioned there; for a discussion of the viceroys of the coregency, see chap. V.

5 Chap. II, year 1-B; the "Sphinx Stela," B. M. 440 (year 1-C), has the same titulary as the Silsileh stela, though it is not in as good a condition.

6 For a discussion of the mythological nature of the royal titulary, as written by the god Thot, see Helck, ZAeS 82 (1957), 133-140.

7 In line 17 of the Quban stela he is called a *r3-ḥry n p3 mš'*, but since the inscription also states that he held this at the age of ten, the title does not indicate that he was engaged in actual military operations during the coregency.

8 See Wb V 95, 6-9.

9 For the particular combination of *w'f ḫ3swt*, see Wb I 285, 10-13, and especially 285, 11-12 for the phrase as used in royal names.

10 The writing of  can be understood as referring not only to "foreign lands" but also the inhabitants of those areas and, therefore, "foreigners." In Papyrus Sallier IV 17, 2, the word is written in Ramesses' titulary with "people" determinatives, which encourage the reading "foreigners."

11 For *'3 nḫt*, see Wb II 316, 10.

12 Throughout his lifetime, Ramesses II did show special concern for the god Ptah, as has been indicated in this study. Even his prenomen could be altered from *Wsr-M3't-R' Stp-n-R'* to *Wsr-M3't-R' Stp-n-Ptḥ* (for example, see Habachi, Deification, 37, fig. 23a and Pl. XIVc).

13 For the composition of the Egyptian army, see Faulkner, JEA 39 (1953), 32-47; Schulman, Military Rank, Title and Organization in the Egyptian New Kingdom, 17-25; and JARCE 1 (1962), 47-53; and Yeivin, JNES 9 (1950), 101-107.

14 We know that in regnal year 5, Qadesh was no longer loyal to Egypt; it probably had severed allegiance upon the death of Seti I; cf. Goedicke, JEA 52 (1966), 71.

15 For *nb-ḫpš*, cf. Wb III 269, 14-16.

16 For *Iṯỉ-t3wy*, see Simpson, JARCE 2 (1963), 53-59.

17 The "Marriage Stela" (34-D). It has been recognized that Ramesses did not employ the phrase *nb Ḥbw-Sd* before he celebrated his second Jubilee; see Roeder, Hermopolis 1929-39, VIII 19f. Though not found in dated inscriptions, Ramesses did use the singular *nb Ḥb-Sd*, which must belong to the time between his first and second Jubilees, for after his second Jubilee (in the dated monuments) he employed the plural only.

18 In the "Dedicatory Inscription" of Abydos, Ramesses II is called "our Re" (line 39); for the King as Re, see Grapow, Die bildlichen Ausdruecke des Aegyptischen, 30; also compare Hornung, MDAIK 15 (1957), 120-133, for the Eighteenth Dynasty.

19 For the word *grg* as "remettre en ordre," see Vandier, Mo'alla, I, α, 2; I, β, 1; also see Faulkner, Dictionary, 291.

20 See the discussion in chap. V, where it was noted that even in Greek times Ramesses' claim to have been engendered by Ptah was remembered.

21 Chap. II, year 42-C. Perhaps there is a mistake, and these two ostraca should have the word *nṯr*.

22 For *ḥḳ3-Iwnw*, cf. Wb III 171, 20-26; the combination of *ḥḳ3* with the city *Iwnw* is not common.

23 Cf. Habachi, Deification, *passim*, and Yoyotte, in Anthes, Mit Rahineh 1956, 66-70. Unless attempts at deification were made as early as year 42; see above.

24 For "Atum Lord-of-the-two-lands-of-Heliopolis" see chap. IV, line 2, of the Alliance commentary.

25 For *grg t3wy* and related forms as royal epithets, cf. Wb V 186, 10.

26 For this see the analysis in chap. III.

27 This tomb was originally begun in the reign of Horemhab but was either never finished or needed restorations by the time of Ramesses' reign; see Daressy, ASAE 18 (1919), 196-210.

28 Ostracon Gardiner 28; cf. Černý-Gardiner, Hieratic Ostraca I 3, Pls. IX-IXA.

29 For the restoration text of the Unis pyramid, cf. Drioton and Lauer, ASAE 37 (1937), 201-211; for the tomb of *Špss-k3.f*, cf. Jéquier, Le Mastabat Faraoun, 12-13, and Douze ans de fouilles, 160-161; and Porter-Moss III 97. Also cf. Helck, ZDMG 102 (1952), 45-46, and Wildung, Die Rolle aegyptischer Koenige im Bewusztsein ihrer Nachwelt, 228.

30 See above in chap. II, under year 16-A; the dates assigned by Mariette to "Apis II" and "Apis III" can no longer be maintained, and therefore there is no evidence for *Ḫ'-m-W3st*'s public activities in year 16 of Ramesses II.

31 For studies pertaining to Ramesses' Jubilees, see Borchardt, ZAeS 72 (1936), 52-59; von Beckerath, ZAeS 81 (1956), 1-3; Gardiner,

Papyrus Wilbour II 13, note 3; Bonnet, Reallexikon, 158-160; and Habachi, ZAeS 97 (1971), 64-72.

For a reference to the celebration of his second Jubilee, cf. Papyrus Anastasi II 5, 5, and Caminos, LEM 47; also see Papyrus Bologna 1094 1, 7 and Caminos, LEM 6. His last Jubilee was probably celebrated in year 66 (66-A).

For the association of Ptah with the Jubilees, see M. Sandman Holmberg, The God Ptah, 87-93.

And for discussions of Jubilees in other periods, see Wilson, JAOS 56 (1936), 293-296; Simpson, JARCE 2 (1963), 59-63; and Uphill, JNES 22 (1963), 123-127, JNES 24 (1965), 365-383, and JNES 26 (1967), 61-62.

32 Once a new element appears in a dated inscription this does not mean that it was always employed from that time onward. The basic titulary could be used at any time in his reign; see, for example, the stela of *St3w* of year 63-C, where the simple nomen and prenomen are used.

33 Porter-Moss, *passim*. This is not to diminish his early activities, especially during the coregency.

34 Bruyère, FIFAO 20 ii.

35 Brugsch, Geographie I 181, Pl. XXXVI (no. 796).

36 Porter-Moss II 15-19, 23-24, and 47-49. For Luxor, *ibid.*, 98-102 and 108-110.

37 The pylon at Armant most likely dates to the reign of Ramesses II instead of Tuthmosis III; cf. Mond-Myers, Armant (Text), 15 and 25. The dates recorded on the pylon, referring to his later Jubilees, are an indication that this construction probably belongs to the latter part of the reign, cf. *ibid.*, 164 and Pl. XCIII.

38 Roeder, Hermopolis 1929-1939, especially VIII 19f.

39 Daressy, ASAE 3 (1902), 22-31. Also see Anthes, Mit Rahineh 1956, 7-9, where it is definitely stated that that particular temple could not be dated before year 30.

40 Naville, Ahnas el-Medineh, 9-10, where a portal must have been erected after year 34.

41 A statue from Mendes has *Nṯr-ḥḳ3-Iwnw* on it and must date towards the last quarter of his reign; Naville, *op. cit.*, 18. Also see Petrie, Tanis I, Pls. IV-V, and Tanis II, Pls. V, VII and XI; and Naville, Bubastis, Pls. XXXVI and XXXVIII.

42 Most recently, Goedicke, CdE 41 (1966), 23-39, with references; Stadelmann, CdE 40 (1965), 46-60. Because an (undated) "Marriage Stela" was used as a base for a statue of Ramesses II, one may reasonably assume that this building activity occurred after year 34; cf. Lefebvre, ASAE 25 (1925), 34-36; Porter-Moss II 95. What does this say for the marriage?

43 Lines 19ff.

44 Roeder, Der Felsentempel von Bet el-Wali, Taf. 31; Ricke, Hughes and Wente, The Beit el-Wali Temple of Ramesses II, Pls. 7 and 9.

45 Not only are the scenes of Ramesses conquering the Nubians similar

in a number of temples in Nubia, even the captions may be repeated; cf. Wente, in Ricke, Hughes and Wente, *op. cit.*, 11, note 1.

46 Porter-Moss VII 21-27.

47 *Ibid.*, 33-37.

48 *Ibid.*, 53-64.

49 *Ibid.*, 82-83.

50 *Ibid.*, 84-89.

51 *Ibid.*, 95-111.

52 *Ibid.*, 111-117; most recently, Desroches-Noblecourt and Kuentz, Le petit temple d'Abou Simbel.

53 Porter-Moss VII 126.

54 *Ibid.*, 127.

55 *Ibid.*, 159-164.

56 *Ibid.*, 215-221.

57 *Ibid.*, 67.

58 *Ibid.*, 81.

59 *Ibid.*, 91.

60 *Ibid.*, 126.

61 *Ibid.*, 133.

62 For the Viceroys of Kush, see Reisner, JEA 6 (1920), 28-55 and 73-88; Gauthier, Rec. Trav. 39 (1921), 182-238; and Habachi, Kush 5 (1957), 13-36.

63 Reisner, JEA 6 (1920), 40.

64 *Ibid.*, 44-45, and Habachi, Kush 5 (1957), 26-33.

65 Porter-Moss VII 118 (17).

66 Habachi, *op. cit.*, 28-31.

67 Reisner, *op. cit.*, 41.

68 Faulkner, JEA 33 (1947), 34-39. For the *wḥm mswt*, see chap. V.

69 Though year 4 must represent the "First Campaign" implied in the Qadesh inscriptions (B 3), we do not know if there were any military encounter at that time between Ramesses' forces and those of the later Hittite opponent.

70 Chap. II, year 5-A, for references. For discussion of the battle of Qadesh, see most recently, Goedicke, JEA 52 (1966), 71-80; and Faulkner, MDAIK 16 (1958), 93-111.
For other aspects of Qadesh, cf. Burne, JEA 7 (1921), 191-195; Yeivin, JNES 9 (1950), 101-107; Edel, Z.A. 15 (1950), 195-212,

and Z. A. 16 (1952), 253-258; Schulman, JARCE 1 (1962), 47-53; and Gardiner, The Ḳadesh Inscriptions of Ramesses II.

[71] Pézard, Syria 3 (1922), 108.

[72] Goedicke, JEA 52 (1966), 71.

[73] Faulkner, MDAIK 16 (1958), 99.

[74] Goetze, OLZ 32 (1929), 832-838; Edel, Z. A. 15 (1950), 195-212, and 16 (1952), 253-258. But also see Helck, Beziehungen, 214.

[75] Breasted, ARE III §356; Helck, *op. cit.*, 222-223; Noth, ZDPV 64 (1941), 39-74.

[76] Ugaritica V 69-79.

[77] Line 14 of the Alliance.

[78] Cf. Helck, Geschichte, 186; Sturm, Der Hettiterkrieg Ramses' II., 182-191; and Gardiner, Egypt of the Pharaohs, 264.

[79] Chap. I.

[80] Cf. Breasted, ARE III §369; Faulkner, CAH^2 II xxiii 15; and Goetze, CAH^2 II xxiv 46-47.

[81] Cf. chap. IV in the commentary on lines 15 to 17. One may conjecture that the "discord" of Hattushilish could refer to his difficulties with Urkhi-Teshub.

[82] Rowton, JCS 13 (1959), 1-11; J. M. Munn-Rankin, CAH^2 II xxv 6-8; Goetze, CAH^2 II xxiv 46-47; and chap. I.

[83] *Op. cit.*, 11.

[84] As Hattushilish did with Babylon, in defense against Assyria (KBo I 10). See chap. I, and especially note 55; cf. Edel JCS 12 (1958), 130-133, and Rowton JNES 25 (1966), 243-249.

[85] For the economic situation in Egypt at this time, see Černý, Cahiers d'histoire mondiale I (1953-54), 903-921, and Helck, Materialien, *passim*.

[86] For the "Apology" of Hattushilish, see Goetze, MVAG 29/3 (1924) and 34/2 (1930), III 38 - IV 32.

[87] For the letter KBo I 10, see notes 83-84 above.

[88] See note 86 above.

[89] For an English translation of this text, see Sturtevant and Bechtel, A Hittite Chrestomathy, 183-193. This is assuming that the Edict was in force, though the chaotic conditions following the death of Telepinush indicate that it had little immediate effect.

[90] Whether this was exile with Hattushilish in control, an uncommon reaction on the part of a usurper in contrast to much of Hittite history, or a continuation of the struggle between the two rivals is uncertain, though the latter appears more likely.

[91] KBo I 10.

92 If Ramesses did pretend to give support to Urkhi-Teshub, then Babylon may have been instrumental in changing the fortunes of Hattushilish.

93 See chap. I; most recently, Rowton, JNES 25 (1966), 245.

94 The phrase "empty years" is adapted from Papyrus Harris I 75, 4, where it refers to a later time. See note 93 for the date of Urkhi-Teshub; Rowton, JNES 25 (1966), 245, equates his reign with regnal years 10 to 17 of Ramesses II.

95 Ramesses' letter to the King of Mira (KBo I 24; most recently, Edel Z. A. 15 [1950], 196, and Indeogerm. Forsch. 60 [1949], 74, with note 1) was probably written during the struggle between Hattushilish and Urkhi-Teshub; it is unlikely that a vassal would correspond with a foreign ruler when his lord was in full control, for such would have broken the normal relationship between suzerain and vassal reflected in extant treaties. Hence, sometime in the latter part of his second decade, probably after regnal year 17, Ramesses still gave ostensible support to the legitimate ruler, Urkhi-Teshub. At the same time, however, he could also have begun negotiations with Hattushilish.

96 It is possible that the military events recorded on the outer face of the east wall of Ramesses' court of the temple of Luxor belong to this time; see Kitchen, JEA 50 (1964), 47-70.

97 Line 17 of the Alliance.

98 Cf. lines 17 and 19 of the Alliance. The "subjects" of Ramesses could refer to vassals, though at this time *b3kw* is not a common term for such. This reference, combined with the lack of dated monuments from Egypt proper, would lead one to believe that the "crime" was committed in Egypt.

99 And thus why Hattushilish could dictate the "Addendum" to the Alliance; cf. chap. IV.

100 Hattushilish and Ramesses most likely arrived at an agreement prior to the time when the final and formal negotiations were conducted; it was this "agreement" (*sḫr*) which eventually led to the formation of the alliance.
According to the "Apology," Hattushilish tolerated Urkhi-Teshub for seven years and then declared war on him. We do not know how long this struggle lasted though a number of years would not seem improbable. For a recent discussion, see Redford, History and Chronology, 199-208.

101 See chap. II, year 18-C; most recently published by Černý, Eretz Israel 5 (ה), 75*-82*.

102 See Černý's commentary, *op. cit.*, 80*-81*.

103 For the use of *ḥsḳ* to cut off an arm or leg, or even a head, see Wb III 168, 14; the use of *ḥsḳ* for cutting off a head is confined to religious literature.

104 In line 1 of the Alliance, Ramesses stressed his legitimate kingship by referring to the *st-Ḥr nt ʿnḫw*; in this instance he is Horus in charge of the Two Lands as a result of having "appeared" upon the throne of Horus.

105 Urk. IV 85, 9-10.

106 Beisan stela, line 12.

107 Lines 14-15.

108 For *ḥf3*, see Wb III 73, 13-16.

109 Line 24, the same word as used in the Alliance.

110 For the composition of the Egyptian army, see note 13 above. The reference to Sherden coming from the midst of the sea and joining his Majesty because of his "fame" on "Stela II" from Tanis (Yoyotte, Kêmi 10 [1949], Pl. VI) may reflect this situation.

111 Cf. Habachi, Deification 12, note 30; Barsanti and Gauthier, ASAE 11 (1911), 64-86; Moret, The Nile, 301; Komorzynski, ASAE 51 (1951), 111-122; and also Revillout, Revue égyptologique 3 (1883), 101-104.
For the Greek source, see Diodorus Siculus I 54 and 73.

112 Most recently, Habachi, ASAE 52 (1954), 527-559, with references.

113 Helck, Materialien, 262.

114 For references, see chap. II, year 5-A.

115 See note 110 above.

116 Porter-Moss II 49 (3).

117 Wreszinski, Atlas II 58.

118 Breasted, ARE III §352.

119 Sometimes Askelon is placed in a separate campaign of either year 6 or 7 (Faulkner, CAH^2 II xxiii 14), or in year 8 because that was the time of a known campaign (Breasted, ARE III §352, with note a).

120 Kitchen, JEA 50 (1964), 47-70. The date of these events is unknown and we cannot even be certain that they represent a single campaign.

APPENDIX

Because of space, certain abbreviations are employed in the following chart:

Bakir	Bakir, The Cairo Calendar No. 86637
BIE III	Legrain, Bull. Inst. Ég., Third Series, 10 (1899)
BMMA	Winlock, Bulletin of the Metropolitan Museum of Art, Part II, The Egyptian Expedition 1922-1923
Cat. des mon.	de Morgan, etc., Catalogue des monuments et inscriptions
C:CC	Černý, Cairo Catalogue
C:DeF	Černý, Documents de fouilles
CG:HO	Černý and Gardiner, Hieratic Ostraca I
C:OH	Černý, Ostraca hiératiques
D:O	Daressy, Ostraca
FQ:Step Pyramid	Firth and Quibell, The Step Pyramid, Vol. I
GW:OM	Goedicke and Wente, Ostraca Michaelides
James	James, Hieroglyphic Texts from Egyptian Stelae, etc., Part 9
J:Deux pyramid	Jéquier, Deux pyramid du Moyen Empire
J:Ship's Log	Janssen, Two Ancient Egyptian Ship's Logs
M. Habu	Medinet Habu, The University of Chicago Oriental Institute Publications
MM:Armant	Mond-Myers, Temples of Armant
MPV:Cat.	Malinine, Posener, Vercoutte, Catalogue
N:Def	Nagel, Documents de fouilles
P-R	Pleyte and Rossi, Papyrus de Turin
S:Aniba	Steindorff, Aniba
S:DeF	Sauneron, Documents de fouilles
Sérapéum	Mariette, Le Sérapéum de Memphis découvert et décrit par Aug. Mariette
S:Graf	Spiegelberg, Aegyptische u. a. Graffiti
S:HOP	Spiegelberg, Hieratic Ostraka and Papyri
W:Atlas	Wreszinski, Atlas
W:Report	Weigall, A Report on the Antiquities of Lower Nubia

Note: All dates discussed in chapter II are listed in chart V, even those which may not properly belong to Ramesses II or be employed in a chronological structure of his reign.

CHART V
CORPUS OF DATED INSCRIPTIONS

Year	Description	Publication	Kitchen	Porter-Moss	Number
1	Abydos, Dedicatory Inscription	Bibl. d'étude 4	II 323-326	VI 3 (34-37)	1-A
1	Gebel Silsileh, "Hymn to the Nile"	ZAeS 11, 129-135	(II 338)	V 217	1-B
1	Giza, Sphinx Stela Fragment	James	II 337	III 9	1-C
1	Abu Simbel, Door Thickness	L.D. III 189 a		VII 108 (92-93)	1-D
1	Theban Tomb 157, *Nb-wnn.f*	ZAeS 44, 30-35		I^2 267 (8)	1-E
1	Theban Graffito, No. 298	S:Graf 26			1-F
1	Luxor, Triple Shrine	MDAIK 22, 68-69			1-G
2	Aswan Stela	(see year 10)			2-A
2	Sinai, Serabit el-Khadim, No. 252		II 339-340	VII 349-350	2-B
2	Nahr el-Kelb, South Stela	(see year 10)			2-C
2	Sai Island	AJSL 25, 98		VII 164	2-D
2	Theban Graffito, No. 225	S:Graf 21			2-E
3	Quban Stela	Bibl. d'étude 9		VII 83	3-A
3	Luxor Pylon, East Wall	JEA 57, 110-119	II 345-347		3-B
4	Nahr el-Kelb, Middle Stela	L.D. III 197 b	II 1	VII 385	4-A
4	Lachish, Hieratic Bowl Inscription	PEFQS 1937, 238		VII 371	4-B
5	The Qadesh Inscriptions	MIFAO 55	II 2-147		5-A
5	Cairo Ostracon 25671	C:CC I 55 (75*)			5-B
5	Thebes, Graffito of *R'-ms*	C:DeF 9, 6 (No. 1140)		I^2 771	5-C
5	Louvre Leather Manuscript	MMAF I 481-510			5-D
7	Aniba, Stela Fragment	S:Aniba II 1, 27			7-A
8	Ramesseum, Asiatic Campaign	W:Atlas II 90-91	II 148-149	II 151	8-A
8	Turin Papyrus	P-R I 41			8-B

Year	Description	Publication	Kitchen	Porter-Moss	Number
8	Heliopolis Stela	ASAE 38, 217-230		IV 62	8-C
9	Papyrus Sallier III, Colophon	MIFAO 55, 208	II 101		9-A
9	Deir el-Medineh, Hathor Stela	FIFAO 20 ii 56-57			9-B
9	Beisan Stela	(see year 18)			9-C
9	Heliopolis Stela	(see year 8)			9-D
9	Cairo Papyrus 86637	Bakir			9-E
10	Nahr el-Kelb, South Stela	L.D. III 197 c	II 149	VII 385	10-A
10	Aswan Stela	L.D. III 175 g	II 334-335	V 245	10-B
13	Apis Stela	(see year 16)			13-A
14	Abydos, Stela of *P3-sr*	ASAE 16, 161-170			14-A
15	Papyrus Cairo 65739	JEA 21, 140-146			15-A
16	Serapeum, Apis Stela, Louvre 3	MPV:Cat., 4		III 206	16-A
17	Theban Tomb 311, Graffito	BMMA		I^2 387	17-A
18	Deir el-Medineh, Ostracon No. 77	C:DeF 3, 21			18-A
18	Saqqara, The Inscription of Mes	ZAeS 39, 1-10		III 129	18-B
18	Beisan Stela	Eretz Israel 5	II 150-151	VII 379	18-C
19	Deir el-Medineh, Ostracon No. 31	C:DeF 3, 7			19-A
20	Giza, Chephren Fragment		II 338	III 6	20-A
21	Thebes, The Hittite Alliance	MVAG 1902/5			21-A
	Karnak		II 225-232	II 49 (2)	21-A
	Ramesseum		II 230-232	II 152 (14)	21-A
23	The Bentresh Stela, Louvre	ZAeS 74, 49-51	II 284-287	II 89	23-A
23	Apis Stela	(see year 26)			23-B
26	Heliopolis, Mnevis Tomb, Stela	ASAE 18, 207		IV 59	26-A
26	Deir el-Medineh, Ostracon No. 250	C:DeF 6, 3 (No. 250)			26-B
26	Theban Ostracon	Currelly, Theb. Ost., 8			26-C

26	Serapeum, Apis Burial "No. III"	(ASAE 18, 207)			26-D
26	Bentresh Stela	ZAeS 74, 49-51	II 284-287	II 89	26-E
27	Medinet Habu, Graffito	M. Habu II 107-108			27-A
30	Bigeh Inscription, First *Ḥb-Sd*	Thesaurus 1127 I		V 256 (5B)	30-A
30	Gebel Silsileh (Duplicates)	(unpublished)		V 212 (42-43)	30-B
30	Gebel Silsileh, Vizier *Ḫ'y*	Thesaurus 1128 III		V 212 (47)	30-C
30	Gebel Silsileh, Great Speos, Niche	L.D. III 175 f		V 209 (4)	30-D
30	Ostracon Gardiner 28	CG:HO I 3			30-E
30	Serapeum, Apis Stela, Louvre 3	MPV:Cat., 4		III 206	30-F
30	Serapeum, Apis Stela, Louvre 4	Sérapéum III 15-16		III 206	30-G
33	Sehel Inscription	Cat. des mon. I 88		V 251 (137)	33-A
33	Sinai, Statue Fragment No. 298			VII 365	33-B
33	Bentresh Stela	ZAeS 74, 49-51	II 284-287	II 89	33-C
33	Ramesseum, Jar Inscription No. 275	S:HOP Pl. 32			33-D
33	Papyrus Anastasi V 24, 7-8	Gardiner LEM 70			33-E
34	Bigeh Inscription	Thesaurus 1127 I		V 256 (5B)	34-A
34	Gebel Silsileh (Duplicates)	(unpublished)		V 212 (42-43)	34-B
34	Gebel Silsileh, Vizier *Ḫ'y*	Thesaurus 1128 III		V 212 (47)	34-C
34	Marriage Stela	ASAE 25, 181-185	II 233-257		34-D
34	Deir el-Medineh, Ostracon No. 447	C:DeF 7, 29			34-E
34	Saqqara, Graffito	J:Deux pyramid 13-15			34-F
35	The "Decree of Ptah"		II 258-281		35-A
35	Faiyum, Fragment, Cairo 42783	Livre des rois III 44		IV 99	35-B
35	Ostracon Gardiner 24	CG:HO I 7			35-C
35	Theban Graffito, No. 988	S:Graf 82			35-D
36	Bigeh Inscription	Thesaurus 1127 I		V 256 (5B)	36-A
36	Papyrus Gardiner 9	(unpublished)			36-B

Year	Description	Publication	Kitchen	Porter-Moss	Number
36	Deir el-Medineh, Jar Inscription	N:DeF 10, 22			36-C
36	Saqqara, Graffito	FQ: Step Pyramid I 85			36-D
37	Gebel Silsileh (Duplicates)	(unpublished)		V 212 (42-43)	37-A
37	Gebel Silsileh, Vizier *Ḫ'y*	Thesaurus 1128 III		V 212 (47)	37-B
37	Thebes, Graffito	(unpublished)		I^2 590	37-C
37	Deir el-Medineh, Ostracon No. 333	C:DeF 6, 25			37-D
37	British Museum Stela 164	James			37-E
37	British Museum Stela 166	James			37-F
38	Abu Simbel, Viceroy *St3w*	L.D. III 195 b, c		VII 118-119 (24)	38-A
38	Ostracon Michaelides 47	GW:OM 17			38-B
38	Cairo Ostracon 25809	C:OH I 95 (116*)			38-C
39	Ramesseum, Jar Inscription No. 321	S:HOP Pl. 38			39-A
40	Gebel Silsileh (Duplicates)	(unpublished)		V 212 (42-43)	40-A
40	Gebel Silsileh, Vizier *Ḫ'y*	Thesaurus 1128 III		V 212 (47)	40-B
40	Sehel Inscription, *Ḫ'-m-W3st*	Cat. des mon. I 103		V 251 (137)	40-C
40	Gebel Silsileh, *Ḥy* Text	BIE III 10, 133		V 211 (30)	40-D
40	Ostracon British Museum 5634	CG:HO I 22-23			40-E
40	Wadi Allaqi, Graffito	JEA 33, 55		VII 318	40-F
41	El-Kab, Temple of Amenophis III	L.D. III 174 d		V 188 (1)	41-A
42	Gebel Silsileh, Stela of *Ḫ'y*	Rec. Trav. 26, 219		V 212 (48)	42-A
42	Abydos, Stela of *Wn-nfr*	Rec. Trav. 31, 209		V 70	42-B
42	Ostracon Louvre 2262	Rec. Trav. 16, 64-65			42-C
42	Aswan *Ḥb-Sd*	ZAeS 97, 64			42-D
44	Gebel Silsileh, Stela of *Ḫ'y*	Rec. Trav. 26, 219		V 212 (49)	44-A
44	Wadi es-Sebua', Stela of *St3w*	ASAE 11, 83-84		VII 55	44-B
44	Abydos, Jar Inscription	Amélineau		V 80	44-C

45	Theban Graffito, No. 1401	C:DeF 9, 28		45-A
46	Papyrus Berlin 3047	JARCE 2, 65-73		46-A
46	Deir el-Medineh, Jar Inscription	N:DeF 10, 50 (a)		46-B
46	Ostracon British Museum 5634	(see 40-E)		46-C
47	Deir el-Medineh, Jar Inscription	N:DeF 10, 18 (11)		47-A
47	Saqqara, Graffito	FQ: Step Pyramid I 82-83		47-B
48	Deir el-Medineh, Jar Inscription	N:DeF 10, 50 (c)		48-A
48	Deir el-Medineh, Ostracon No. 294	C:DeF 6, 14		48-B
48	Saqqara, Graffito	FQ: Step Pyramid I 83-84		48-C
49	Deir el-Medineh, Jar Inscription	N:DeF 10, 18 (28)		49-A
50	Abu Sir, Graffito	Rec. Trav. 26, 152-154	III 79	50-A
51	Armant, Temple Pylon Fragment	MM: Armant, 164		51-A
51	Asyut Stela	(see year 61)		51-B
52	Papyrus Leiden I 350 *verso*	J: Ship's Logs		52-A
52	Qantir, Jar Inscription	ASAE 30, 43-45		52-B
53	Ostracon Louvre 2261	Rec. Trav. 16, 65		53-A
54	Armant, Temple Pylon	MM: Armant, 163		54-A
54	Papyrus British Museum 10447	Gardiner RAD, 59		54-B
54	Deir el-Medineh, Ostracon No. 351	C:DeF 7, 4		54-C
55	Papyrus British Museum 10447	Gardiner RAD, 59		55-A
55	Serapeum, Graffito	Sérapéum III 15	III 204	55-B
56	Papyrus Sallier IV *verso* 17, 1-4	Gardiner LEM 98		56-A
56	Aniba, Jar Inscription	S:Aniba II 1, 220		56-B
56	Theban Graffito, No. 857	S:Graf 70		56-C
57	Armant, Temple Pylon	MM: Armant, 163		57-A
57	Ramesseum, Jar Inscription No. 323	S:HOP Pl. 38		57-B
58	Ramesseum, Jar Inscription No. 300	S:HOP Pl. 35		58-A

Year	Description	Publication	Kitchen	Porter-Moss	Number
59	Cairo Ostracon 25619	C:OH I 40			59-A
60	Armant, Temple Pylon	MM: Armant, 164			60-A
61	Papyrus Gurob, Fragment N	Gardiner RAD 27			61-A
61	Asyut Stela	ASAE 28, 175		IV 264	61-B
61	Armant, Temple Pylon, Fragment	(see year 51)			61-C
62	British Museum Stela 163	James			62-A
63	Armant, Temple Pylon, Fragment	MM: Armant, 164			63-A
63	Deir el-Medineh, Ostracon No. 285	C:DeF 6, 12			63-B
63	Tonqala (Tomas), Stela of *St3w*	W: Report, 113			63-C
64	Deir el-Medineh, Ostracon No. 621	S:DeF 13, 14			64-A
65	Sesebi, Votive Tablet	JEA 23, 147		VII 173	65-A
66	Armant, Temple Pylon, Fragment	MM: Armant, 164			66-A
66	Cairo Ostracon 25237	D:O 60-61			66-B
66	Coptos Stela, *B3k-wr*	Rec. Trav. 9, 100		V 129	66-C
67	Papyrus Gurob, Fragment L	Gardiner RAD 30			67-A
67	Abydos Stela, Ramesses IV		VI 17-20	V 44	67-B

BIBLIOGRAPHY

Note: The bibliography is limited to the full titles of articles quoted and to those works which have been abbreviated because of frequent occurrence.

Albright, W. F., Further Light on the History of Israel from Lachish and Megiddo, BASOR 68 (1937), 22-26.

_____, James Llewellyn Starkey, Excavator of Lachish, BASOR 69 (1938), 6-7.

_____, The Chronology of the Divided Monarchy of Israel, BASOR 100 (1945), 16-22.

_____, The Evolution of the West-Semitic Divinity 'An-'Anat-'Attâ, AJSL 41 (1925), 73-101.

Aldred, Cyril, The Beginning of the El-'Amārna Period, JEA 45 (1959), 19-33.

_____, Two Theban Notables during the Later Reign of Amenophis III, JNES 18 (1959), 113-120.

_____, Year Twelve at El-'Amārna, JEA 43 (1957), 114-117.

Bakir, Abd el-Mohsen, *Nḥḥ* and *ḏt* reconsidered, JEA 39 (1952), 110-111.

Barsanti, Alexandre and Henri Gauthier, Stèles trouvées à Ouadi es-Sabouâ (Nubie), ASAE 11 (1911), 64-86.

von Beckerath, Juergen, Das Thronbesteigungsdatum Ramses II., ZAeS 81 (1956), 1-3.

_____, Die Lesung von "Regierungsjahr": Ein neuer Vorschlag, ZAeS 95 (1969), 88-91.

_____, Ein neues Monddatum der aegyptischen Geschichte?, ZDMG 118 (1968), 18-21.

_____, Noch einmal die Lesung von  "Regierungsjahr," ZAeS 84 (1959), 155-156.

Birch, Samuel, Upon an Historical Tablet of Ramesses II., 19th Dynasty, relating to the Gold Mines of AEthiopia, Archaeologia 34 (1852), 357-391.

Bittel, Kurt, Bemerkungen zu dem auf Bueyuekkale (Bogazköy) entdeckten hethitischen Siegeldepot, Jahrbuch fuer kleinasiatische Forschung 1 (1950-51), 164-173.

Blackman, A. M., Preliminary Report on the Excavations at Sesebi, Northern Province, Anglo-Egyptian Sudan, 1936-37, JEA 23 (1937), 145-151.

Borchardt, Ludwig, Jahre und Tage der Kroenungs-Jubiläen, ZAeS 72 (1936), 52-59.

Boscawen, W. St. Chad, The Monuments and Inscriptions on the Rocks at Nahr-el-Kelb, TSBA 7 (1882), 331-352.

Bouriant, Urbain, Notes de voyage (le traité de l'an XXI entre Ramsès II et le prince de Khéta), Rec. Trav. 13 (1891), 153-160.

_____, Petits monuments et petits textes recueillis en Égypte, Rec. Trav. 9 (1887), 81-100.

Breasted, James Henry, Ancient Records of Egypt. 5 vols. Chicago, 1906-7.

_____, Oriental Exploration Fund of the University of Chicago. First Preliminary Report of the Egyptian Expedition, AJSL 23 (1906), 1-64.

_____, Oriental Exploration Fund of the University of Chicago: Second Preliminary Report of the Egyptian Expedition, AJSL 25 (1908), 1-110.

Brugsch, Heinrich, Beitraege zu den Untersuchungen ueber Tanis, ZAeS 10 (1872), 16-20.

_____, Ein neues Sothis-Datum, ZAeS 8 (1870), 108-111.

_____, Le mot *Àdon*, Revue égyptologique 1 (1880), 22-32.

Bruyère, Bernard, Deir el Médineh. Cairo 1924-53. (=FIFAO 1/1, 2/2, 3/3, 4/3, 4/4, 5/2, 6/2, 7/2, 8/3, 10/1, 14, 15, 16, 20, 21 and 26.)

Burne, A. H., Some Notes on the Battle of Kadesh, JEA 7 (1921), 191-195.

Černý, Jaroslav, A Note on the "Repeating of Births," JEA 15 (1929), 194-198.

_____, Catalogue des ostraca hiératiques non littéraires de Deir el Médineh. Vols. 1-5. Cairo, 1935-1951. (=Documents de fouilles, 3-7.)

_____, Datum des Todes Ramses' III. und der Thronbesteigung Ramses' IV., ZAeS 72 (1936), 109-118.

_____, Deux nouveaux fragments de textes littéraires connus depuis longtemps, Revue de l'Égypte ancienne 1 (1927), 221-226.

_____, Graffiti at the Wādi el-'Allāḳi, JEA 33 (1947), 52-57.

_____, Graffiti hiéroglyphiques et hiératiques de la nécropole thébaine. Cairo, 1956. (=Documents de fouilles, 9.)

_____, L'identité des "serviteurs dans la Place de Vérité" de des ouvriers de la Nécropole royale de Thèbes, Revue de l'Égypte ancienne 2 (1929), 200-209.

_____, Ostraca hiératiques. Cairo, 1935. (=Catalogue général des antiquités égyptiennes du Musée du Caire, Nos. 25501-25832.)

_____, Papyrus Salt 124 (Brit. Mus. 10055), JEA 15 (1929), 243-258.

_____, Prices and Wages in Egypt in the Ramesside Period, Cahiers d'histoire mondiale I (1953-54), 903-921.

_____, Stela of Ramesses II from Beisan, Eretz Israel 5. Jerusalem, 1958.

_____, Three Regnal Dates of the Eighteenth Dynasty, JEA 50 (1964), 37-39.

_____, in Richard A. Parker, A Saite Oracle Papyrus from Thebes. Providence, Rhode Island, 1962. (=Brown Egyptological Studies 4.)

Chassinat, Émile, Textes provenant du Sérapéum de Memphis, Rec. Trav. 21 (1899), 56-73.

Christophe, Louis-A., Quelques remarques sur le Grand Temple d'Abou-Simbel, La Revue du Caire 47 (1961), 303-333.

Daressy, Georges, La tombe d'un Mnévis de Ramsès II, ASAE 18 (1919), 196-210.

_____, Le temple de Mit Rahineh, ASAE 3 (1902), 22-31.

_____, Notes et Ramarques, Rec. Trav. 14 (1893), 165-185.

_____, Quelques ostraca de Biban el Molouk, ASAE 27 (1927), 161-182.

Dawson, W. R., and T. E. Peet, The so-called Poem on the King's Chariot, JEA 19 (1933), 167-174.

Drioton, Étienne, and J.-P. Lauer, Une inscription de Khamouas sur la face sud de la pyramide d'Ounas à Saqqarah, ASAE 37 (1937), 201-211.

Edel, Elmar, Die Abfassungszeit des Briefes KBo I 10 (Hattušil -- Kadašman-Enlil) und seine Bedeutung fuer die Chronologie Ramses' II., JCS 12 (1958), 130-133.

_____, Die Rolle der Koeniginnen in der aegyptisch-hethitischen Korrespondenz von Boğazköy, Indeogerman. Forsch. 60 (1950), 72-85.

_____, Die Teilnehmer der aegyptisch-hethitischen Friedensgesandtschaft im 21. Jahr Ramses' II., Orientalia N.S. 38 (1969), 177-186.

_____, Ein neuer Beleg fuer "Niniveh" in hieroglyphischer Schreibung, Orientalia N.S. 37 (1968), 417-420.

_____, KBo I 15 + 19, ein Brief Ramses' II. mit einer Schilderung der Ḳadešschlacht, Z.A. 15 (1950), 195-212.

_____, Neue keilschriftliche Umschreibungen aegyptischer Namen aus den Boğazköytexten, JNES 7 (1948), 11-24.

_____, Neues Material zur Beurteilung der syllabischen Orthographie des Aegyptischen, JNES 8 (1949), 44-47.

_____, Untersuchungen zur Phraseologie der aegyptischen Inschriften des Alten Reiches, MDAIK 13 (1944), 1-90.

_____, Zur historischen Geographie der Gegend von Ḳadeš, Z.A. 16 (1952), 253-258.

_____, Zur Lesung von  "Regierungsjahr," JNES 8 (1949), 35-39.

_____, Zur Schwurgoetterliste des Hethitervertrags, ZAeS 90 (1963), 31-35.

Edgerton, William F., Critical Note. On the Chronology of the Early Eighteenth Dynasty (Amenhotep I to Thutmose III), AJSL 53 (1936), 188-197.

_____, On the Late Egyptian Negative , AJSL 48 (1931), 27-44

_____, The Government and the Governed in the Egyptian Empire, JNES 6 (1947), 152-160.

Emery, Walter B., The Order of Succession at the Close of the Nineteenth Dynasty, Mélanges Maspero, I 1, 353-356. (=MIFAO 66.)

Erman, Adolf, Beitraege zur Kenntnisz des aegyptischen Gerichtsverfahrens, ZAeS 17 (1897), 71-83 and 148-154, with Taf. I.

_____, Das achte Jubilaeum Ramses' II., ZAeS 29 (1891), 128.

_____, Gebete eines ungerecht Verfolgten und andere Ostraka aus den Koenigsgraebern, ZAeS 38 (1900), 19-41.

_____, Neuaegyptische Grammatik, Second Edition. Leipzig, 1933.

Fairman, H. W., A Block of Amenophis IV from Athribis, JEA 46 (1960), 80-82.

_____, Preliminary Report on the Excavations at 'Amārah West, Anglo-Egyptian Sudan, 1938-9, JEA 25 (1939), 139-144.

_____, Preliminary Report on the Excavations at Sesebi (Sudla) and Amārah West, Anglo-Egyptian Sudan, 1937-8, JEA 24 (1938), 151-156.

_____, The supposed Year 21 of Akhenaten, JEA 46 (1960), 108-109.

_____, and Bernhard Grdseloff, Texts of Ḥatshepsut and Sethos I inside Speos Artemidos, JEA 33 (1947), 12-33.

_____, in J. D. S. Pendlebury, The City of Akhenaten, Part III. London, 1951.

Faulkner, Raymond O., A Concise Dictionary of Middle Egyptian. Oxford, 1962.

_____, Egyptian Military Organization, JEA 39 (1953), 32-47.

_____, The Battle of Kadesh, MDAIK 16 (1958), 93-111.

_____, The Battle of Megiddo, JEA 28 (1942), 2-15.

_____, The Wars of Sethos I, JEA 33 (1947), 34-39.

Fisher, Clarence S., Bethshean, Pennsylvania University Museum Journal 14 (1923), 227-248.

Foucart, George., Études thebaines, BIFAO 24 (1924).

Friedrich, Johannes, Staatsvertraege des Ḫatti-Reiches in hethitischer Sprache, MVAG 31 (1926), 34/1 (1930).

Gaballa, G. A., and K. A. Kitchen, Ramesside Varia I, CdE 43 (1968), 259-270.

Gardiner, Alan H., A late-Egyptian use of the older absolute pronouns, ZAeS 50 (1912), 114-117.

_____, A Lawsuit arising from the Purchase of Two Slaves, JEA 21 (1935), 140-146.

_____, Ramesside Administrative Documents. London, 1948.

_____, Ramesside Texts relating to the Taxation and Transport of Corn, JEA 27 (1941), 19-73.

_____, Regnal Years and Civil Calendar in Pharaonic Egypt, JEA 31 (1945), 11-28.

_____, Some Reflections on the Nauri Decree, JEA 38 (1952), 24-33.

_____, Tanis and Pi-Ra'messe: A Retraction, JEA 19 (1933), 122-128.

_____, The Coronation of King Ḥaremḥab, JEA 39 (1953), 13-31.

_____, The Delta Residence of the Ramessides, JEA 5 (1918), 127-138, 179-200, 242-271.

_____, The Graffito from the Tomb of Pere, JEA 14 (1928), 10-11.

_____, The Harem at Miwēr, JNES 12 (1953), 145-149.

_____, The House of Life, JEA 24 (1938), 157-179.

_____, The Reading of the Word for Regnal Years, JNES 8 (1949), 165-171.

_____, The So-called Tomb of Queen Tiye, JEA 43 (1957), 10-25.

_____, and H. I. Bell, The Name of Lake Moeris, JEA 29 (1943), 37-50.

Gauthier, Henri, La grande inscription dédicatoire d'Abydos, Bibl. d 'étude, 4 (1912).

_____, Les "fils royaux de Kouch" et le personnel administratif de l'Éthiopie, Rec. Trav. 39 (1921), 179-238.

Gelb, I. J., Two Assyrian King Lists, JNES 13 (1954), 209-230, Pls. XIV-XVII.

Glanville, S. R. K., Book-keeping for a Cult of Rameses II, JRAS 1929, 19-26.

Goedicke, Hans, Considerations on the Battle of Ḳadesh, JEA 52 (1966), 71-80.

_____, Die Laufbahn des *Mṯn*, MDAIK 21 (1966), 1-71.

_____, Early References to Fatalistic Concepts in Egypt, JNES 22 (1963), 187-190.

_____, Ein Brief aus dem Alten Reich (Pap. Boulaq 8), MDAIK 22 (1967), 1-8.

_____, Hieratische Ostraka in Wien, WZKM 59/60 (1963-64), 1-43.

_____, Some Remarks on the 400-Year-Stela, CdE 41 (1966), 23-39.

_____, The Abydene Marriage of Pepi I, JAOS 75 (1955), 180-183.

_____, Was Magic used in the Harim Conspiracy against Ramesses III?, JEA 49 (1963), 71-92.

Goetze, Albrecht, Ḫattušiliš, MVAG 29/3 (1925).

_____, Kizzuwatna and the Problem of Hittite Geography, New Haven, 1940.

_____, Neue Bruchstuecke zum Grossen Text des Ḫattušiliš und den Paralleltexten, MVAG 34/2 (1930).

_____, On the Chronology of the Second Millennium B.C., JCS 11 (1957), 53-61.

_____, Zur Schlacht von Qadeš, OLZ 32 (1929), 832-838.

Grapow, Hermann, Wie die alten Aegypter sich anredeten, wie sie sich grueszten und wie sie miteiander sprachen, Abhandlungen der Preuszischen Akademie der Wissenschaften, Philo.-hist. Klasse, 1942, No. 7.

Griffith, F. L., The Abydos Decree of Seti I at Nauri, JEA 13 (1927), 193-208.

Gueterbock, H. G., Die Siegel, MDOG 75 (1937), 52-60.

_____, The Predecessors of Shuppiluliuma Again, JNES 29 (1970), 73-77.

Habachi, Labib, Khatâ'na-Qantîr: Importance, ASAE 52 (1954), 443-562.

_____, La Reine Touy, femme de Séthi I, et ses proches parents inconnus, Revue d'égyptologie, 21 (1969), 27-47.

_____, Setau, the Famous Viceroy of Ramesses II and his Career, Cahiers d'histoire égyptienne 10 (1967), 51ff.

_____, The Graffiti and Work of the Viceroys of Kush in the Region of Aswan, Kush 5 (1957), 13-36.

_____, The Jubilees of Ramesses II and Amenophis III with Reference to Certain Aspects of their Celebration, ZAeS 97 (1971), 64-72.

Hall, H. R., Édouard Naville, JEA 13 (1927), 1-6.

Hamada, A., A Stela from Manshîyet eṣ-Ṣadr, ASAE 38 (1938), 217-230.

Hamza, Mahmud, Excavations of the Department of Antiquities at Qantîr (Faqus District), ASAE 30 (1930), 31-68.

_____, The Identification of 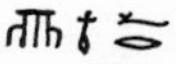 "Khent-Nefer" with Qantîr, Mélanges Maspero I, 647-655. (=MIFAO 66.)

Harris, J. R., How Long was the Reign of Horemheb? JEA 54 (1968), 95-99.

Hayes, William C., Inscriptions from the Palace of Amenhotep III, JNES 10 (1951), 35-56, 82-111, 156-183, 231-242.

Helck, Wolfgang, Bemerkungen zu den Thronbesteigungsdaten im Neuen Reich, Analecta Biblica 12 (1959), 113-129.

_____, Das thebanische Grab 43, MDAIK 17 (1961), 99-110.

_____, Der Papyrus Berlin P 3047, JARCE 2 (1963), 65-73, Pls. IX-XII.

_____, Die Aegypter und die Fremden, Saeculum 15 (1964), 103-114.

_____, Die Bedeutung der aegyptischen Besucherinschriften, ZDMG 102 (1952), 39-46.

_____, Die Sinai-Inschrift des Amenmose, MIO 2 (1954), 189-207.

_____, Die soziale Schichtung des aegyptischen Volkes im 3. und 2. Jahrtausend v. Chr., JESHO 2 (1959), 1-36.

_____, Feiertage und Arbeitstage in der Ramessidenzeit, JESHO 7 (1964), 136-166.

_____, Review of Campbell, The Chronology of the Amarna Letters, OLZ 60 (1965), 559-563.

_____, Soziale Stellung und Grablage (Bemerkungen zur thebanischen Nekropole), JESHO 5 (1962), 225-243.

_____, *Ṯ*KW und die Ramses-stadt, Vetus Testamentum, 15 (1965), 35-48.

_____, Urḫi-Tešup in Aegypten, JCS 17 (1963), 87-97.

_____, Zur Geschichte der 19. und 20. Dynastie, ZDMG 105 (1955), 27-52.

Hornung, Erik, Neue Materialien zur aegyptischen Chronologie, ZDMG 117 (1967), 11-16.

_____, Untersuchungen zur Chronologie und Geschichte des Neuen Reiches. Wiesbaden, 1964. (=Aegyptologische Abhandlungen, 11.)

_____, Zur geschichtlichen Rolle des Koenigs in der 18. Dynastie, MDAIK 15 (1957), 120-133.

Iversen, Erik, Horapollon and the Egyptian Conceptions of Eternity, Rivista degli Studi Orientali, 38 (1963), 177-186.

Kaiser, Otto, Das Orakel als Mittel der Rechtsfindung im alten Aegypten, Zeitschrift fuer Religions- und Geistesgeschichte 10 (1958), 193-208.

Kamal, Ahmed-Bey, Stèle de l'An VIII de Ramsès II, Rec. Trav. 30 (1908), 213-18.

Kitchen, K. A., Further Notes on New Kingdom Chronology and History, CdE 43 (1968), 313-324.

_____, On the Chronology and History of the New Kingdom, CdE 40 (1965), 310-322.

_____, Review of Campbell, The Chronology of the Amarna Letters, JEA 53 (1967), 178-182.

_____, Some New Light on the Asiatic Wars of Ramesses II, JEA 50 (1964), 47-70.

Korošec, Viktor, Hethitische Staatsvertraege. Leipzig, 1931. (=Leipziger rechtswissenschaftliche Studien 60.)

Krall, J., Der Kalender des Papyrus Ebers, Rec. Trav. 6 (1885), 57-63.

Kuentz, M. Charles, La Bataille de Qadech, MIFAO 55 (1928-34).

_____, La *Stèle du Mariage* de Ramsès II, ASAE 25 (1925), 181-238.

Landsberger, B., Jahreszeiten im Summerisch-Akkadischen, JNES 8 (1949), 248-297.

Langdon, Stephen, and A. H. Gardiner, The Treaty of Alliance between Ḫattušili, King of the Hittites, and the Pharaoh Ramesses II of Egypt, JEA 6 (1920), 179-205.

Lefebvre, Gustave, Fouilles à Abydos, ASAE 13 (1914), 193-214.

_____, Une version abrégée de la *STÈLE DU MARIAGE*, ASAE 25 (1925), 34-45.

Legrain, Georges, Notes prises à Karnak, Rec. Trav. 22 (1900), 51-63.

_____, Notes Prises à Karnak, Rec. Trav. 26 (1904), 218-224.

_____, Recherches généalogiques, Rec. Trav. 31 (1909), 1-10, 201-220.

_____, Sur l'ordre de succession au trône de Ramsès II, Bull. Inst. Ég., Third Series, 10 (1899), 133.

_____, Un miracle d'Ahmès Ier à Abydos, ASAE 16 (1916), 161-170.

Lods, Adolphe, Le rôle des oracles, Mélanges Maspero I, 91-100. (=MIFAO 66.)

Loret, Victor, Le grande inscription de *Mes* à Saqqarah, ZAeS 39 (1901), 1-10.

_____, Pour transformer un vieillard en jeune homme, Mélanges Maspero I 2, 853-877. (=MIFAO 66.)

Luckenbill, D. D., Hittite Treaties and Letters, AJSL 37, (1921), 161-211.

Malinine, M., G. Posener, and J. Vercoutter, Catalogue des Stèles du Sérapéum de Memphis. Vol. I. Paris, 1968.

Maspero, Gaston, Notes sur quelques points de grammaire et d'histoire, ZAeS 19 (1881), 116-131.

Matthiew, Militza, A Note on the Coronation Rites in Ancient Egypt, JEA 16 (1930), 31-32.

Meissner, Bruno, Die Beziehungen Aegyptens zum Ḫattireiche nach ḫattischen Quellen, ZDMG 72 (1918), 32-64.

_____, Synchronismen, OLZ 20 (1917), 225-228.

Meyer, Eduard, Geschichte des Alterthums. Third Edition. Stuttgart, 1910-13.

Mond, Robert, and Oliver H. Myers, Temples of Armant. 2 vols. London, 1940. (=Egyptian Exploration Society, Memoir 43.)

Montet, Pierre, La stèle de l'an 400 retrouvée, Kêmi 4 (1931), 191-215.

_____, Tanis, Avaris et Pi-Ramsès, Revue biblique 39 (1930), 5-28.

de Morgan, J., U. Bouriant, G. Legrain, G. Jéquier, and A. Barsanti, Catalogue des monuments et inscriptions de l'Égypte antique. Vol. I. Vienna, 1894.

Mueller, W. Max, Der Buendnisvertrag Ramses' II. und des Chetiterkoenigs, MVAG 7/5 (1902).

Nagel, Georges, La Céramique du Nouvel Empire à Deir el Médineh. Cairo, 1938. (=Documents de fouilles, 10.)

Nassouhi, Essad, Grande liste des rois d'Assyrie, AfO 4 (1927), 1-11, Pls. I-II.

Neugebauer, O., Die Bedeutungslosigkeit der 'Sothisperiode' fuer die aelteste aegyptische Chronologie, Acta Orientalia 17 (1939), 169-195.

_____, The Chronology of the Hammurabi Age, JAOS 61 (1941), 58-61.

Newberry, Percy E., Akhenaten's Eldest Son-in-law 'Ankhheprurē,' JEA 14 (1928), 3-9.

Nims, Charles F., An Oracle Dated in "The Repeating of Births," JNES 7 (1948), 157-162.

_____, Places about Thebes, JNES 14 (1955), 110-123.

Otten, Heinrich, Die hethitischen "Koenigslisten" und die altorientalische Chronologie, MDOG 83 (1951), 47-71.

_____, in Ernst Weidner, Die Inschriften Tukulti-Ninurtas I. und seiner Nachfolger, Graz, 1959. (=AfO Supp. 12.)

_____, Inschriftliche Funde der Ausgrabung in Bogazköy 1953, MDOG 87 (1955), 13-25.

Parker, Richard A., Once Again the Coregency of Thutmose III and Amenhotep II, in Studies in Honor of John A. Wilson, 75-82. Chicago, 1969. (=SAOC 35.)

_____, Review of Hornung, Chronologie, Revue d'égyptologie 19 (1967), 185-189.

_____, Sothic Dates and Calendar "Adjustment," Revue d'égyptologie 9

(1952), 101-108.

_____, The Lunar Dates of Thutmose III and Ramesses II, JNES 16 (1957), 39-43.

Pézard, Maurice, Mission archéologique à Tell Nebi Mend (1921), Syria 3 (1922), 89-115.

Ranke, Hermann, Eine Bleitafel mit hieroglyphischer Inschrift, ZAeS 74 (1938), 49-51.

el-Razik, M. A., Some Remarks on the Great Pylon of the Luxor Temple, MDAIK 22 (1967), 68-69.

Read, John G., Early Eighteenth Dynasty Chronology, JNES 29 (1970), 1-11.

Redford, Donald B., Exodus I 11, Vetus Testamentum 13 (1963), 401-418.

_____, History and Chronology of the Eighteenth Dynasty of Egypt, 1967.

_____, On the Chronology of the Egyptian Eighteenth Dynasty, JNES 25 (1966), 113-124.

_____, Some Observations on 'Amārna Chronology, JEA 45 (1959), 34-37.

_____, The Coregency of Tuthmosis III and Amenophis II, JEA 51 (1965), 107-122.

_____, The Earliest Years of Ramesses II, and the Building of the Ramesside Court at Luxor, JEA 57 (1971), 110-119.

Reisner, George A., The Viceroys of Ethiopia, JEA 6 (1920), 28-55, 73-88.

Reisner, George A., and M. B. Reisner, Inscribed Monuments from Gebel Barkal, ZAeS 69 (1933), 73-78, Tafel VIII.

Riemschneider, Kaspar K., Hethitische Fragmente historischen Inhalts aus der Zeit Ḫattušilis III, JCS 16 (1962), 110-121.

Roeder, Guenther, Zwei hieroglyphische Inschriften aus Hermopolis, ASAE 52 (1954), 315-442.

de Rougé, Emmanuel, Étude sur une stèle égyptienne, Journal asiatique, 5. Série, 1865-68.

_____, Inscriptions hiéroglyphiques copiées en Égypte, Études égyptologiques 9-12 (1877-78).

de Rougé, Jacques, Le poème de Pentaour, Revue égyptologique 3 (1885), 149-161.

Rowe,A.,The Two Royal Stelae of Beth-Shan, Pennsylvania University Museum Journal, 20 (1929), 89-98.

Rowton, M. B., Comparative Chronology at the Time of Dynasty XIX, JNES 19 (1960), 15-22.

_____, Manetho's Date for Ramesses II, JEA 34 (1948), 57-73.

_____, The Background of the Treaty between Ramesses II and Ḫattušiliš III, JCS 13 (1959), 1-11.

_____, The Material from Western Asia and the Chronology of the Nineteenth Dynasty, JNES 25 (1966), 240-258.

_____, *Ṭuppū* in the Assyrian King-Lists, JNES 18 (1959), 213-221.

Sauneron, Serge, Catalogue des ostraca hiératiques non littéraires de Deir el-Médineh. Cairo, 1959. (=Documents de fouilles 13.)

_____, La tradition officielle relative à la XVIIIe dynastie d'après un ostracon de la Vallée des Rois, CdE 26 (1951), 46-49.

Schaefer, Heinrich, Die kupferne Zielscheibe in der Sphinxinschrift Thutmosis des IV., ZAeS 67 (1931), 92-95.

Schulman, Alan Richard, The *N'rn* at the Battle of Kadesh, JARCE 1 (1962), 47-53.

Sethe, Kurt, Die Berufung eines Hohenpriesters des Amon unter Ramses II., ZAeS 44 (1907), 30-35.

_____, Die Jahresrechnung unter Ramses II. und der Namenswechsel dieses Koenigs, ZAeS 62 (1927), 110-114.

_____, Ramses II. als 'erster Prophet des Amun,' ZAeS 58 (1923), 54.

_____, Sethos I. und die Erneuerung der Hundssternperiode, ZAeS 66 (1931), 1-7.

Shorter, Alan W., Reliefs showing the Coronation of Ramesses II, JEA 20 (1934), 18-19.

Simpson, William Kelly, Studies in the Twelfth Egyptian Dynasty: I-II, JARCE 2(1963), 53-63.

_____, The Single-Dated Monuments of Sesostris I: An Aspect in the Institution of Coregency in the Twelfth Dynasty, JNES 15 (1956), 214-219.

Spiegelberg, Wilhelm, Beitraege und Nachtraege zu Daressys Publikation der hieratischen Ostraca des Museums von Gizeh, OLZ 5 (1902), 307-335.

_____, Bemerkungen zu den hieratischen Amphoreninschriften des Ramesseums, ZAeS 58 (1923), 25-36.

_____, Ostraca hiératiques du Louvre, Rec. Trav. 16 (1894), 64-67.

_____, Varia, Rec. Trav. 15 (1893), 141-145.

_____, Varia, Rec. Trav. 26 (1904), 143-154.

Stadelmann, Rainer, Die 400-Jahre-Stele, CdE 40 (1965), 46-60.

Starkey, J. L., Excavations at Tell ed-Duweir, PEFQS 1937, 228-241.

Stern, Ludwig, Die Nilstele von Gebel Silsileh, ZAeS 11 (1873), 129-135.

Struve, W., Die Aera "ἀπὸ Μενόφρεως" und die XIX. Dynastie Manethos, ZAeS 63 (1928), 45-50.

Tadmor, Hayim, Historical Implications of the Correct Rendering of Akkadian *dâku*, JNES 17 (1958), 129-141.

Thausing, G., Die Ausdruecke fuer "Ewig" im Aegyptischen, Mélanges Maspero I 35-42. (=MIFAO 66.)

Thomas, Ernest S., Oracular Responses, Ancient Egypt 1921, 76-78.

Tresson, Paul, La stèle de Koubân, Bibl. d'étude 9 (1922).

_____, Mélanges, Un curieux cas d'exorcisme dans l'antiquité, Revue biblique 42 (1933), 57-78.

Uphill, Eric P., Pithom and Raamses: Their Location and Significance, JNES 27 (1968), 291-316.

_____, The Date of Osorkon II's Sed Festival, JNES 26 (1967), 61-62.

_____, The Egyptian Sed-Festival Rites, JNES 24 (1965), 365-383.

_____, The Sed-Festivals of Akhenaton, JNES 22 (1963), 123-127.

Varille, Alexandre, La stele égyptienne n° 1175 du Musee de Toulouse, Kêmi 3 (1930-35), 39-43.

Virolleaud, Charles, L'Orient au temps des Ramsès, L'Ethnographie 50 (1955), 3-15.

Wainwright, G. A., The aniconic Form of Amon in the New Kingdom, ASAE 28 (1928), 175-189.

Weidner, Ernst F., Aus den hettitischen Urkunden von Boghazköi, MDOG 58 (1917), 53-78.

_____, Die Kaempfe Adadnāraris I. gegen Ḫanigalbat, AfO 5 (1928), 89-100.

_____, Die neue Koenigsliste aus Assur, AfO 4 (1927), 11-17.

_____, Politische Dokumente aus Kleinasien, Boghazköi Studien 8 (1923).

_____, Wasašatta, Koenig von Ḫanigalbat, AfO 6 (1930-31), 21-22.

Weigall, Arthur E. P., A Report on the Antiquities of Lower Nubia, Oxford, 1907.

_____, A Report on the so-called Temple of Redesiyeh, ASAE 9 (1908), 71-84.

Wente, Edward F., On the Chronology of the Twenty-First Dynasty, JNES 26 (1967), 155-176.

_____, The Suppression of the High Priest Amenhotep, JNES 25 (1966), 73-87.

Wiedemann, Alfred, Ein Fund thebanischer Ostraka, ZAeS 21 (1883), 33-35.

Wilson, John A., Illuminating the Thrones at the Egyptian Jubilee, JAOS 56 (1936), 293-296.

_____, The Oath in Ancient Egypt, JNES 7 (1948), 129-156.

Winckler, Hugo, Vorlaeufige Nachrichten ueber die Ausgrabungen in Boghaz-köi im Sommer 1907, MDOG 35 (1907), 1-59.

Winlock, Herbert E., The Museum's Excavations at Thebes, in The Bulletin of the Metropolitan Museum of Art, Part II, The Egyptian Expedition 1922-23, 11-39.

Yeivin, S., Canaanite and Hittite Strategy in the Second Half of the Second Millennium B.C., JNES 9 (1950), 101-107.

Yoyotte, Jean, Le nom de Ramsès "Souverain d'Héliopolis," in Rudolf Anthes, Mit Rahineh 1956, 66-70.

_____, Trois généraux de la XIXe dynastie, Orientalia N.S. 23 (1954), 223-231.

GENERAL INDEX

Wine Jar Inscription, 43, 48, 50
55, 58, 60, 66, 105
Winlock, 35

Yuni, viceroy, 160

EGYPTIAN WORDS AND NAMES